Fire that Kindles Hearts

Aroharui,

Linda Tuhiwai Smith

Kia Ora Taima

Na Graham Smith

Fire that Kindles Hearts

TEN MĀORI SCHOLARS

edited by

SELWYN KĀTENE

STEELE ROBERTS
AOTEAROA

A catalogue record for this book is available from the National Library of New Zealand.

ISBN 978-1-927242-88-9

Production assistance: Gerry Te Kapa Coates, Mark Derby, Andrew Robb & Diana Russell. Thanks to Waimatua Morris of Huia Publishers, the University of Waikato, and all others who supplied illustrations.

Tohutō (macrons): Where known, macrons have been retrospectively added to citations, whakapapa and names, for consistency and to assist pronunciation.

Please advise the editor or the publisher of any errors or omissions in this book; they can then be corrected in any future printings.

STEELE ROBERTS PUBLISHERS
Box 9321, Wellington, Aotearoa New Zealand
info@steeleroberts.co.nz • www.steeleroberts.co.nz

Contents

WĀHINGA KŌRERO

by Sir Tīpene O'Regan, Ngāi Tahu

Saying anything useful about leadership is always something of a challenge and saying anything useful about academic leadership even more so. By any definition leadership requires followers, but leaders are not recognised as such merely by appointment to the front. That's enough for managers or functionaries, but recognition as a leader is far more than that.

Selwyn Kātene, in his introduction, draws eloquently on Ngata's description of the late Pei Te Hurinui Jones as demonstrating scholarly leadership. However, Pei Te Hurinui, with whom I was fortunate enough to have had some contact in his latter years, never saw himself as an academic and would not, I suspect, have described himself as a scholar. Although one of our greatest sources of Māori scholarship and literary accomplishment, he would have been happy to see himself listed among the pantheon of tribal scholars and respected kaumātua of his day. I suspect his role as the trusted advisor to more than one generation of the Kāhui Ariki of Tainui meant more to him than the various emblems of scholarly respect that he wore with such consummate grace.

Indeed, few of the more important sources of Māori scholarship that we rely on so heavily today as the primary feedstock of academic pursuit would have seen themselves as academic leaders or have been seen thus by others. However revered within the Māori world of my own and earlier generations, their studies and researches were almost entirely undertaken in a non-academic frame. Their primary terms of reference were the maintenance of the heritage and identity of their own iwi. Interest in their work by others was very much a secondary consideration — if at all.

It has been only relatively recently that our universities have even recognised Māori Studies or te reo Māori as proper subjects of academic inquiry or as being of substantive scholarly interest. In the academic generation preceding my own any such pursuit was shielded behind the skirts of various Western divisions of knowledge such as anthropology, linguistics or history. Māori had no status in its own right or on its own terms in the academy. Today that is changing — and it is changing, at least in part, through the efforts of the scholars represented in this volume and by a number of their colleagues.

However respected within te ao Māori, though, few Māori academics have themselves pretended to be leaders. If they have achieved distinction in the academy it has been by a process of selection and appointment within a very Western institution and on terms and conditions established and maintained by a Western power culture. The wider Māori community tends, like most New Zealanders, to view the academy with suspicion, however much it rejoices, at a whānau level, at the increasing success of Māori tertiary students. The tendency to question the relevance or significance of academic pursuits may be heard being vociferously debated around the table in the marae kitchen at the same time as the hākari is being prepared for a graduation celebration. Ambivalence abounds, then, on the marae and beyond in the wider community. Whatever we may think of the relevance of the academy there is general Māori satisfaction at the fact of culturally proficient tribal members being elevated to senior positions.

Selwyn Kātene strongly reinforces the point that Māori scholarship has a much broader sweep — with its own history and record — well beyond its present recognition by the academy. He emphasises the respect in which the scholar has traditionally been held. He explores a range of thinking about the evolution of the process by which the blending of traditional Māori scholarship and the Western academic model has taken place. His contributors reflect that evolutionary process. The ten professors are all well known participants in it. It is a process which is now well advanced but yet far from complete. I suspect it will be another generation before it can be said that things Māori stand within our universities squarely on their own terms.

The MANU AO Academy was instituted in an attempt to advance, indeed accelerate, that evolution. It is a matter of regret that this is its final publication. The process, though, will continue. Māori scholarship is expanding at a near exponential rate in our contemporary universities. The advance of a culturally autonomous standing for Māori scholarship within the wider academy is unstoppable. The dream of TE MANU AO will be realised.

MANU AO leadership course of emerging Māori academics
held at Te Herenga Waka Marae, Victoria University, Wellington,
2 September 2011

Selwyn Kātene.

KUPU WHAKATAKI

'The torch-bearer will I think be Pei Jones — a good man, with plenty of vision, a first-rate Māori scholar, steeped in West Coast folk lore &c. and a very competent master of English ... And he has the fire that kindles hearts.'[1]

Āpirana Ngata's description of Ngāti Maniapoto leader Pei Te Hurinui Jones reminds us that Māori scholarship is not just about academics studying, researching and teaching at tertiary education institutions but recognises the significant contributions from community-based traditional scholars as well. Although Jones had spent some time at Wesley College, he had no further formal education, yet many of his works such as *Ngā Mōteatea* were profound contributions to Māori literature. Even before Jones, Ngāti Kahungunu's Whatahoro Jury — one of the founders of Pāremata Māori (Māori Parliament) at Pāpāwai marae in the Wairarapa during the 1890s — was also a prolific writer and scholar of ancient Māori oral traditions and customs. Educated by tohunga at traditional whare wānanga, Jury's scholarly works included the seminal manuscript *Lore of the Whare Wānanga*.

Māori scholarly tradition has its origins in several millennia of experiences journeying and living throughout the Pacific. Mātauranga Māori (Māori knowledge) evolved in parallel with changing times. Having no written language and record as such, early scholars relied on oral narratives and artwork such as drawings, pottery-making and wood-carving to express themselves, including their past and future. Sir Mason Durie wrote about this in his tribute to renowned scholar and paramount chief of Ngāti Whātua, Professor Sir Hugh Kāwharu:

> Human existence was essentially contextualised as part of a wider environmental framework within a timeframe that extended over a score or more generations. Metaphor, allusion and the juxtaposition of past and future added depth and meaning to literary endeavours contributing to the emergence of a Māori world view within which knowledge and its application had a genealogy of its own and scholars were entrusted to safeguard the integrity of the learning process.[2]

In Aotearoa, the change in the 19th century from a focus on oral tradition to written language and historical record enabled widespread collection and dissemination of knowledge that would benefit future generations. In parallel, the role scholars had played as guardians of mātauranga Māori and its importance regrettably diminished over time. Early ethnographers such as Elsdon Best and Percy Smith often misunderstood tribal traditions. They sought to convey a uniform, romanticised view of Māori history. The value of rich oral narratives honed by rangatira, tohunga, kaumātua and kuia on the marae over many years was undermined in favour of the prevailing view that the written word was more reliable and aligned better with Western ideology.

Early in our history it was common for Māori scholars (and others, e.g. tribal leaders) of note who had passed on to be revered by their whānau, hapū and iwi. Their accomplishments were often remembered in word and song in the form of powerful rhetoric that gave an indication of their mana, esteem, and values. Hirini Moko Mead suggests images of leadership included being compared to a 'sheltering rātā tree', 'a tōtara tree standing tall in the forest', or 'a rock dashed by the waves of the sea'.

> The language of metaphor in songs and in orations emphasised the importance to a group of people … of having dedicated leadership to guide them through the challenges of life. The loss of a great leader is a tragedy and composers of song used very striking images to carry the message. The lightning flashes, the thunder resounds, and these images very clearly signal that the loss of a leader is an earthshaking event that causes uncertainty about the future and may plunge the tribe into a period of internal unrest.[3]

What does scholarship mean? Four types of scholarship have been discerned: discovery, integration, application, and teaching.

> There are aspects of scholarly activity and purpose in addition to discovery/genesis research, and any understanding of academic purposes must take them into account. Thus the focus is on, in addition to discovery research, the creative use of the outcomes of discipline-based research, the quality enhancement of

teaching, the application of knowledge to key issues of societal significance, and the importance of dissemination through teaching.[4]

Māori scholarship focuses on participation and excellence in the Māori world and also being responsible global citizens. Graham Smith, in this book, suggests that Māori scholarship "requires a critical understanding of the reality of our lives now and where we are up to in respect of our contemporary existence while simultaneously remembering that Māori still need the knowledge and skills to be Māori citizens." Scholarship has to be not only ethical but also practical, with the endpoint leading to clear gains for Māori.

However, Māori scholars themselves disagree on what exactly it means. Atholl Anderson defines it as

> often by Māori, although not just by Māori, but particularly as scholarship about Māori. I don't think there is a paradigm of Māori scholarship in any more profound sense, and I don't think that there could be. Others disagree and the conundrum between Western scholarship and what are perceived as Māori ways of thinking and acting in an academic context is still unresolved.

Contemporary Māori scholars are no less important than their illustrious predecessors. The Young Māori Party, a product of the Te Aute Old Boys Association, included a new generation of Māori scholars who were tasked with articulating, disseminating and verifying mātauranga Māori in ways that accorded with both the written word and Māori oral tradition.

This first wave of intellectual leaders included Sir Āpirana Ngata, Rēweti Kōhere, Te Rangi Hīroa (Sir Peter Buck) and later Dr Maharaia Winiata. With their university training, coupled with tribal experiences, they acted as intermediaries between the different modes of scholarship: Māori and Western. Of them, Durie writes:

> They were inevitably answerable to critical Māori readers, and were not able to avoid marae standards of proof. But nor were they immune from the standards demanded of serious academic writers. In short, they lived and worked at the interface between two systems of knowledge and two sets of accountabilities, creating in the process a space for later generations of Māori intellectuals.[5]

As professionals and intellectuals, they were determined to improve the spiritual and material conditions of Māori by political means. With missionary zeal they advocated a message of adaptation and survival through social and religious reform. Their leadership style was typically transformational in that they had vision, recognised that they needed to be the agents of change, and they set themselves far-reaching goals of self-determination.

A second wave of intellectual leadership came about half a century later with the advent of scholars such as Hirini Mead, Ranginui Walker and Mason

Durie. As Aotearoa became increasingly exposed to global competition there was a need for high-calibre Māori academic leadership. The first wave of intellectuals had backgrounds in medicine, law and religion; the next had medical and teaching backgrounds. To attain high levels of professionalism and continuing professional development, they maintained active links between their scholarly pursuits and the wider dimensions of Māori social, cultural and economic advancement.

Today, the emergence of a distinctive Māori brand of indigenous scholarship challenges universities to respond by providing opportunities for ongoing theoretical and methodological development.

Māori leadership and scholarship need to build on a capacity to tolerate ambiguity and value diverse realities. The responsibilities of scholars are to document their findings, which can be replicated or elaborated and are open for critique and peer review. Advancing Māori scholarship is a key goal that takes into account the increasing numbers of well qualified Māori across a range of subject areas and their interest in using Māori concepts and philosophies alongside perspectives from other bodies of knowledge.

At a MANU AO Academy seminar at Victoria University of Wellington in 2010, Labour MP Shane Jones lamented how few Māori academics are being used as commentators by both mainstream and Māori media. Yet there is a growing need for evidence-based information from scholars' analysis to assist Māori in forming opinions on, for instance, the merits of political parties or the interpretation of public policy and legislation. Commentary on public affairs, without fear or favour, is part of the job of being a scholar.

The influence of Māori intellectuals in the latter decades of the 20th century was at its height with the likes of Ranginui Walker, Patu Hōhepa, Tīpene O'Regan and Hirini Mead in regular demand to comment in mainstream media on a range of issues affecting Māori. Other leading thinkers such as Kāterina Mataira, Api Mahuika, Rose Pere and Whatarangi Winiata were pre-eminent in te ao Māori. These scholars were at the forefront of the Māori renaissance period. They moved easily between topics, drawing on a variety of positions and contextual understandings, as advocates for (or against) reform, or as educators and champions of civil rights.

Māori scholars at universities continue to accept that they have a part to play in their institution's role as critic and conscience of society.[6] They help the public to gain greater understanding of social issues and to make progress towards socio-economic and cultural well-being. Māori scholars are members of a community of leaders who will readily identify and challenge assumptions, seek alternative ways to interpret situations, remain sceptical about what is seen and heard, and be unafraid to make judgements, as appropriate.

When Professor Margaret Mutu of the University of Auckland said, in response to a Department of Labour report, that white immigration to New Zealand should be restricted because it poses a threat to race relations due to immigrants' white supremacist attitudes, her university stood by her controversial remarks notwithstanding claims that she was racist and calls for her dismissal. Vice-Chancellor Stuart McCutcheon issued a statement: [7]

> The vice-chancellor understands the concerns raised over Professor Margaret Mutu's reported comments but believes very strongly in the right of academics to comment on issues in which they have expertise, even when those comments may be controversial.
>
> The Education Act protects the right of academics, within the law, to question and test received wisdom, to put forward new ideas and to state controversial or unpopular opinions. That is an important right in a free society.

Academics are always under scrutiny from their own community. Moana Jackson, for instance, suggests that Māori academics could help to better fulfil their role by considering, "Who is still controlling our learning?" At a MANU AO seminar he challenged them to make space to continue developing independent Māori thought, and shared his hope that scholars "will actually plant your feet again in the sands and on the rocks of our own intellectual tradition." [8]

Fire that Kindles Hearts is about the formative experiences and leadership of a selection of senior Māori academics. It chronicles the changes they went through as they forged careers for themselves, whether producing knowledge, teaching, furthering their research, or as leaders and administrators. The ten scholars in this book were educated in both the Māori and Pākehā worlds. Some were simultaneously providing leadership within their family and tribal communities. They were imbued with all the expectations and responsibilities that entails, inevitably a source of conflict for some.

Māori leadership champions high ethics, moral values, and sets standards and benchmarks for others to reach or surpass. The scholars in this book are all models of leadership. They are comfortable living as Māori; they take care of their own well-being and acknowledge their positions of responsibility; they have a strong sense of camaraderie with their peers; they value the rich diversity of other minority cultures, nationalities and religions. They have entrepreneurial dispositions to adapt and flourish in an ever-changing wānanga or university environment in New Zealand and overseas.

Leadership is essentially everyone's business. Anyone is potentially a leader in his or her own right. Nowadays, leadership is concerned about people being given the opportunity to realise their innate potential to move society forward, and to develop that capability in each other. Leadership competencies are not just possible but essential at every level of tertiary education institutions where everyone's contribution can be valued as part of the community's overall success.

How do you go about being a good scholar and leader? The experience of these ten senior academics points to being transforming — aiming to do things continuously and better, to welcome change, and seize whatever opportunities may arise. They made things happen because they were prepared to challenge the status quo, inspire a shared vision, and act with courage according to well considered principles. They have been able to bring people together as cohesive groups despite differences such as age, gender, religion or socio-economic status. Being themselves, surrounding themselves with people who positively care, and treating people the way they wanted to be treated are hallmarks of these ten leaders. While they gained success according to Western standards of achievement they never lost their cultural identity or the esteem of their people.

What stands out is that these scholars trace their success to early training and experiences, dreaming big, hard work, and the support of whānau at home and among peers at teachers' college and university. Many of them came from rural, materially poor backgrounds. They were encouraged by some caring individual teachers, but overall found the education system was set up in such a way that they were not expected to succeed, whereas their Pākehā compatriots were encouraged, supported and expected not to fail. Their experiences in universities were generally similar. Tertiary institutions market themselves as being proud of their academic traditions, but too often are intent on maintaining their elite status, and in so doing advantage the powerful and help them to remain influential. Those who are not 'of their kind' find the experience alienating and isolating. If universities are serious about their claim to be open-minded bastions of free thought and the conscience of society, they need to undergo a major transformation to make the tertiary experience welcoming, rewarding and beneficial for all communities.

Young and emerging Māori scholars need to be encouraged and rewarded for their efforts, not overlooked or under-utilised by people in leadership. The words *encourage* and *courage* have the same origin — heart. Scholars need heart. There is no bravery, boldness or sacrifice without heart. Enlightened leadership is needed to support emerging scholars, because the struggle to the top is arduous, requiring courage and thriving with encouragement.

Today, more so than ever before, education is the key to a better and more prosperous world and the best means by which individuals and institutions can address the challenges that come before them, and take advantage of the opportunities that arise. As the world changes around us a new Aotearoa is emerging. Māori scholars are carving out their futures, confident that they have something unique to offer the world. They aspire to break new ground, foster new communities of interest, advance new ways of working together, and promote a distinct and valued Māori world-view.

For Māori scholarship to advance and succeed during these challenging times, though, scholars must not only be culturally, academically and technically equipped but also creative, innovative, connected, inspiring and willing to transform the lives of others. They need to build on their traditional values and strengths to contribute to addressing the big issues of our age, such as sustainable resource use, community resilience in times of natural and induced environmental disasters, health and wellbeing, to name but a few.

Māori scholars are whānau-focused leaders who accept responsibility, value people, understand relationships and share aspirations. The dual accountability of Māori scholars and academics is common and challenging, given the propensity of both the tertiary institution and the community to place demands on those well equipped but rare individuals. While possible, it is difficult to juggle those twin responsibilities, i.e. to meet academic expectations and tribal/community obligations. Each role is important for the scholar. Success in one can often lead to failure in the other. Success in both comes after much practice, experience and fortitude. Leadership is the result.

As academics and scholars, Māori have a responsibility to take upon themselves multiple tasks when in academia. First, they have to be good teachers, researchers and administrators at their chosen institution. Next, they are required to be role models of good standing, attitudes and behaviour, mentoring and providing pastoral and academic support to other Māori staff and students, when required.

Another role of a Māori scholar is being prepared and willing to be used as an instrument and servant in the hands of their people, regardless of whether the timing and scope of the task may be beyond their control. And, finally, there's an educational role and acting as a go-between, interpreting Māori needs to their institution and likewise explaining to Māori the benefits of academia and the importance to the tribe of an effective working relationship and partnership with an educational institution.

Pursuing common goals through the power of people working together, greatness through collaboration, and empowerment and breakthroughs by harnessing ideas are leadership traits that successful Māori scholars/academics possess.

It is the 'soft stuff', the relationships and interactions, that are at the heart and soul of leadership. Referred to as emotional intelligence, it is concerned with being willing to self-reflect from time to time, and to commit to making connections with others. These interpersonal, relational skills sometimes have to be learned. Much more is required nowadays to develop personal abilities in order to confidently wear the mantle of leadership. No one is born with leadership in their DNA — everyone has to work at it, improving attitudes, accumulating knowledge and gaining experience. Leaders learn from their own mistakes, from mentors, and from examples all around them. They practise and enhance their skills in the pursuit of perfecting their craft.

To advance iwi development, Māori scholars need to move towards ever more interdependent and collaborative ways of working to address challenges in health, employment, education and housing. A cadre of young, innovative, creative and energetic Māori leaders, confident and skilled in te ao Pākehā while proud and proficient in te ao Māori, can be active change agents within Aotearoa New Zealand, and in taking the best of what we offer to the world.

⁂

The idea to document a selection of contemporary scholars' leadership experiences came about as a result of discussions in 2010 at wānanga held by the MANU AO Academy, an inter-university Māori academy established to advance Māori leadership and scholarship.

Apart from the people who feature in this book there were others I would have liked to include, but for various reasons was not able to. Professors Whatarangi Winiata and Sir Hirini Moko Mead were not considered as their experiences had been well covered in *A Fire in Your Belly: Māori Leaders Speak* (Huia Publishers, 2003)

Advances in Māori academic achievement owe a lot to the efforts of these ten professors, among others. They took on difficult challenges. They took advantage of opportunities presented to them. They are the torchbearers, visionaries, each one distinguished in their own way. They leave a legacy from which we can all draw inspiration and strength. When we remember their stories and experiences they become part of our own and help us to live richer lives.

As we become increasingly distanced from early visionaries there is a pressing need for contemporary leaders and scholars to be acknowledged, for them to share what they have learned, and for their achievements and insights to be documented. This will create a source of knowledge and encouragement for those seeking to advance their education, and especially for emerging scholars in search of inspiration and direction.

Toi tū te kupu, Toi tū te mana, Toi tū te whenua [9]

This whakataukī by Tinirau of Whanganui is a plea to hold fast to our culture, for without language, mana and land, the essence of being Māori would no longer exist. It is also a reminder of the importance of nurturing and maintaining wisdom, understanding and knowledge if we are to continue to live quality lives with good health and a decent standard of living, and to actively participate as global citizens.

Acknowledgements

E ngā iwi huri noa i te motu, tēnā koutou katoa.

First and foremost, thanks and congratulations to the ten scholars who agreed to share their backgrounds, experiences and visions for inclusion in this book.

Others I acknowledge include members of Te Kāhui Amokura (chaired by Professor Piri Sciascia), the Māori Committee of Universities New Zealand – Te Pōkai Tara acting as the governance entity for the MANU AO Academy, which was disestablished in 2012 when its leadership and scholarship promoting activities became integrated within the eight universities.

Important also were the contributions from my hard-working colleagues in the production of the book — Rāwiri Tinirau for his assistance with several interviews and early editing tasks, and Taniya Ward for providing administrative support.

Notes

1   Bruce Biggs. 'Jones, Pei Te Hurinui', from the Dictionary of New Zealand Biography. Te Ara — the Encyclopedia of New Zealand, updated 29-Oct-2013 www.TeAra.govt.nz/en/biographies/4j11/jones-pei-te-hurinui — quoted from A Ngata, PH Buck & MPK Sorrenson (1986). *Na to hoa aroha: From your dear friend: The correspondence between Sir Apirana Ngata and Sir Peter Buck, 1925-50* (Vol. One), Auckland University Press in association with the Alexander Turnbull Library Endowment Trust and the Māori Purposes Fund Board, p. 87

2   Mason Durie, 2007, Academy Yearbook, Royal Society of New Zealand, Wellington (A tribute written after the death of Sir Hugh Kāwharu, 19 September 2006)

3   Hirini Mead *et al* (1985), Scoping Paper: Māori Leadership in Governance, Hui Taumata, Wellington, pp 6-7

4   Brigid Heywood, 20 November 2013, 'Academic Scholarship in the 21st Century', Massey University Academic Board, p 4

5   Mason Durie *op cit*

6   Section 162 of the Education Act (1989), clause (v)

7   www.stuff.co.nz/national/education/5571101/Racist-Mutu-must-be-accountable

8   Moana Jackson, 29 July 2009, *Plant Feet not Flags*, MANU AO Seminar, Wellington

9   www.maori.cl/Proverbs.htm

RANGINUI WALKER

Professor Ranginui Walker, of Te Whakatōhea, was educated at St Peter's Māori College, Auckland Teachers' College and the University of Auckland. He taught in primary school, held a lectureship at Auckland Teachers' College, then took up a temporary lectureship in the Anthropology Department at the University of Auckland, where he completed his PhD in 1970. He then took up a permanent post in the Centre for Continuing Education at Auckland, serving there for 15 years at the interface of community relations between Māori and Pākehā. Dr Walker was secretary (and chairman) of the Auckland District Māori Council, and a member of the New Zealand Māori Council. In 1993 he was appointed professor and head of Department of Māori Studies at the University of Auckland. Now retired, he holds several local and national positions of responsibility. He and wife Deidre have three children and are grandparents to 22 mokopuna.

I had a traditional upbringing in an isolated valley in the Bay of Plenty. The Crown had confiscated our land in 1865, and our people were pushed onto a reservation up against the bush. In our household I had two grand-aunts, and nannies with moko on their chin. There was also a grand-uncle who lived with us and he seemed to spend most of his time in his room saying karakia and chanting away. We had a little farm of about 40 cows, and it was basically a subsistence existence. My father used to go hunting in the bush, coming back with pigeons and wild pigs to supplement the larder. The income from the dairy cows was used to buy goods from the local store.

We lived about 12-15 miles from Ōpōtiki in a valley full of my relations. My mother always planted her vegetables according to the phases of the moon and the Māori calendar. At harvest time they would have the first food ceremony and when it was time to harvest the kūmara and the potatoes, my relations would come around and help, and would leave laden with food in their sacks.

The valley was a little world of its own, and that was the Māori world I lived in up to age five. It was a traditional whānau and hapū living situation. My family life was characterised by love all around me. When we were on the farm my mother was constantly baking, cooking and preserving, and her pantry was full of preserves and baked goods. My parents were hard workers and we have a high work ethic in our whānau.

We were living in a safe part of the world, and it was a kind of utopia. There was always plenty of food: kaimoana, food from the bush, and the vegetables and fruit that you grew. Although we were not rich, we were never hungry. We were very fortunate, and our people were very fortunate, right around the East Coast; what remnant of coastline we had, we could see that most people had a garden in the period between 1932 and 1939. That's a part of our history that's gone. My parents went to share-milk among Pākehā farmers, among the descendants of military settlers who took our land. The owner of the farm was actually a Syrian, and he was related to us — one of his cousins was reputed to have been my father's father. This Syrian looked after my parents and eventually we became owners of this farm. We were milking about 80 to 100 cows. We were relatively well off from then on. We were among the landed gentry, but living among Pākehā. We had hunts going across our land, and my father joined the hunts. Later when I was a teenager I loved going on the horses to the hunts.

Primary education

When I went to school I learned that there were Pākehā around, and that they were different from us, and had control of everything. In fact the first Pākehā I ever saw was during the Depression of the 1930s. He was a swagman looking for work, who came to our place and was given a room in the potato house. They put down a bed for him there and I woke up in the morning and went out and saw this apparition. It scared the daylights out of me. He had a red face like cooked crayfish. That was the first Pākehā I'd ever seen. The other Pākehā I came to know was the district nurse, who would come in and check up on us. Afterwards, I met Pākehā authority figures at school and elsewhere in town.

At the age of five I went to the convent school in Ōpōtiki, which was a huge shift from this utopian valley where the Māori way of life dominated, to the town where the Pākehā dominated. We lived about four miles from town. I caught the bus to the school and the first day at school I'm dragged before the nuns for speaking Māori. As a five-year-old, you learn quickly that Māori language was considered inferior and disallowed. I'd go home, my parents would talk Māori to me and I'd answer in English. That is how my Māori language started to fade away — the assimilationist process of the educators, those who control the education system, worked on me. The nuns and priests were Irish, so we learned about Ireland, the Emerald Isle, sang the Irish songs and there were Christian icons of Mary and Joseph and Jesus. That is the imposition of a foreign culture on vulnerable five-year-olds. The convent taught me the unhealthy teachings of suppression, oppression, and domination of my mind. I realised that Pākehā dominated the world, the local council and the police. None of my relations were in positions of power and my townie cousins couldn't speak Māori. When I went to school I realised why this was so.

Secondary education

When I was 13 my parents decided they didn't want me to go to the local high school because the young students were smoking, running around the streets at lunchtime and so on. They chose Hāto Pētera, St Peter's Māori College, which was just being opened in 1946 for the first time as a secondary school. My uncle had been there when it was a rural training school for young men and one of its objectives was to train young Māori men as catechists, but ideally to recruit them for the priesthood. That hardly ever happened. More often than not they'd have 12 to 15 young men in training. St Peter's had quite a big piece of land at that point. It was over 200 acres and the college was farming cows and pigs, and the boys were taught those manual and agricultural training skills together with elementary English and arithmetic.

The Māori Catholic community wanted a secondary school because Governor Grey had given 270 acres to the Catholic Church. Apparently Whina Cooper sold some of her own land up at Hokianga to help support the school and get it going. I remember them opening the school with Whina up on the stage. She had this little pine tree sitting on the stage with money on it and getting donations from the people. I was 13 going on 14 at the time. St Peter's started with only 46 pupils, and we fielded two rugby teams. It was very religious, dominated by the priests — the Marists did the teaching and the Mill

Hill priests took the religious aspects. They were very strict and authoritarian. I liked the Marist brothers. They were good teachers. I also admired the headmaster, Brother Patrick, affectionately known to the students as Patty. He liked softball, so he trained us to play it.

There was no problem with the brothers — they were all good teachers — but the Mill Hill fathers were strict, spiritual disciplinarians. No newspapers were allowed in the school in case our minds were contaminated by stories of rape and untoward material like that. Prayer in the mornings, karakia at lunchtime, karakia in the evening, and there was also Mass. I knew the Jesuit axiom was true; give me a child for the first seven years, and he's mine for life. That's what the Catholic Church does to you. It was indoctrination, and I rebelled internally against the lack of intellectual freedom. For instance we were taught that there were certain books you must not read, like Darwin's *Origin of Species*, Huxley's *Brave New World* and Karl Marx's *Das Kapital*. This didn't make sense to me.

When we arrived at school we had to surrender all our money to the priests. Saturday was the only day we had off, and it was like living in a monastery really. We'd be allowed to go and walk about Takapuna, Northcote, and some of us used to get as far as Devonport and Milford, having a look around. Of course, some boys kept some of their money. We hid money in our shoes and would go to the pictures in the afternoon. The priests would come and wait outside the picture theatres and take our names down. The next Saturday you weren't allowed out. You were put on the roster to rub down the walls. It's this authoritarian domination of your liberty. It took me 30 years to get the Catholic Church out of my system. The only thing it taught me is right from wrong, but you can learn that anyway without it being imposed on you from the outside by an outside kind of philosophic system.

Early Māori academic involvement

The year 1894 saw the first Māori graduates, with Āpirana Ngata followed by Peter Buck, and later Māui Pōmare and Tūtere Wī Repa. Those men went into Parliament, but these educated graduates were a challenge to the nexus of power dominated by Pākehā. From 1910 there was a deliberate policy in the Education Department to shut Māori out of the professions. The directors of education, including William Bird, the inspector of Native Schools, were adamant they did not want Māori to enter the professions. Instead, they wanted Māori men to be trained in manual work, such as agricultural workers, and Māori women to become domesticated. That was a deliberate policy of tracking Māori downwards and away from the professions. Te Aute College was encouraged to change its curriculum, and to discontinue the matriculation curriculum. When they refused to comply with the department's policy, scholarships were suspended for boys going to Te Aute. That's why there is a gap between the first wave of Māori graduates and the second wave, and I am a part of this latter wave.

We came in the 1950s: Hugh Kāwharu, Pat Hōhepa, Matiu Te Hau, Hirini Mead, all those people. After secondary school, there were very few options for people of my generation. For many of us, the only option we had was to go into teaching. The policy of steering Māori away from the professions led to a shortage of assistants for the native schoolteachers. The native schools were in isolated rural Māori communities, in the tribal hinterlands. Māori was the number one language of the children going to those native schools, but all the teachers were Pākehā. Imagine the culture clash that went on there, and so the headmaster had to resort to recruiting a local person as a junior assistant, invariably Māori, to help the Pākehā teacher with the infants and to induct them into school routines. Suddenly the headmaster finds that these assistants are quite clever and that they would make good teachers. It was recommended to the Department of Education that they be trained as teachers and that's when the department changed its policy to introduce the Māori quota to teacher training, just before the 1939 war. The first intake included people like Matt Te Hau and Johnny Waititi, Bruce Biggs and his wife Te Aroha, but when the war intervened they went off to war. Those that survived came back, completed their teaching and then went out into the rural schools. When they did their country service, three years, they would be integrated into the general education system, and one of the first to do so was my uncle, Matt Te Hau. He had spent three years down at Ruātoki, then he came to Auckland and taught at Ōrākei Primary School and later the prestigious Normal Intermediate School. At that time I had arrived in Auckland as a student in 1950-51. There were about 30 of us, from all around New Zealand. That's how we managed to break into teaching.

The curriculum at St Peter's Māori College was not great. Imagine a small school of 46 students. We were not taught maths or chemistry — there was not enough capacity in the school, so we were denied these subjects. I sat School Certificate in Māori, English, horticulture, geography and general science. The profession I wanted to go into was medicine, but we did not have the relevant subjects at St Peter's, so the only place for me to go into was teaching. Uncle Matt at Normal Intermediate became uncle to all the students of that intermediate school, and also at training college. He also became uncle to all the students that managed to make it into university. He taught Māori at Wesley College on Saturday mornings. He was a perfectionist, and an amazing teacher.

Creating space within the academy

Āpirana Ngata campaigned from 1925 to establish a lectureship in Māori Studies. He got the University of Auckland Council to agree, but they did nothing. He fought for 20 years to get funding for a lectureship, but couldn't get the funding. In 1939 the Young Māori Leaders Conference agreed that should happen but the war interrupted further work. After the war, in 1949, Maharaia Winiata, who was a former Methodist minister, was appointed lecturer in adult education at Auckland University. That was the first foothold Māori got into the university system and it was in adult education. Why? Because that was one recommendation of the 1939 Young Māori Leaders Conference organised by Ngata at Auckland University. The conference agreed to a Centre for Māori Studies and they wanted adult education as well. In 1951 Ralph Piddington, the first professor of anthropology, recruited Bruce Biggs, who was teaching at Manutahi, to be a junior lecturer in Māori. This was an important step in our initial breakthrough into the academy. This showed us how power works. The candidates for that job would have been Matt Te Hau, Bruce Biggs, Maharaia Winiata and possibly Johnny Waititi. The system chose Bruce Biggs. This is what the system does — chooses someone like themselves. They would rule a person like Maharaia Winiata out as too pro-Māori, and being pro-Māori is interpreted as having a chip on your shoulder. That's the way politics work. So our first appointment was in adult education, an unthreatening place.

When Bruce Biggs was recruited, the Romance languages department opposed the appointment because as the French language professor said, Māori is a language with no literature, with no scholarship around it. Dr Bill Geddes, who was the senior lecturer in anthropology, a new department at the time, sent Bruce to the library to gather various books, such as *Ngā Mōteatea*, *Te Paipera Tapu* (Māori Bible) and *Ngā Mahi ā Ngā Tūpuna*. He did a collection, and then he tabled them as proof of scholarly literature. After much opposition, a resolution was passed for Māori to be taught. That's part of a fight to get the

Ranginui Walker's biography of Sir Āpirana Ngata.

breakthrough into the system. Bruce won the position in a racist mêlée. Bruce said later that he realised it was racist, but he thought that what gave him the edge against Matt Te Hau was that he had an idea about research, which is what the university liked. Matt never held it against Bruce. He supported him and taught in the department, as did John Waititi and all the other people, and of course Bruce became the pre-eminent scholar in linguistics in the South Pacific and helped grow the Department of Anthropology.

Importance of unions

At teachers' training college, out of 1000 students there were only 30 who were Māori, and we hung about together. We were all mates. We went to the dances together, to the socials at the college. We went to rugby matches, to the pubs, and occasionally we had Pākehā mates as well. I had a Pākehā mate who grew up on the North Shore and he was a bit older than me. He took me down to the wharves to work on the ships at night and earn some pocket money. We worked along with the union guys when they were shorthanded. One time we went there, there was a little hubbub going on, and we found out that there was to be a strike, and that the union guys would be shut out. That event was the 1951 waterfront strike. I was horrified at what was done to the wharfies because a lot of Māori were working on the wharves at that time. All our relations were working there, and they were shut out. Employers in Auckland were prohibited from employing them. The soldier boys from military training were brought in to man the wharves. Māori in Auckland survived by going out to Kawakawa Bay getting mussels and watercress and eels and other kaimoana. It was a bad time in our history, but it was just another symptom of the oppressive nature of power in this country, which has a long history from the time of the King Movement, Parihaka, Maungapōhatu, to the waterfront strike. I could see that the state had this power to oppress working-class people and they were being branded as communists.

The unions at that time were perceived as getting too powerful and there was a class war on. They fought it in terms of class war. I was astonished at how well paid we were on the boats. Being a farmer and a hard worker, I would work like hell and the wharfies would tell me to slow down, so that the work would be drawn out. We were working out at the Onehunga wharves and we were told that if we finished before lunch, we could go home. But if we didn't finish before lunch and stayed for an hour after lunch, we would get paid for the rest of the day. This was all good experience and I learnt a lot.

When I went out to work in the freezing works in Westfield, the union men turned up on payday asking for me to pay the union subscription and I saw no reason to pay it. I asked why I should pay the subscription. I was told that the steel caps, fleecy jackets and gloves I wore were all conditions negotiated by the union. The timeout from the chillers was another condition. I understood, and paid them the money. That's all a learning process and at that time the wharfies and the freezing work unions were strong. They were getting dirt money, they were getting danger money, they were getting double and triple time. There was a ship that had a broken back in the harbour; the decks were also buckled and we had to clean it out. As wharfies we were paid triple time on a Sunday to do that. Those conditions are gone now. The unions have been de-powered by both the Labour and the National governments. It's a different world now, from those times. My generation lived in the fat years. I feel sorry for the current generation of students. There was always plenty of work between the 1950s and the 1960s. You could always get work during the holiday periods. That's not the case now because of mechanisation.

Teaching career

Teachers' college was not really intellectually challenging, but you learned how to teach when you went out in the schools on section. After I graduated I went up north to teach for three years. I taught at Pipiwai, about 30 miles from Whāngārei, and I loved it up there. I was teaching primer three and four, and what an experience. I then spent about 18 months at Whangaruru. When I would go home to Ōpōtiki for my holidays, this Syrian relation who had married into our whānau would welcome me in Māori. He would say "Haere mai Rangi Te Pākehā."

"What are you talking about?" I'd reply.

"You know," he'd say. That's what the education system had done to me, turned me into a Pākehā, so he was teasing me. It wasn't until years later I understood, but of course what the Pākehā had done was to create a weapon to be used against them later in life. They didn't realise what they had spawned, because I came to understand the Pākehā mentality, the Pākehā system.

At Pipiwai I realised there was a dissonance between me, 'Rangi Te Pākehā', coming into this Māori community. The valley was jammed with people living at a subsistence level, contract working, working in the freezing works at Moerewa, fencing and shearing. Here we had these kids with their different culture, and the separate culture of the school. I had put the sums up on the board and one of the Shortland kids within a minute or two was sitting up, as if he had finished. I said, "Have you finished?"

"Yes sir." Big smile on his face, beautiful dimples, and I looked at his work and he'd written one, two, three down the side but he had not computed the

Ranginui Walker
with his class at
Mt Eden.

sums. I thought, there's a lot of teaching to do here. Here I was trying to teach
these kids how to be like Pākehā. There's a real distance between us and the
culture foisted on us. I went to Whangaruru and then to Punaruku.

I was put into the district high school to teach; I went from teaching the
primers to teaching third to fifth form, maybe 15 or 16 children in the high
school. I loved it and I thought that this is where I would like to make a
future for myself, in secondary school. That required a degree, so I enrolled
for a degree at the University of Auckland, part-time. I soon realised it was an
impossible mission, because books were hard to come by, and were either out
of print or unprocurable.

University study and work

My wife Deidre and I returned to Auckland in 1955 and I enrolled at university.
I only did two papers the first year, getting an A for anthropology and a B for
Māori. I thought, gee, I worked too hard because the anti-intellectual culture
of students at that time was, oh so and so got an A, they sucked up to their
lecturer. From then on I just set my sights low to just get Cs, and pass that way,
never dreaming about the consequences of competition later on, on your CV.
So I'm teaching day school at Mt Eden and going to lectures in the afternoon.
A lot of the lectures were after three o'clock so we could do degrees part-time,
but to supplement the poor pay we teachers had to take on extra jobs. For me
it was to teach English and arithmetic to new immigrants at Seddon Tech,
mainly Pacific Island people. That was a night job. Then Johnny Waititi tapped

me on the shoulder and asked if I would help out at Queen Victoria Girls' School. Because of our camaraderie and the nature of the struggle I couldn't say no.

John Waititi and I were like soulmates, and he needed someone to teach at Queen Victoria, so I took it on. My Māori language was poor. It was in recovery mode from learning at the university. Here I was put in the position of having to teach the language, and I had been trained to do that at Queen Victoria Girls' School. I had three jobs, a day job and two night jobs, and luckily they were on different nights. I was going to university at the same time. Deidre would give me bread and fill a flask up with soup, laden with bacon bone leftovers, and I would sit in my car at night and have my dinner between lectures and teaching, and get home at 9 o'clock. Those are the hard yards that one does.

Lecturing and doctoral study

It took me seven years part-time to complete my bachelor's degree. I was then asked to lecture at teachers' training college, and again I witnessed the use of power. They established a lectureship there, and appointed Harry Lambert. He was a nice man but like many of us, not a native speaker of Māori, whereas there were better candidates like Johnny Waititi, Maharaia Winiata and others. During this time, Maharaia and Matt Te Hau had expanded the footprint of adult education. Matt had subsequently been recruited into university as well, where they both worked hard and backed up Bruce Biggs in the development of Māori Studies. Te Hau and Winiata went out into the communities and worked on the ground. They had their lectures on marae. Matt lectured in Northland, and Maharaia throughout the Waikato and Bay of Plenty. They shared what they had and worked hard. We had those influential people opening the doors for us, pioneering the way, and we followed, expanding and building on their efforts.

I was shoulder-tapped to replace Harry Lambert, because I was conservative at the time, and thought of as a 'safe' Māori. I went there to do my best to improve the situation at teachers' college. I would go down the motorway and cut bundles of flax and teach the students how to make kits and other items like that. Student enrolment grew and when I left it was ready to be taken to another level by the person who followed me, Vernon Penfold. I then decided to do a master's degree part-time, while teaching at teachers' college. I loved teachers' college, the training, the age group. It felt very comfortable, a good job to have. But after five years, I realised it was intellectually unchallenging and that I was in danger of stagnating.

Guest lecturer
at North Shore
Teachers' College.

I was over 30 years old, so I decided to return to university and do a doctorate, after being encouraged to do so by Bruce Biggs, who was leaving for Hawai'i. He put in place a temporary lectureship for me and I was pitchforked into teaching anthropology. The lecture room was crammed, people were spilling out the doorway and I was right in among them. They had come to listen to me, so I made sure that I prepared well. That's one thing you learn at training college, to prepare your work thoroughly before you go in front of a class. People still come up to me and say how they enjoyed those lectures.

When I went to see the professor about doing a doctorate he looked at my academic record and could see this string of Cs in the bachelor's. He wasn't too pleased, but he let me enrol. It was a different world then, because the universities were laissez-faire. There wasn't the training that you give students now. They didn't teach you anything about bibliographies, or how to write essays. While enrolled for a doctorate I was teaching at the university and then I'd go straight out to Ōtara and do the fieldwork. I would spend all day out there, well into the night, because Māori hui at night time for the local marae or whatever the organisation, and hui would go on until late. At weekends I would participate in sport with rugby and basketball teams. There were a lot of Māori working in local industry who would organise sports teams. They would all come together at weekends to fraternise, have a hāngi, and so on.

I made myself part of the community out in Ōtara while I was doing my research. I had to choose a role that didn't compromise my position as an observer, the classic anthropological participant observer. I took notes and recordings and I would come back late at night and write up some of my thoughts of the day. Within 18 months, I had enough material to start writing. I wrote about 70 or 80 pages. No one taught you how to write a thesis; you just looked at other theses. I took my first piece of writing to Professor Piddington and he asked me who my supervisor was. I told him that it was him. That's how laissez-faire it was. He said "No, but who are you seeing?" In other words, I'm too busy to see you. "Go and see Hugh Kāwharu," he said. I saw Hugh and gave him my writing. He told me that I had a thesis, and to finish it. All pretty laissez-faire.

In my third year of my doctorate I won the Queen Elizabeth II Scholarship. I removed myself from university lecturing and concentrated on finishing writing. That was the only time I had the luxury of a full-time year at university. I completed my thesis at the end of 1969 and handed it in.

Further work and community experiences

Within no time at all my uncle, Matt Te Hau, recruited me to work in adult education. The interesting thing here is what a doctorate does for you. I had no idea where I was going once I'd completed the doctorate. I had resigned from my job at training college, and the temporary lectureship at university. But I didn't wait long till I had a job. Matt offered me the job in adult education. He also told me that there had been trouble in the Auckland District Māori Council and he wanted me to take on the role of secretary. Arapeta Awatere came to me with the same request. These elders coming to me, identifying me as a person with a doctorate who had the skills and abilities to do these jobs, flattered me. My job was to resurrect the Auckland District Māori Council after a string of scandals.

I was also lecturing on Māori things in Continuing Education. I'd organise my lectures, present them at night to a mainly Pākehā audience from the garden suburbs of Titirangi and the like. They were lovely middle-class people, but there were no Māori. I'm teaching them about Māori. Māori were not enrolling in adult education unless their courses were on the marae. Therefore, I would do my bit teaching there, then turn my attention to the work of the Auckland District Māori Council. We had no money or resources, so I would use my wife's typewriter. I'd call a meeting of the council and few would turn up, and I had this long list of marae committees. The council was the kēhua. Uncle Matt was the chairman, and Titewhai Harawira and Syd Jackson would turn up for hui, and occasionally Dennis Hansen and some others. When I read the Welfare Act, I soon realised that the Māori Council was a paper tiger. I would write up the minutes, come home, Deidre would help type them, and

I'd take them into Māori Affairs because we didn't have any copying systems. Then I'd bring the minutes of hui home, and we'd put them into envelopes and post them. Having done the hard yards at the very first hui I called, I was attacked by one of the members — he perceived me as having come in off the street and taken this important position. I couldn't believe it, but that's the nature of politics — you are tested. I stood up to them and one day, after about the third meeting, it was so bad that Matt closed the meeting. So I thought the only way to re-organise this council is to go out to the people. The following year I organised hui so that we would go to marae around the region. We learned from the grassroots what was expected of the Auckland District Māori Council, including that the council had been charging marae $40 for their annual subscription, instead of the normal $20 fee!

When I saw a Māori being slammed in the press, I felt it. Here I was, given the job to try and straighten things out, and we were down in the dumps. When this marae subscription fiasco happened I wrote back to inform marae that the subscription was only $20. That's when they realised they had a secretary with integrity, and that's when the marae started to come to our hui and engage with the council. We slowly started to grow as we went from marae to marae. Over the next two or three years we built up attendance at the council's monthly hui so that at our height we had 36 Māori committees across the Auckland metropolitan area, from Wellsford down to Pukekohe. Now we had a political platform to attack the system, but we had no resources to deal with the resource consents that came in from the local bodies. There were multiple local bodies across the region at that time and we were getting planning consents and deviations from the regional plan, and they were coming to me and I was trying to get back to them and meet their timelines. I didn't have the resources or time to do this, but luckily I identified Peter Rikys, a young lawyer, and he willingly joined the council and took up a lot of the local body planning consents. I decided that the council had to be more efficient. We organised a planning committee and saw that even they found the workload heavy. The only way to do this was to become part of the system; because being outside of the system, the power structure is oppressive. I decided to get onto the relevant committee on the Auckland Regional Council. I read the Town and Country Planning Act and in Section 3 (1G) it refers to matters of cultural importance to Māori. I then wrote to the Auckland Regional Council and I told them the Auckland District Māori Council wants a place on the Planning Council for Māori. Fortunately the head of the Planning Council at that time was Barry Curtis, who had worked in Tūhoe as a surveyor and understood where I was coming from. He argued in the Planning Council and they agreed to support Māori representation and took the matter to the Regional Council for approval. It was won only on the casting vote of the chairman. They agreed to have a person on the Planning Council and we put Pauline Kingi on as our representative. That's how you use power to kick doors open.

I'm teaching about Māori to the middle-class elite of Auckland at night school and in the weekends I'm busy on council business rousing up Māori on the ground. I would read in the paper that a secretary or person, too often a Māori, had absconded with funds. I would run training hui on organisation and administration of committees and management of funds. Then there was the gang problem. They too were hitting the headlines, so I'd organise a seminar on the gangs, and they would come to the university and we'd talk the problems over. Then there was the business of Māori getting arrested for taking shellfish beyond their quota. I would organise a conference on fisheries and we had the Ministry of Agriculture and Fisheries come and we would try talking to them about Māori conservation practices, about the principle of rāhui and other issues. We knew we were dealing with a mono-cultural power structure and we were trying to bring about understanding and transformations that way.

I also started organising big national conferences on land use for Māori leaders because Māori were stuck on sheep farming and dairy farming. We had a person from up north come and talk about three-tier farming in microclimate areas. We were trying to introduce alternative scenarios to Māori people on the ground. Those are the sorts of things I would do at weekends, and I decided the best place to run those national hui was at Tūrangawaewae Marae in Ngāruawāhia, supported by the Māori Queen and the Kīngitanga movement.

The most influential hui I ran was the 1984 conference on Māori educational development. It had come to my notice that the Department of Education had organised a development conference around the curriculum, which had not been looked at for over 20 years, and that no Māori had been invited to participate. I then wrote to the department and asked why. They said that they were not to blame, rather it was the fault of the Post Primary Teachers' Association, and that they should nominate people on to this committee. Instead of writing to the PPTA, I thought that we would have our own education conference. This was about Māori doing it for ourselves, empowering ourselves. I organised this hui in 1984, and many people came. This conference was a major development for Māori. I can recall Whatarangi Winiata coming, and he would tease me and say that I had already organised what the resolutions were. I said no, it came out of the conference.

I was involved in Continuing Education, and the university regards it as not a proper academic discipline, but on the periphery. I didn't regard it as the periphery. I regarded myself as being in a key position where I could interface between the university and the Māori community and I had a free rein to do what I thought was necessary to improve the situation for Māori. That is why I stayed in Continuing Education for 18 years. I had no particular wish to teach in an academic department, as I had already tasted that. I was using the position that I had to the maximum. I knew that I had tenure and academic freedom — the right to be the critic and conscience of society — and I espoused that role in the Auckland District Māori Council and in the New Zealand Māori Council. Like for instance when a young 17-year-old, Daniel Houpapa, was shot outside the police station in Taumarunui, the father was very conciliatory. However, when a reporter went down and investigated the situation, he found that it was like an extra-judicial killing. At that time we had an oppressive system in place. We had an authoritarian, dictatorial prime minister in Rob Muldoon. I thought to myself, I'm prepared to take this on, because I'm in a secure role. Syd Jackson and Ngā Tamatoa kept talking to the father, but by this time the trail was growing cold. Finally, the father changed his mind and decided to request a judicial inquiry. He came to Auckland with a motion to ask me for support. I was prepared to take it on, and took the motion to the Māori Council calling for an inquiry into the shooting. To my surprise Ben Couch MP turns up at the hui and attacks me. My brother-in-law, Graham Latimer, who is chairing the hui, lets Ben continue, and he referred to us as radicals from Auckland. When the motion was put, the New Zealand Māori Council voted against having an inquiry. I challenged their decision, given that the matter had been brought before them with pain and tears: heke o te roimata, te hupe. I returned to Auckland and reported to my council. Eddie McLeod, the secretary of the Māori Council at one time, reminded me that Ben Couch was not a member of the council and that he should not have been at the meeting. We put the motion again and we argued the case. One by one the District Māori Council representatives voted for it. A very conservative group went to Wellington to present the case for an inquiry, and Muldoon turned them away. If I had gone, I would have argued against Muldoon, but that's how it all works. We didn't have an inquiry, and the consequence of not having an inquiry at least provided the basis for action for subsequent cases, such as the events that saw shootings in Wellington and Waitara later on. The conditions are still there and we suffer the consequences of not having had a commission of inquiry into police procedures.

Whānau role modelling

When your parents and elders give a name to a person, there's a point to the name. Ranginui, my name, belongs to everybody, so I work for everybody. I

Three generations: Ranginui Walker with his son Michael (left) and grandson Curtis.

put 100% of my effort here in Auckland on behalf of all Māori. At one point the people back home said to my mother, "Why doesn't your boy come back here to help with his own people?" Now, my mother was the pillar of our marae and I'm sure she felt the pain of that. I've since done that for her, over the last 20 years, and I've been a member of the Whakatōhea Māori Trust Board.

Whānau is everything to me. If you have a good, safe upbringing, then all the potential within you will just unfold naturally. A good home background is fundamental to success. For the first time we have intergenerational graduation. My three children are all graduates. Two of them are doctors: one an anaesthetist and one a paediatrician. The anaesthetist, Stuart, is much admired in his field. My daughter, Wendy, is the paediatrician. She's the clinical director at Middlemore Hospital. My other son, Michael, is a professor of biology and he is at the top of his field. He's a member of the Royal Society, a singular achievement for a Māori. In the next generation, all of Stuart's children are graduates. Three of them are doctors, one is an architect and one a teacher at Selwyn College. Michael's daughter is doing a doctorate at the moment in science, and his son is doing an engineering degree, completing his fourth year. He started work in the Christmas holidays at Fisher & Paykel. Hopefully he'll get a permanent job there. So we have inter-generational graduation now. So it's now a tradition in our whānau to follow a certain path. I've got two mokopuna at the University of Otago. One is going to do medicine; the other business studies. Our whānau numbers thirty-two people when we are together, counting the in-laws. We've planted our tūrangawaewae up north at Pipiwai. We are Ngāti Ranginui at Whananaki. My son bought ten acres and my daughter and her husband bought 60 acres, so we've got a standing in the north. We're the new tribe of Northland. They don't know it yet.

Further tertiary experiences and commentary

The University of Auckland was the pioneer of Māori Studies, and when Bruce Biggs returned to New Zealand he became the expert in linguistics in the South Pacific. Gradually the department grew and grew. When I was in Continuing Education, I applied for a job at Massey University. There was a professorship in anthropology, and applicants were required to demonstrate some knowledge of Māori. I applied for the position to test the veracity of that statement. They didn't know that. I was shortlisted and there were other candidates as well. In the end, Massey decided not to make an appointment. Later, they contacted me and asked whether there was any merit in splitting the position between anthropology and Māori Studies, and whether I would consider the appointment in Māori Studies. I said yes, to keep the door open

With Deirdre and eight mokopuna tuarua.

With Graham Hinangaroa Smith at Nanaimo Bay, after the opening
of the long house at University of British Columbia, Canada.

by testing the veracity of what was tagged in that anthropology professorship.
I had no intention of going to Massey. Mason Durie was on the appointments
committee at that time, so to avoid going to Massey, I went to Hugh Kāwharu.
I told Hugh that I had been in Continuing Education for 18 years, making a
mark, and that Massey was likely to offer me a chair in Māori Studies. I asked
if there was an alternative offer, and the University of Auckland came back with
an associate professor position.

In 1987 I returned from being on leave, and Bruce Biggs asked me to
teach the post-Treaty components within the Introduction to Māori Society
paper. I agreed to do that. This is what you do when you do the hard yards —
pukumahi, ringa raupā — you take on the jobs, no matter what. I had my own
jobs, but here's an additional one that is good for the people. Bruce taught the
first half of the course, and I taught the latter. He taught that Māori were at
the last end of the line, that they had lost their ability to navigate. They had
from Bruce the negative, deficit-theory perspective and I offered hope and
positive affirmation from a post-Treaty perspective. When I started teaching
this large audience of students, I could sense the negativity and the anger
among them, from the nature of the questions, especially from the Pākehā
students. I told them that what they had heard comes from various sources,
written by Pākehā authors. Most historiography is Pākehā, but when you put

it together it doesn't make a pretty picture and that's what the angst was from the Pākehā students. One thing I did when teaching post-Treaty issues was to make the lectures relevant and topical. I was involved on the ground with the post-Treaty machinations myself, going to all the hui, including the hui hosted by Hepi Te Heuheu to establish the tribal-focused National Māori Congress. I was feeding those experiences into my lectures. The students appreciated getting fresh material, hot off the press. Gradually I decided there was an even greater need for this. I lifted the cap on student enrolment for this course and it exploded. Other departments were sending their students to do my course. By that time Bruce had left, and I had taken over the entire paper. By the end of the course, Pākehā students would thank me for opening their eyes. This Stage I course became the basis of my book *Ka Whawhai Tonu Mātou: Struggle Without End.*

There had been a real enthusiasm and development in the 1990s at universities in the Māori Studies area — it hasn't been looked at since. The whole drive, immense enthusiasm and vitality which were there, somehow seems to be gone now. It dissipated and it hasn't come back at all, and while we tend to think, well, perhaps a change of leadership is needed or a different personality, there's something else missing. It's not quite there at the moment.

I was immersed, interfaced with the community as well as the university. I was going to many hui and on the Māori Council; I was in a key position and this was informing my teaching. Everything was happening around us in Auckland, and outside in the political arena, I was not afraid to challenge political leaders. You have to have the guts to stand up and speak the truth to those in powerful positions. I had the guts to do that because I know what it is like and I was in a secure job. Muldoon once wrote to the vice-chancellor of the University of Auckland about me, calling for me to be dismissed for teaching subversive views. Fortunately the university stuck by its principle of intellectual freedom, critic and conscience of society. That is one of the beauties of working in the academy. There are very few people who had the guts to come out and espouse that role. Most people are very conforming.

I am glad I decided to give up my Māori Council work in 1990, because I felt my career was important to me. I was an associate professor but I wanted to be a full professor one day and my career was stalling because I was doing too much outside. At the 1987 Auckland District Māori Council elections the radicals came in to try and take this mana that I had. A whole lot of committees came with their money to register to be able to vote, and Deidre was the secretary taking the money, and after the hui the cheques bounced. This was Māori politics at its worst. They filibustered, trying to win the chairmanship, but in the end I got voted back. At the next election I announced I was going to retire. I didn't tell them I was going back to attend to my professional roles. The Māori wardens wanted to honour me so they suggested they nominate me for a knighthood. Deidre and I are not in favour of knighthoods, but I didn't have the heart to discourage them. That nomination lay on the table from 1990 through to 2000 when Labour came to power, but by that time the knighthoods had gone. I was contacted about whether I would accept the DCNZM, which I accepted, because that's a New Zealand award. It's not the old imperial award. When the imperial awards were reinstated, people had the option to reclaim them. I stood out against the imperial award system, and I am glad I did. The British Empire has a lot to answer for: they stomped all around the world ruining the cultures of indigenous people who had their own culture and design for life. What we had worked, it was successful, and it was environmentally friendly. They came around and ruined that.

At the Ngā Pae o te Māramatanga award for excellence in research, 2007: (standing) Stuart Walker, Rosemary Pohio, Philip Beattie, Wendy Walker, Leilani Walker, Punahamoa Walker; (sitting) Rātana Walker, Deirdre Walker, Ranginui Walker, Michael Walker.

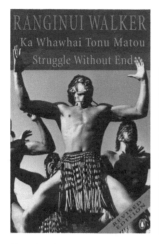  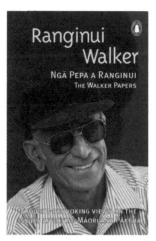

More books by Ranginui Walker.

In 1990 I had already started writing the first edition of *Struggle Without End*, then I went overseas on leave looking at our Pacific Island connections. I learned a lot there and came back and concentrated on teaching and expanding Māori Studies at Auckland. I had to teach classes twice per week, and there were many tutors to support the programme. Deidre used to help me mark the many scripts. I was doing the hard yards in the Department and of course in 1993 when Hugh Kāwharu left I slotted in as professor. It was a hard slog to get there.

We need to look after ourselves, and our fellow colleagues and be the independent voice of reason, a critic and conscience of society.

Ngāhuia Te Awekōtuku

Ngāhuia Te Awekōtuku was Professor of Research in the School of Māori and Pacific Development at the University of Waikato until 2014. With other degrees in Art History and English, her PhD (1981) was in Psychology. This experience contributed to her writing an early (1991) monograph on Māori research ethics. For years she worked in the heritage and creative sectors as a curator, governor, and activist/advocate. Her many publications include two works of fiction: *Tahuri: Stories* (1989) and *Ruahine: Mythic Women* (2003) and the prizewinning *Mau Moko: the world of Māori tattoo*. Her research interests include sex and gender issues, museums, body modification, power and powerlessness, spirituality, ritual and exploring Māori ways of death.

Where did it start for me and what about my whānau? My whānau is a very complicated organism. He mea whāngai ahau e tētahi whānau i Ōhinemutu i a Ngāti Whakaue. I was adopted, raised by a family in Ngāti Whakaue, Ōhinemutu, Rotorua, because my biological parents were quite old at the time of my birth. My paternal half-sisters are now in their late 80s, my maternal siblings all in the 70s. My mother was from Ngāti Pikiao and Ngāti Rangiteaorere, as well as Ngāti Mahuta of Waikato, and my father from Ngāti Whakaue, and Tamakaimoana of Tūhoe. They were my biological parents and once lived in the area where I grew up in Ōhinemutu. I mention my whakapapa because it had quite a significant impact on me later.

My whāngai family were weavers. They were wāhine whāwhā harakeke; singers, entertainers, haka people and tourist guides. My mother, Paparoa, whom I call mother although she was tōku whāea ātawhai, my adopted mother, was the daughter of Hera and Ruapotakataka Tāwhai. Hera of course was of Ngāti Whakaue, and Ngāti Rangiwewehi. Ruapotakataka was from Waimā, up north, so my mummy was of mixed iwi heritage and my kuia was this magical being who lived in the pā harakeke, her flax plantation, and was an extraordinary person. My first teachers were my kuia Hera and Paparoa. Her husband was from Ngāti Toa and Ngāti Raukawa ki Ōtaki, and probably the less said about him the better. He moved in and out of the household over the years. But my real learning and initial introduction to how you learn and how you teach was my kuia and my mother, in the family.

Now, how did they do it? They were both notable weavers, particularly Hera. She made the korowai cloak for Queen Elizabeth II on the occasion of her visit here to New Zealand in 1953. So I was this little girl growing up surrounded by flax, tukutuku, pīngao, tāniko, whatu and raranga, in this amazing household, in the pā, Ōhinemutu. Stuff hanging from the ceilings, stuff hanging off the walls, and stuff underfoot, yet I was not a weaver. I wasn't really interested in it, or good at it at all. I had ten left fingers and thumbs, but I grew up with my kuia who not only did the kākahu for the British Queen, but she was — I know this sounds whakahīhī or vain — one of the principal weaving tutors and experts during the Ngata revival of the 1920s and '30s. She used to travel all around the country with him. One of her major works is the tukutuku (panel work) and the tāniko pulpit at St Mary's at Tikitiki as well as the tukutuku and the tāniko pulpit in St Faith's Anglican Church in Ōhinemutu. Most of the work was a collective effort as she taught many others well but those two pulpits, that was solo work, i.e. her own work. Why I mention Hera is that she had this strong sense of excellence — a particularly uncompromising view about what she considered to be good.

In our house in Ōhinemutu is a beautiful panel of tukutuku originally prepared for the restored Tamatekapua in the late 1930s. My kuia Hera withheld it. I asked her why it wasn't in Tamatekapua and she said to me, "Me āta titiro, look closely at it and start counting and then you'll know." I looked at the design and a line was one cross out. One māwhitiwhiti or cross-stitch was missing. From a distance you'd never know. You would only know if you went there and you counted the lines. For my kuia, that was not good enough. It could not go in to a prestigious whare rūnanga, so it ended up at home. It was slightly flawed but there it was in our sitting room, and it's still there today.

My kuia was equally critical and compulsive about the people that she taught. My mummy, who worked in later life at the Māori Arts & Crafts Institute at Whakarewarewa with Emily Schuster and others, had the same rigour. She was notorious, as was my kuia, for unpicking people's work. They were perfectionists. If they saw something out of the ordinary in someone's tāniko belt or kete they would pull it all apart. They'd sit there and undo it. They'd find the ara (line of plaiting) or the aho (weft) and they'd say, "Back you go. We won't accept work that is not perfect." So those were my grounding values in a way from my mummy, my aunties, who were also weavers, and most of all my grandmother, my kuia Hera. For all of her notions of excellence, she was the most humble, easygoing, sweet-natured, wouldn't say boo to a goose, worker. She certainly did not have airs and graces. On the marae she was a real ringa raupā, a hard worker, in the kitchen, at the back. She was the real deal and so was Paparoa. Those were my early years as a little child. However, I observed an unhappy marriage. Our whānau were sometimes in and out of the pā at Ōhinemutu. We tried it out for a year or so in the suburbs to please the husband, but went back to the pā quickly because life imploded. My mother really tried. Anyway I ended up down in Wellington with my aunt, who was my mummy's cousin.

Early education at Mt Carmel and St Michael's

I was in Hātaitai, Wellington, for a year with my Aunty Nuki, who was married to a senior specialist at Wellington Hospital. It was a rich educational experience for me. Suddenly I was exposed at eight years old to classical music from Mozart and Vivaldi, and people reading poetry! Aunty Nuki would go to Ngāti Pōneke marae in Thorndon religiously every Sunday night to meet and associate with her dear friends, and in so doing maintain her Māoritanga. A loving and passionate woman, my aunt had three sons, Derek, Jacky and Richard. They played piano, violin, and cello! They were a little bit older than me. They went to extremely exclusive and expensive Catholic boys' schools and so little Miss Muffet from the pā also attended a similar private school. I was sent up the road to Our Lady of Mt Carmel Convent in Hātaitai, worlds away from my Rotorua Primary School where I had heaps of relations and close whānau around me.

The nuns at Mt Carmel spoke French and Latin. They were wonderful. It was another extraordinary experience for me, a young child. As one quirky building, it was an elaborate three-floored brick structure on a ridge overlooking the harbour. It also had extraordinary views of Cook Strait and the South Island, all the way to the mountains. I was the only Māori child in the school, which was weird. It was at that school that I got a sense of ethnic difference, even though there were Italian, Portuguese and Greek children who were the same colouring as me. I was there for only two terms, but my experience with nuns as inspired teachers and mentors began there. Everything was so formal. We wore uniforms that were incredibly costly, with one outfit imported directly from France, if you can imagine. It was taupe silk and cobalt blue linen, so beautiful. The education we got from Mt Carmel was typically staunch and Catholic. But what I remember most clearly about that school was the intense music — Mozart, Bach, Monteverdi — which I still enjoy. We also went to the cathedral, Sacred Heart, on Holy Days. This glamorous adventure suddenly stopped, all over in less than a year. I was sent back to Ōhinemutu and they decided to put me in a Catholic school. I was enrolled at the St Michael's Convent School where I went with my Kereopa, Morrison and Corbett relations from home.

One of my cousins and I would regularly walk to school together and then her father got a transfer to Auckland. Her leaving Rotorua broke my heart. It was Donna Awatere. She and I were like sisters. She had her father as her teacher; I had my kuia as mine. Donna was at St Michael's with me. She was fiercely competitive. We lived on the Ōhinemutu side of the Utuhina stream and Donna's house was on the other side, in Koutu. We yelled at each other over the water, we would fight — she would bully me and the other kids and would always win. I missed her terribly when they left. We didn't see each other again until we were both at the University of Auckland. Which is another saga!

At school I enjoyed Latin, and enjoyed aspects of Christian doctrine. I can probably still recite entire pages of the catechism because it was so programmed into us. Again, there at St Michael's I enjoyed music and creative writing. There were two nuns to whom I owe a great deal. One was the principal, Sister Mary Annunciata, a remarkable teacher and extraordinary woman. The Catholic school system had its own curriculum, and we'd get proficiency tests in English, geography, and social studies. I was good at those subjects. My other favourite nun was a brilliant, tall and fabulous creature who could do all sorts of stuff like pick up tables and chairs, load the truck then drive the truck, coach the boys' football, concrete the tennis court. All of it, this nun could do easily. Her name was Sister Mary Bertrand. They wore the complete nun outfit with the heavy veils, their pale faces framed by ivory-white wimples, their wide pectoral collars and yards of clunky rosary beads in great big belts, and their laced-up leather boots. They had this sense of capability and competence and they lived in a world without men, which appealed to me.

At the age of eight at Mt Carmel I knew I was different because I had a Māori name and I was a Māori kid. At St Michael's I was with the whānau, which was great. As I approached puberty, however, another way of being different emerged: my passionate, hopeless, unrequited crush on one of the nuns. She read to us from books. One was *Carve Her Name with Pride,* which became a film, about Violette Szabo who worked in the resistance in World War II, and how she spied for the Allies and sent secret information, and shot Germans! Her courage won her a Military Cross. That's hero number one. Hero number two was St Joan of Arc, leading the troops into battle wearing lots of armour and being fabulous. At school we also had lots of commentary on Irish nationalism, the IRA, what was happening in Ireland, how similar that was back home in Aotearoa, and so on. Was it similar to Māori history, and why? These are the questions asked in our Christian doctrine classes. We had a black baby fund too where we put aside a penny for the black babies in Africa and then suddenly there was a thing called apartheid, which fascinated me. Here we were relatively innocent 10–13-year-olds in a provincial Catholic school talking about apartheid, talking about the unfairness and the horror of that regime. Talking or thinking about the British invasion of Ireland and did that happen in a similar fashion to Māori.

These things are what the nuns taught us in my school environment; but at home it was different. At home there was an abusive man living with us. My mother was keeping down three jobs and saying things like, "If you can't pay cash, don't buy it," and "Everything you do has got to be your best. You don't have to be good in a big way but be the best in small ways and they'll all add up in the long run, you'll go forward, you'll move onwards." I will never forget what she wrote in my autograph book when I was eleven: "Tama tū, tama ora; tama noho, tama mate." She explained that it meant, "If you stand up for yourself, you will prosper; if you don't, then down you go." Yet my whānau were also drinkers, party people — clink, clink, clink after six o'clock most evenings. We were not righteous or saintly people, although ironically the abuser was regarded as righteous, as he never drank at all. We were certainly not a clean-living pious Christian family in the pā, and very few of the families were like that anyway. We got along, because we had to.

We'd go to church from time to time. My mother had a strong sense of social justice, of social equity. I did have the sublime privilege of growing up in a Māori-speaking home even though they never, ever encouraged us kids to speak and that was sad. There were three of us: my older brother Joseph, adopted in when he was about 9, and my little sister Vicki, seven years younger than me. Even more complicated: Joe and I had the same birth mother, and Vicki was a mokopuna tuarua of my kuia Hera. We were never encouraged to kōrero, but we would always listen and it was a household full of women, aunties and girl cousins visiting, and a happy one when the husband wasn't around.

One thing I did at Mt Carmel was to start writing stories. In Standard 3 aged nine my first series of stories was published in a wee Catholic school magazine. My poetry was also published and some ended up in overseas publications. During this period, after the bliss of Hātaitai, the home front was rugged, and so I buried myself beneath my books, although we didn't have that many in the house. One amazing Christmas, a set of Arthur Mee's *The Children's Encyclopaedia* appeared. I was in heaven! The nuns were also good to me and they'd often keep me back from school because my mother was working and there were other nasty circumstances as well. At 12 I entered the Ngārimu Essay Competition and won it, and it looked like I was going to be a successful budding scholar.

Secondary school

When I went to Rotorua Girls' High School I was a year ahead, so I was one of the youngest in the class, 3 Professional A, French and Latin. There were terrible pressures, a sense of being different, brainy, all that. I wasn't able to do my homework on a particular weekend because of family drama, and the maths teacher, an obnoxious racist, pulled me up and snarled, "You didn't do your homework. Do you know what? You are a black abomination!" This was in front of everybody in the class that comprised 39 snooty girls. Well, I actually didn't know what she meant, though her words sank in and stayed there. That's the funny bit but I knew it was horrible and this would have been my second or third week at school. I'd already had a hard time because all my good mates that were at St Michael's were at the co-ed school across town at Western Heights, but because I lived at Ōhinemutu we were obliged to go to Rotorua Girls' High.

At Rotorua Girls' High I met another whole extended whānau from all over the Rotorua Lakes area and we ran wild. They were my cousins, and I ran wild with them. I got an A for Latin and in every other subject I got less than 10% for that year. I was also experimenting with girls. All my mates were straight and they were getting pregnant. One pivotal moment in my life is that I started having a kind of fling with a Pākehā girl and she suggested we run away together. I was 12 going on 13, it was March 1962, and I was so enraptured with her that we did just that! I had to get away from home anyway. Things were horrible because 'the husband' had come back. Jae and I were on the run for nearly a week. We were juvenile delinquents and the cops finally caught up with us but by then we'd done some quite criminal things to get from Rotorua to the north of Hamilton. My girlfriend had a blossoming sex addiction. She was happily servicing chaps who gave us rides in their cars and so I saw a lot of stuff then. What she did was much worse than what I was used to seeing in the baths in Ōhinemutu. When the police brought us back to Rotorua her parents were mortified and sent her away to a posh boarding school. They were both high-profile Pākehā and all the blame was on me, of course, "the black abomination". Again. I thought, "I'm not black. I'm the fairest in my family and Māori aren't black." It was a weird thing to say to a kid like me because, although it was like a knife going through my gut, it was also an interesting intellectual challenge to unpack what that phrase meant, especially after learning about apartheid and black babies from the nuns. Anyway I was in trouble with the police. I was constantly on the street, constantly out there and fooling around with alcohol and whatever. Just as well methamphetamines had yet to arrive in Aotearoa; I was one hard little nut to crack. My friends, my cousins were getting hapū but not me, so I ended up wanting to stay at school. However, I got expelled in September that year.

I still wanted to go to school. Fortunately I won a scholarship to a Catholic School, only to have a sordid but swift encounter with a priest. I confronted him, and subsequently told my mother. He blamed me, saying "One rotten apple in the box turns all the other little apples rotten!" I ended up missing out on the Catholic school even after his groping me. Back into the state school system I went. However, that's a decision I'm proud of, telling my mother what he did to me.

I ended up at Western Heights High School. The headmaster, Derek Lake, looked at my Catholic school reports, and at the Latin mark, then said "You're obviously a very clever girl. If I come halfway to meet you, will you come halfway to meet me?" We were in his office and he stood up and he was a 6 foot tall Pākehā in his faded academic robe and he walked around his desk and I literally collapsed in this puddle of tears and hupe and just cried and cried and said "You know, I'm just a Māori, and I'm bad." He said "No, you're very clever," and then he shook my hand! More tears. And so I got another Ngārimu Scholarship that same year, an essay prize, and sadly had to ditch the Latin because they didn't teach it at Western Heights. I had some interesting teachers, some of whom got me aside and said, "As a young Māori woman, you have a great responsibility to your people," and I was still quite keen on all the social justice stuff, but after that encounter with the priest I was becoming a bit disillusioned too. I was deeply ashamed about the expulsion as well, and felt that the Mt Carmel and St Michael's primary school nuns would never forgive me. Yet I suspect they'd be quite proud of me now. Despite that, I chucked in Catholicism.

Western Heights High School was where I did most of my secondary education. The other part of my life, my home life when it was settled and the man was away, involved my grandmother and my mother and my aunties doing concerts, and weaving. My kuia, the weaver, had also been a guide at Whakarewarewa. So there was an emphasis in the whānau on speaking properly, on performance, on manaaki tangata. It was also about always being ready to look your best, and to meet new people and to show them the beauties of our wonderful land, the geysers, the mud pools, the lakes, the bush, and us, as Māori. My biological mother Erana passed away in 1963 and I was just getting over my abomination period and beginning to straighten out at Western Heights. I'd just got the Ngārimu Scholarship. I was becoming much more settled and then she passed away and I ended up sitting with her in the wharemate and I found out who she was and who the family were. King Korokī came to her tangi with five buses from Waikato. Her sister, my aunt Te Aho o te Rangi, was a prominent local personality, ran her own business, and was on 15 different land trusts. They were a well-to-do Māori family with whom I had absolutely no contact at all.

On gaining my MA, my maternal whanau gifted me with the name, Te Awekōtuku; it was a singular honour, as my grandmother was the last to hold it. Having her name still awes me. She married a scientist with three Oxford degrees. He came to Rotorua in the early 1900s. His family included many scholars and writers, and his sister our great-aunt Ada was a bluestocking poet and suffragist. This is my birth whakapapa on that side; they were active intellectuals, both male and female.

As a little child I couldn't do flax. I was just hopeless at it, but I could remember whakapapa and waiata, I could repeat stories and I could make up my own. So of course I wonder about the nature and nurture stuff. I still felt incredibly inadequate around my whānau ātawhai whom I regard as my immediate family.

On the death of my biological mother, I spent some time with that family. They had all been to private schools, and were schoolteachers, business people, really up there. Anyway, my social justice awareness kicked in, and I looked at their big flash cars, Cadillacs, Pontiacs, Chevrolets, whatever. It was just too hard to figure out; so I was happy to go back to the pā with my humble kuia who was a weaver and my mummy who had various jobs. One job was in a sewing factory, others involved her cleaning in the night and in the morning, and she also did concerts — performed on the tourist stage. I helped her whenever I could. This work ethic never left me. I got my first job at age eleven, in my aunty's milk bar/dairy. I never did much sport because I worked every weekend and my mummy was at work; we all worked and if I got a particular kind of job like the milk bar I could take my book and read it. Much better than cleaning!

However, my mummy and my adopted family couldn't really get it that I wanted to study. They just couldn't get it. I never had a real desk at home until much later. I'd sit in the corner with my books, sometimes with people singing, yahooing and drinking around me, and they'd all laugh. "Who does she think she is? Little Miss Smart-arse. Miss Whakaparanga! Brains too big for her boots!" It was weird. I wonder if my intellectual obsession is actually genetic, because I grew up in an environment not exactly conducive to being an academic.

All through high school I had jobs. Some of them of course embarrass me acutely now because I modelled for Pākehā. There are still postcards, calendars, record covers, all sorts of stuff with me on them with long hair, pale skin, wearing a piupiu, posing. It was common in the pā; a lot of us did that, it was like being in the concerts. That's an integral part of my upbringing and that's also how I was able to fund my schooling. Then I got School Certificate and I did well and my mummy said "Oh good, now you can work in the post office!" I didn't want to work in the post office.

"No, you go and work in the post office, you got School Certificate, now you are well qualified, miss!"

"No, I want to go back to school," I said. "Right, well you've got to get a good job to go back to school. So mahi atu!"

At Western Heights the 6th form had a special uniform so I had to make good money to buy myself one. I could never afford the blazer, so I altered my uncle's old blue jacket and it passed. Most of my work was modelling and special tourist gigs and concerts, all that to get through the 6th form years. One such job exposed me to the horrors of tourism. I became one of two girls appointed as Miss Rotorua Māori Meter Courtesy Maids. The other was the beautiful June Northcroft-Grant, now a prominent artist. We had to wear piupiu all day long in the summer holidays. I sang, I smiled, I did the poi and haka. I made big money and worked with the National Film Unit and the Tourist Department, and Rotorua Progressive Businessmen's Association. I even went on a 3-week promotional trip to Australia!

When I got University Entrance accredited my mummy said "Oh, great, now you can go to training college and be a teacher!" This is my mummy and her aspirations for me. You can be a teacher. But I didn't want to be just a teacher. I was more ambitious.

My mummy Paparoa had a younger sister, Lydia Tāwhai. She was a trained teacher and boarded with us for a while. I was three or four years old then. She had me reading and writing at four. This is my adopted mother's baby sister, now Lydia Tāwhai O'Leary. A major force in the primary education sector in her sadly short lifetime. She used to say to me, "You were like a sponge, you were three years old, just absorbing it all, and you couldn't get enough." She had me reading and writing at four, and making stories at five, which is how I came to skip a year at school. She was a important positive influence for me.

While I was having my troubles as a mad juvenile delinquent, someone else floated through the pā. She was elegantly dressed and had this amazing voice, like the BBC. She had long hair, in one single curl over her shoulder and across her front and she came to interview my grandmother about her book, which was *The Art of Piupiu Making*. That woman was Ngāpare Hopa and she was not only beautiful, but she could sing too, and she was an Educated Māori Woman. I was completely struck by her. She had this notebook, and wrote in it constantly. She was a great influence for me in wanting to learn more and stay at school. She inspired my winning essay in the Ngārimu competition that year.

Another important teacher was my Aunty Dorothy, actually my cousin, and she married a Pākehā man, Dudley Blomfield. He was the grandson of the painter and while I was running mad and being defiant they offered to take me into their home, which was on the margins of the pā, and care for me. It was more fabulous Baroque music, fine arts, high (Western) culture all around me and Ngāpare Hopa would visit them! Uncle Dudley, who taught me to drive, said I could be like Ngāpare but I thought I could never be like that. They'd both tell me, "You're clever, you're clever." Well, I thought I wasn't that clever at that time, too busy playing up, but they kept saying I was. That was the encouragement I needed at the time. So Ngāpare Hopa and my Aunt Dorothy were pivotal women in my life and good role models. And Uncle Dudley, old colonial Auckland family — along with Aunt Dorothy — instructed me on how to hold my fish knife and fork, and the difference between a martini glass and a brandy snifter. Things a young lady ought to know. Ha!

Promoting Rotorua tourism at Surfers Paradise, in 1965: "I was 16 in this photo, taken over 50 years ago! The image speaks to its time, but still reflects the lives of many young Arawa women today."

I finally got through high school and the social justice issues kept lingering. I also followed the apartheid struggle. I maintained an active interest in current affairs, and wondered about suburban neurosis. In 1965 I wrote to Dr Fraser McDonald, and his wife Jacquie Fahey the painter actually remembered that when we met as feminists years later! I was in the 6th form at the time and he was the Superintendent of Carrington Mental Hospital, with this theory about women in the suburbs getting this thing called suburban neurosis because of the pressure of children and being isolated and I thought he didn't include Māori. What about Māori neurosis? I was aged sixteen. I had this fire burning inside me from a young age, like from baby time, and it was always *why*? Why is it like that? One of my questions was "Why did Hinemoa swim?" A profoundly ironic question when my kuia Hera Tāwhai was in the first-ever New Zealand full-length moving picture, film, made in 1913, *Hinemoa*. Her poster is a flagship image for the National Film Archive. From a young age I was also conscious of Maggie Papakura and her scholarly Oxford achievements. Her *The Old Time Māori* was one book my kuia had at home, as she had travelled to England in Maggie's concert party.

University

When I got to Auckland University I wanted to do law. It was probably the most painful time of my life, even worse than puberty. It was 1967 and I was the only Māori girl in the whole law school, one of eight women in an enrolment of about 400 men. Also the only Māori girl in O'Rorke Hall, where you had to wear a dress to dinner and the boys had to wear a jacket and a tie. The Paki brothers also stayed there, and they were at law school too. Another important person came into my life at that time: Merimeri Penfold, a gentle and genuine kuia. She took me to the university Māori club. I was the only student that year from a state school. There were the boys from Te Aute, and St Stephen's, and the girls from Hukarere, Queen Victoria and St Joseph's. Scattered about were those from Sacred Heart and St Mary's. I didn't belong to any of those schools and so it was horrible for me. There were the Hāto Petera and Hāto Pāora boys and of course all these people knew each other. And, then in the corner was a Pākehā student with a guitar, singing her Māori translation of 'Kumbaya', and expecting everybody to sing it with her. Here am I raised and nurtured in haka, in Māori music and here's this Pākehā and there are all these twittering, beautifully groomed, stuck-up Māori only talking to each other. None of them talked to me. I thought, I'm not coming back to this. At the hostel that night I made friends with the domestic staff. The toilet cleaners, the sweepers, the dishwashers, the cooks and the bedmakers were all Māori women, so I hung out with them. Four of them were ship girls — "tima girls", part-time wharf prostitutes. They became my best friends. They knew where the camp crowd hung out, and they took me there. That was my first year and introduction to Auckland University.

I was seventeen, going to law school, yet getting stoned out of my brain. By the end of the third term I was down the road. One reason I got thrown out of O'Rorke was for fraternising with the staff. Most of them came from the North and when they heard that my mother was a Tāwhai from Waimā, well what did I expect! Anyway, I could never get in with the university Māori club scene. I was just a penny diver from Rotorua, and it was hard to fit in. It was just excruciatingly lonely and horrible and being gay, being a camp girl, wasn't easy. Also, I wasn't the stereotypical Māori camp girl, with my perfect teeth, long hair, and being petite, conventionally nice looking. I didn't fit the mould in the camp world of Gleason's Pub, the wharves, the Embers nightclub, the ships; but I liked the rough trade, because a lot of it was familiar to me. However, I kept applying myself. I was doing a double degree, law and English. I was getting A's in English but I was consistently failing my law subjects. In my second year I befriended another woman who was taking law. We both wondered why I kept failing and getting really low marks. We worked together on this one particular project and we used the same case law, and used the same arguments yet she got an A+ grade and I got graded a C–. We bravely confronted the lecturer who reluctantly changed my grade to a B–. So it was that kind of racist behaviour that I experienced. At the same time Syd and Hana Jackson, this amazing couple whom I admired enormously, became my friends. Hana also knew a lot of my relations from her time in Rotorua. Others were Hone Ngata, from the East Coast, and fiery Maxine Rēweti from Tauranga. Both couples were part of the original *No Māoris, No Tour* movement and I felt good with them because they talked about and promoted social justice. I was also at Auckland University law school the same time as Mick Brown, Winston Peters, Stephen Bryers, Satch Satyanand and various others. No women had appeared yet, and there was an absolute resistance to any mention of Māori in the course content or in the way they taught law.

In Māori land law classes I became continually disruptive. I intervened and challenged the lecturer and when we had our final exam I wrote a 40-page essay on Treaty of Waitangi case law and argued that it should have been taught as the core of land law at Auckland instead of learning British, Irish, English, Scots land law. I ignored the exam questions and constructed my own. I learned all the case law, I cited the lot and wrote a complex essay ending with a flourish and predicting things like the percentage of Māori land remaining in Māori hands and being subject to future development within the capitalist framework, and the ongoing alienation of Māori land through the recently passed Māori Affairs Amendment Act. I did all that and I said to the law lecturer that there is powerful commercial potential for lawyers to become well versed in the laws of our own land rather than what's happening over in Europe. I also said that the university law school is concealing and being an apologist for the prejudices of a colonial government. What happened is that my booklet — my 40-page essay — was passed around the law school. It was then cross-marked by a senior academic in Political Science, who professed that my essay deserved an A grade. The Pākehā conservatives in the law school just failed me and that was that. I didn't go back. I got 14 units of the 21 units required for a law degree, but I couldn't do it any more and I was getting A's for English. There was a sequel, however. They did use my 40-page booklet of case law in developing Māori Land Law at Auckland. That was 1969.

I finished my undergraduate degree and started a master's degree majoring in English. I was also very involved in theatre, and the university drama club; I've always enjoyed the stage. Anyway, I proposed Hone Tūwhare as my thesis topic. "What? That man's not a real poet. You're joking!" huffed the pompous white professors and their creeping ponces in the English Department. And so I submitted an embarrassing and execrable thesis on Janet Frame and acquired an honours degree, so I suppose I did well. Throughout that period, though, from my second year I became more and more involved with the anti-Vietnam movement and by 1970 women's liberation and gay liberation. As an opinionated young Māori lesbian woman, I was also passionate about gay rights; I published on this topic as early as 1971.

Agitating, teaching, researching

Ngā Tamatoa had emerged by that time. I participated in that movement with lots of others; we huddled under the generous wings of Amīria and Eruera Stirling, and breathed fire with the Jacksons and the Harawiras. We would go to schools like St Stephen's and Wesley to promote our cause. And often our own people would say to us, "You're not real Māori. Go back to your marae that's where you learn to be a Māori and know what tikanga, real Māori values are. It's not about running down the street with placards. Grow up!" And on and on they went. Some of those same men and women who rubbished us became significant leaders, politicians, Māori personalities and educators. I have since confronted them and reminded them of the origins of institutions like Te Taura Whiri (Māori Language Commission), the Waitangi Tribunal, Māori radio stations, kōhanga reo and kura kaupapa, and so on. If we radicals were not prepared to do the hard yards as protestors, what would have happened? Ironically, we did not get the elite kaupapa Māori jobs. Instead, those very people who criticised us or hid in mumbled shame when we were protesting reaped the benefits of our outrageous risk taking, our arrests and our [criminal] convictions. And with my English degree, even though I had no teacher training at all, I got a part-time job teaching at St Peter's — yes, at Hāto Petera on the Shore.

In my class at the time were people who became significant Māori leaders and they were good boys. I was only young, a 21-year-old, and these boys were men at 18 years old taking sixth-form English. They thought I was a real scream because I'd turn up with my girlfriend on a motorbike. With the boys, I figured out our special curriculum. What was amazing was that they all passed their exams. They were only two terms with me but I turned it upside down and taught them about Māori people who were role models such as Hone Tūwhare, Rowley Habib and Jacquie Sturm, and we did plays like *Pōhutukawa Tree* and *Othello*. I really went searching. *Te Ao Hou* magazine was a fantastic resource but I also used material the boys could relate to. Then I got the sack there for being a known sexual deviant. I appeared on the front page of the *New Zealand Herald* with a group of other women and also on the national television news making statements about lesbian lifestyles and women's rights. It wasn't long before I got a telegram from St Peter's saying my services were no longer required. I lost my job there at Hāto Petera. It was a pity because the boys were much safer with me than with those other people teaching them. Of course, I became unemployable after that.

I continued agitating, politicising, and writing about Māori women and lesbian identity and I published a number of articles on Māori issues in university in the early 1970s. I returned to Rotorua and realised, because my kuia had died in 1970, that no one had captured the stories of her generation. Around that time Tainui's Robert Mahuta and Prof James Ritchie had set up a Centre for Māori Studies and Research at Waikato University, with my uncle John Rangihau. So I'd hang around with them on the way home to Ōhinemutu, and we'd debate topical issues and also discuss them at Ngā Tamatoa events. By late 1974 I had an unpaid position at the research centre in Hamilton, which enabled me to do work on my kuia and put together the life stories of the unique and unstoppable women of her generation.

I started the research project interviewing lots of my kuia and other older aunties. I also had to do various menial jobs just to make ends meet. One such job in parallel with the research was acting. I was in various productions as an actor with the university drama club. For years I'd waited for my big break; whether I was going to be a serious actor or just a exotic minor walk-on, the coloured maid on call. I'd also heard that there was a possibility of a tourism-focused scholarship at the University of Hawai'i. It was a joint doctoral internship, supervised between Mānoa and Waikato. By then I had gathered a lot of stories of my many kuia, and the narrative of Te Arawa tourist guides was emerging. So when that overseas opportunity came along, I applied for it. Meanwhile I'm doing an assortment of rough jobs and doing part-time acting. Then out of the blue, it was one of those crazy hideous moments, I got cast as Beatrice alongside George Hēnare, who was cast as Benedick in the Summer Shakespeare season of *Much Ado About Nothing*. The same week I got that part, I was offered a doctoral fellowship at the East-West Center, University of Hawai'i. The fellowship was to begin in February 1975. The season of Shakespeare's *Much Ado About Nothing* began in February 1975. I wanted to be a good actor and share the stage with the talented George Hēnare, another Māori, a person I respected. By then my mother was beginning to get it from the wider whānau about my antics, my rough jobs and my being a profound embarrassment to her. All those brains and letters after my name, and huh? Of course she said, "Haere, e kō! Go to Hawai'i!" I also saw it as an opportunity I couldn't refuse, so I picked up my guides' narratives and went to Hawai'i in 1975. They were the basis of a doctoral proposal on the social and cultural impact of tourism on Te Arawa. That was primarily through the efforts and support of Professor James Ritchie, Robert Mahuta, Uncle John, and my beloved early mentor Ngāpare Hopa. They always had faith in me. But for me it was like, oh, I've ended up here by default and this isn't true. You know this can't be me. This is weird. How did I end up here when I grew up in a household where achievement was conveyed through the work you did with your hands? The notion of creating or achieving intellectually was foreign, was alien, completely out there, not us, the whānau I grew up with. So again there's that sense of I am different. I'm not like other people and sometimes being a different person is actually a good thing. It's wonderful. It motivates you. I mention fire burning inside me — well, that's the fire that keeps me going but sometimes it gets a bit low and that's the downside to being different and I certainly felt it at that first meeting I attended at the Māori Club and my orientation to Auckland University and introduction to the Māori students of that time. And of course, the alienation I experienced in the Law School.

My doctorate

My PhD experience was the result of another kind of politically motivated direction. I went into it as a rampant Ngā Tamatoa activist, staunchly convinced that tourism was destroying Māoridom and especially Te Arawa. Yet I was aware that tourism got me through high school; I couldn't deny that.

Nevertheless, I had this notion that tourism was a capitalist white construct. Having seen and experienced the Hawai'i context made me firmly of the view that tourism was poisoning and polluting us. I later developed the realisation, which can be applied in any Māori economic analysis, that if an industry or a business or its resources are under Māori ownership, with effective and careful Māori management, it works and it benefits the people. Certainly, the tourism that existed up to that time in my communities was well managed, craftily constructed and the domain of a group of elderly women. That changed in the 1980s. That's when we had the warehouse approach to mass tourism, a complete paradigm shift. That's when the Māori economic summit was held, 1984. We witnessed the mutation of cultural institutions like the Māori Arts and Crafts Institute and professional guiding, which had been the responsibility of certain families for generations. Incrementally, in stages, the tourist concert performances as the domain of Te Arawa, the tangata whenua, were completely transformed. Incursions took place. A new world of tourism was developing before our eyes.

When I did my masters, a generous scholarship from the Trust Board of Tūhoe-Waikaremoana purchased my textbooks. I still have most of them. I also applied year after year to Te Arawa Māori Trust Board for financial aid, and every year I was turned down. I never received a single cent of support from Te Arawa Māori Trust Board, or the Māori Education Foundation, for my tertiary degrees. From the early years I was told, "You are the child of a wealthy family, they should support you." My biological whānau? No way! Doing the PhD, again Te Arawa consistently declined assistance, so after the fourth unsuccessful year, my mummy and a couple of my aunties went to the board chairman and secretary to ask for an explanation. They replied, "We consider it unseemly for an Arawa woman to have such ambition." My whānau couldn't believe what they heard. They were shattered. And the message was that I should have been a high school teacher like every other good, clever Arawa girl, or maybe do something practical like be a nurse or a physiotherapist.

Meanwhile on the other side of my whakapapa, through the door came Te Kotahitanga Tait, John Rangihau and others, and they said to me, "You're our girl. We're so proud of you. We want to give you more money to do your big tohu." However, and I know this sounds weird, but I couldn't take the money. I could not take Tūhoe, Te Urewera funds to support my work on a kaupapa that was essentially Te Arawa. No. It just felt wrong. There was awful disappointment for them and real pain for me because I was the one that was pōhara but I didn't want my Tūhoe people laughing at my Te Arawa people. So I basically paid my own way through my PhD studies, taking quite extraordinary jobs when I was at home like cutting scrub, washing dishes, cleaning swimming pools, hosing down walls, cleaning cars, making beds in motels. I did these jobs while I was doing fieldwork, collecting stories. The East-West Center scholarship covered fees, international travel and accommodation on campus, but the stipend was very small. It was hard because I was back and forth to Hawai'i over a five-year period and also spent a year in Sāmoa. I was quite lucky because I did have good relationships with people. I was also a bit out of control as well. In the final months of my doctoral project, I got cancer, had lots of surgery, and nearly died. It looked like I was going to be no longer on this planet.

The viva examination for my doctorate was something memorable. It was in Jim Ritchie's office with Robert Mahuta and John Rangihau, and the external examiner who was a monkish eccentric Oxbridge professor, Peter Wilson. The office was on the third floor of the building, and Jim's ceiling was a mass of spinning mobiles — seedpods, fish, tiny umbrellas, silk flowers, ossified sea creatures, bells, glass shapes, coral, splinters of wood. As we went inside, the darkening clouds dropped ominously low. When the interrogation began the clouds pushed against the windows; it was a corner office with two walls of glass windows. As I started answering questions, the lightning started. Bright searing flashes. Jim's mobiles all spun, dancing skittishly above our heads. Suddenly we were surrounded by thunder and then it went away and then the clouds were pressing against the windows again. It was so eerie. To open the thesis I cited "Ko whatitiri ki te rangi, ko Te Arawa ki te whenua," and there they all were, in the office with us! I was asked to go out of the room while the examiners deliberated. Eventually I was allowed back in and as I walked through the door the entire room exploded with lightning and thunder and John Rangihau started to karakia and I just sat there blubbing like a newborn baby. It was just awful. Anyway I got the doctoral degree. I passed the exam. And then the iwi requested that the doctorate be conferred at Tamatekapua Marae in Rotorua, as I was the first one of Te Arawa to get a PhD, and also because everyone thought I was dying.

Looking for work

I was young when I got my PhD. I was 32. However, I couldn't get a job. I was unemployable and I guess this is where the bitterness and the rage surfaced within me. I applied for something like 28 jobs. I was the only Māori woman in the country with a PhD. I applied to every university. I would have been happy with a minor tutor's job. "No!" was the answer given me. "You're queer," they said. "You're unreliable. You've got a bad background. You're too political for us. You've got a poor reputation." It wasn't that I hadn't published either, but I had been sick in 1982. I couldn't get a job. I ended up packing kiwifruit in

Cousins and friends at Ngāhuia's PhD graduation in Tamatekapua house, on the Papaiouru marae, Ōhinemutu: Atareta Poananga, Donna Awatere, Ngāhuia, Donna Hall, Ama Rauhihi, Rangitunoa Black, Hana Te Hemara. Photo by Mereana Pitman.

Te Puke for a year and doing seasonal work. Then I was on the dole in Te Puke with my cousins in the Mongrel Mob. I fronted up to a snooty little bureaucrat girl at the front desk, and she said, "Oh, that's not a real PhD, is it? Hmm? Are those real qualifications?" Then she'd get a senior colleague to check them! "Oh, maybe you should take this office job at an insurance agency." I'd reply, "No, no, I'm happy to do kiwifruit when the season comes back. I can dive for agar with my cousins!" It was utterly extraordinary. I could not get a job.

At the end of 1983 I did apply for and get a postgraduate fellowship, which took me to Oxford, England. Makereti — Maggie Papakura at Oxford — was my research topic. When I came back home I thought I would easily get a job, but again I applied for lots and was repeatedly turned down. I was totally bewildered; I was still the only female Māori PhD in the country! At this time two senior Māori men, one a cabinet minister, and the other a very elevated lawyer on the rise said to me, "As long as you live the way you do and you continue those unnatural associations, our men will hate you and our women will despise you, so fix yourself up," and "You are not the sort of leader Māoridom wants. Straighten yourself up, sort out your life and you might have a future here." That was hard to take.

So I went back to Maketū in the Bay of Plenty. My mummy, the weaver, was living at Maketū. I did more kiwifruit picking and then a job came up at the museum in Rotorua. My background working at the Bishop Museum in Hawai'i, and the Pitt Rivers in Oxford gave me the confidence to apply for the position. And I had a PhD! However, I got a call from one of my uncles who was on the selection committee. He advised, "Oh my dear, you'd better not apply for that position, take your name out — ki a mātou nei, kāore e pai ana ngā wāhine ki te whāwhā taonga. He mea tapu ērā. He mahi tapu. Take your application out, my dear, because you are not suitable for that job at the Rotorua Museum". He told me that for them, it's not appropriate for women to care for taonga that are tapu, or sacred. I was shattered again. But this time, it was because for that particular job, I was the wrong sex. I was back in the kiwifruit packhouse with a PhD and I wasn't going to conform or do whatever was required — dress like a fashionable lady, wear make-up, and swan about in high heels and pretend I was heterosexual just to please so-called Māori leaders for whom I had not much respect anyway. I held to this, even if those leaders were the ones who were doing the employing, who were in control of some elements of the Māori academy and the Māori economy. And continue to be. And of course, in the sacred museum sector, I could possibly change my gender, but not my sex.

Waikato Museum

Another job came up. I was still hurt by the rejection in Rotorua early in 1984, and then a job came up in April at the Waikato Museum. I'd already had a lot of contact with the Waikato people and Tainui. At my birth mother's tangi King Korokī and his family revealed their strong kinship with her family. There was an ongoing connection with Waikato, and I'd also had a lot of contact with Te Arikinui Dame Te Ātairangikaahu when she visited Hawai'i as well as at home. She was someone I could talk to and she was always interested in what I was doing. I thought, this is a woman who is a paramount chief. Surely she won't mind if a female — me — applied for that job at the Waikato Museum. I was cheeky, I rang her, I actually rang the Māori Queen. What a cheek! But I thought, ring her. So I rang her. To my horror I got through to her. I wasn't expecting to get through to her but I did, so I told her my story. She said to me, "Have a go. You just have a go. It never hurts to have a go, girl. Put your hat in the ring." So my hat went in the ring, I wore my mother's clothes to the interview, and I got the job.

My first major challenge was an intellectual one but also an extraordinary and awesome task. It was to do with the dismantling, restoration, conservation and reconstruction of *Te Winika*, a carved waka taua built in the 1830s. Te Arikinui herself had gifted her to the Waikato Museum. As the new Curator of Ethnology, I was in charge of this waka. I had recently become intimately involved with a luminous personality from Tūrangawaewae marae. She's a composer and visionary writer, a descendant of the original builders and owners of the canoe. We put together a team with the blessing of Te Arikinui. They were all young females and we took the waka apart into 66 different component pieces. We removed concrete, tin, clay, bitumen, tar, rocks, plastic, iron from her. We took off seven layers of paint. We worked with the men of the Tūrangawaewae canoe crews, and they did all the heavy lifting and grunt work, and we learned so much from each other. We made 1,600 metres of muka as cordage. The men lashed this all back into the waka, their raw strength reassembling her. We researched in the most profound and gratifying way the history of *Te Winika*, the means of early construction. We looked at parts of the waka that were hand-carved, that were carved with pounamu, that were carved with argillite, that were carved with iron and steel. Specialist conservators from Auckland Museum assisted us. It was a major community research project, and it was absolutely brilliant the way we worked together, until a disagreement arose with the museum director over publishing the text. We had two manuscripts prepared, with dazzling images. We had also curated a major exhibition of taonga Māori, specifically of Tainui origin. With no explanation to us, he cancelled all the funding for the two books. His hostility was septic. I had to move on. Fortunately, another opportunity presented itself to me. I was shoulder-tapped by University of Auckland to design and teach the history and theory of Māori and Pacific art. I enjoyed teaching these courses. And I love Auckland.

In July 1991, I applied for the inaugural chair of Women's Studies at the University of Auckland. I had just published *Mana Wahine Māori*, a book of Māori feminist theory and other revelations. There were 12 people on the selection panel. There were three other contenders from Australia, the US and Canada. Of that selection committee, ten members recommended my appointment and two objected vehemently. Those two women, both Pākehā, are now in positions of real status and power. They sabotaged the process. The chairman agreed that with such an overwhelming majority like ten versus two, the appointment should be made in my favour. What happened is that these two women went to the vice-chancellor and said that I was politically and emotionally unstable, and had a bad research record, which was untrue. I had more publications than most of the other applicants. Anyway they persuaded the vice-chancellor to stop the process, and a decision came through on the 19 December that no one was to be appointed. Then a year later, one of those women's cronies got the job. It's hard to talk about and not many people know that story. I should have been a professor in 1991.

My first professorship

Eventually I did gain a professorship but it was at the Victoria University of Wellington, after Sid Mead. I was appointed to the professorship, as dean of the Māori Department, at Victoria University on 1 May 1996. I remember that because it was my birthday. I was offered the job mid-April. I accepted on 1 May. I didn't want to leave Auckland at all, but I was in a relationship which was not working out. I was in Wellington for nearly five years. During this time we established an autonomous Pacific Studies Department, and set up the Pro Vice-Chancellor Māori position. It was a challenging environment. In 2001 I won a Marsden Grant worth half million dollars to study the history and meaning of moko, traditional Māori tattoo. I took it to Waikato University, where I have been a professor for the last few years.

Māori scholarship and leadership

I have written eight books, two of them my short story collections, and three are co-authorships, so productive scholarship is important to me as a Māori academic. Māori scholarship is about making a positive difference, taking responsibility, seizing the moment, preparing for the future, lighting up the darkness of doubt for our tamariki. Māori scholarship is about joy, it's about knowing that you understand the Obama statement, "Yes we can!" Knowing that the way we look at the world as Māori is special and valid and exciting and legitimate. I think of my kuia and her commitment to excellence and it was uncompromising. She taught me that, and so for me the effect of Māori scholarship or being a Māori scholar is about knowing how to learn and then with confidence and generosity knowing how to share what you have learned with others, to elevate others and to make a difference for a better world.

I am lucky to have been influenced by many great leaders and mentors. Leadership is about courage, the sense of risk, the absence of doubt, and yet keeping a genuine sense of humility and service. It's about serving others to the best of your ability. Serving the people is an honour and privilege. Every true leader and luminary is there for the people, not for themselves. I think of Te Arikinui, and there was an intellect. She had a mind like a steel trap. She was an extraordinary thinker and she was critical, she was careful, she was uncompromising too. The common aspect or quality of all those inspiring people is their courage, and that colouring their courage is humility. It is about having a strong sense of *ehara taku toa i te toa takitahi — it's not just about me, it's about all of us.* I am not the centre of attention; everyone is. With this in mind, I stress that I could not be here if I didn't have the kuia I had, if I didn't have a mother who put up with my antics, if I didn't have my aunty who taught me

Ngā Kupu Ora Māori Book Awards, Book of the Decade Award Winner, 2009. Earlier in 2008 *Mau Moko* had won the lifestyle and contemporary culture category in the Montana NZ Book awards. *Mau Moko* was the result of five years' work by University of Waikato's Professor Ngāhuia Te Awekōtuku; Linda Waimarie Nikora, director of the university's Māori and Psychology Research Unit; and student researchers Mohi Rua from the research unit and Rolinda Karapu from the Centre for Māori and Pacific Research and Development.

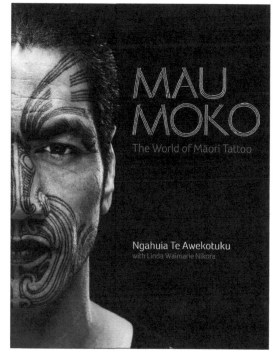

to read, if I didn't have Te Arikinui telling me to put my hat in the ring. I am so grateful to them. I don't know where I'd be; possibly a struggling creative writer at home in Ōhinemutu. Or an eccentric character actor in a foreign city! I don't know.

Moments to remember

If there is one thing I'd want to change in my life if I had it all over again, it would probably be to finish my law degree. The law lecturer who took the 40-page booklet to Political Science for cross-marking saw me a few years later, when I'd started lecturing in Art History. He said, "My dear, you should be on the [judge's] bench" and I burst into tears. I just cried and cried, and said "No, I couldn't do that, but I did get a PhD." Then he just looked at me and said "We lost, you know; we are the worse for it, because we lost you." I often think about that, about finishing that degree because I started the same year as my awesome cousin Georgina Te Heuheu, who was at Victoria University. And she was the first Māori woman to qualify as a lawyer! Yay!

Another moment is when a Mātaatua elder in Wellington once berated me in public and called me tamaiti wāwāhi tahā, that I break calabashes. I'm proud of that. I'm proud of that. I cherish that moment even though it was hurled at me as a kanga or curse. Take the risk. Break the calabash.

However, one of my greatest ever moments was processioning with the berobed university officials into Tamatekapua when I got my PhD, and hearing the robust pōkeka and the searing karanga, and feeling deathly ill, and thinking of my kuia, and remembering all the hard times, and seeing my uncles and aunties there from Tūhoe. They were doing their haka and Robert Mahuta and the crew from Waikato were there too, and leading the local pōkeka was my wonderful Uncle Hamuera Mitchell, whom I also honour as a mentor. He never lost faith in me, that koroua. That was a moment. I've got lots of good moments, but just crossing the verandah and coming into the house, and seeing the poutokomanawa with Ngātoroirangi there, and then feeling that I had to look up to see that dog Pōtakatāwhiti above me with Īhenga, and knowing I was home in my house, and the work I'd done was done for this particular place, like the PhD thesis was written for and about Te Arawa. That was another big moment for me.

I'd like to conclude by mentioning Bonnie Amohau, a very special aunt, who recently turned 90. She was at my graduation, in Tamatekapua. Fifty years ago, when I was at my most dejected and delinquent, she said, "Huia, never give up!" And I haven't yet, and I never will.

MASON DURIE

Emeritus Professor Sir Mason Durie is from Ngāti Kauwhata, Ngāti Raukawa and Rangitāne, and was raised on a whānau farm at Aorangi, near Feilding. After attending Te Aute College he studied medicine at Otago University, and later completed postgraduate study in psychiatry at McGill University, Canada. After an extensive medical career, focusing on mental health, Professor Durie was approached to lead the School of Māori Studies at Massey University, holding a Chair in Māori Research and Development. He has retired from his role at Massey as the Assistant Vice-Chancellor (Māori & Pasifika) and Deputy Vice-Chancellor. He continues to hold a number of local and national positions and responsibilities, and is actively involved in marae and iwi activities. He and his wife, Professor Lady Arohia Durie, have four children and twelve mokopuna.

Whānau influences

As a child I'm not sure that I had strong ambitions to follow any particular career path. Like others at the time, my parents had experienced the hardships following the Great Depression, and in their minds it was important to get a job that would be secure all year round. My father thought that I might be a wool classer. It would provide year-round employment, because wool classers were not seasonal workers; when the shearing season was over, they would work the larger wool stores. My mother thought I should go into government — in those days a government job was considered to be 'for life'. Before my father came back to the farm, he worked mainly at the Feilding freezing works. In winter he would find part-time jobs around the place, working on construction, planting marram grass on the west coast, and similar jobs. Uppermost in our parents' minds was the fear of unemployment and the need to have jobs that offered security.

It was our grandfather, Hoani Meihana Te Rama Apakura Durie, who suggested that we might look beyond today. He was my father's father, who left Te Aute wanting to study medicine. He had come through the era where Māui Pōmare and Te Rangi Hīroa were already leaders and role models for Te Aute boys and he thought he might pursue a medical career. However, his father was opposed, mainly because Dunedin was a long way from Feilding and seemed too far away from home. In the event, after a brief period in Wellington studying law at Victoria, he returned to the family farm to take over from his ailing father. He spent virtually all his adult life farming. So when my brothers and I were about to go to college — I would have been 12 or 13 at the time — he asked the three of us what we were going to do when we grew up. When we seemed unsure he suggested that "One of you should be a doctor, one a lawyer and one a farmer." So for me it was medicine. Looking back, it's quite amazing that when we went to college we already knew that's what we would do. The idea had been planted, it grew, and became the aim right from the third form at Te Aute.

My parents and grandparents had come through the Depression years and a World War in the 1930s and '40s and took nothing for granted. I suspect that was one reason why the work ethic was instilled into us from early years. Our four grandparents would be uneasy if they saw us doing nothing, so as soon as we arrived we would be given a spade, a fork, a rake, a shovel or an axe. At times I thought they overdid it, but to their great credit that approach taught us how to work and that was the same thing I learned at Te Aute — how to work, and how to study.

Secondary education

I had all my secondary education at Te Aute College. That wasn't necessarily my first choice, but it was my grandfather's first choice, because that is where he had been to school. He had good memories of it and thought it was a place to obtain a good education, but also to be educated within a Māori context. I started Te Aute in 1952. My older brother came with me and subsequently my younger brother too; at one point we were all together at Te Aute. It was a good decision and I was fortunate to have had a sound educational opportunity there. It wasn't a big school; there were about 120 students, so that meant a narrow range of subjects, but there was an expectation that we would succeed. When we went to Te Aute I received the Ōtaki Porirua Trust Board scholarship. In those days it paid the whole fee, about £112. Then in the summer holidays from the third form we worked in the Feilding freezing works so that we could get enough money to cover clothes and be fairly independent.

In those days we used to sit an exam called School Certificate in the fifth form. Even in the third form the boys talked about School Certificate and some would get up at five o'clock in the morning to study. The subject that was beginning to interest me most was science. Our science teacher was Bill Mataira from Rongowhakaata, a graduate of Victoria University. He was a fastidious teacher. The work he gave us in the fourth and fifth form formed the basis for notes when I went to university. He probably over-prepared us, but I enjoyed the approach and it was to stand me in good stead, giving me an appreciation of the biological sciences. I also had a good maths teacher, Sam Dwyer, and had a good English teacher, Watson Rosevear, who later became Bishop of Waiapu. He was also the chaplain at the school.

At Te Aute there were a large number of boys from the east coast, native speakers, and there were a small number of boys from the west coast, who were generally not native speakers. We were second language learners, although we knew enough Māori to be able to play rugby, where all the conversation tended to be in Māori, to befuddle the opposition as much as anything. The Māori teacher was Harold Wills, who had previously been principal of the Ōtaki Māori Boys' College. He wasn't Māori, but he had been a student at Te Aute at the same time as my grandfather. In his classes we had two textbooks. One was *The Pilgrim's Progress*, written in Māori and the other was the Māori translation of the Holy Bible. We would read a section of the Bible or *Pilgrim's Progress* and then translate it.

All told, if it was not a totally rounded education, it had depth, and I appreciated the opportunity.

Tertiary experiences

By the time I had been accepted to the University of Otago I had learned enough to be able to hold my own with others from the larger schools. I was one of a handful of Māori students there — only about 50 across the whole university. University life was quite a different experience for me. I had come from a small school that had been dominated by Māori views and worldviews.

Although I stayed in a hostel, Selwyn College, I not infrequently felt somewhat estranged from others because of the lifestyle, a different way of interacting and relating, coupled with some reticence on my own part. We had to work hard to get into medical school. You were not accepted until year two, and to enter second year medicine high grades were required in all four papers for the medical intermediate exam: botany, physics, chemistry and zoology. Once in medical school things were a little more relaxed and the work was increasingly interesting, but nonetheless required ongoing study and still more exams. I had been awarded a Ngārimu tertiary scholarship that was helpful, and during holidays it was always possible to obtain work at the Feilding freezing works.

In my second year I made contact with the other Māori students. Most of them were not in medicine, they were doing other courses including law. We started a Māori club and that became important to us. I was the secretary and treasurer of the club and the chair was another Te Aute old boy, Te Pākaka Tāwhai, who had left Te Aute the year before I started so his name was well known to me. He'd been head prefect there. People used to think he was the patron of the club because he looked older, and in fact he was a bit older than the average student, but it was good to work with him. Years later the same relationship continued when I came to Massey and he was a lecturer there.

While still a second year med student, I was beginning to feel there was a wider mission than medicine alone. Our grandfather's intention for us was that we would be useful to Māori. He didn't say that, but that's what he meant. For Māori doctors that meant there would be an expectation to make a difference to Māori health. That was probably one reason why we formed the Māori club; not just to socialise, but to consider how Māori students might contribute to Māori, beyond getting a degree. We organised the national Māori students' meeting in Dunedin one year. Those conferences had only started a few years before. In 1961 a group of us travelled to Wellington and were impressed with the commitments evident by Māori students at Victoria and agreed to host a similar event in Dunedin in 1962 — it was a great success and involved most of the Otago Māori students — then only about 50.

The most important point to mention about Dunedin was that Otago University was where I met my wife, Arohia. She was studying nutrition and home science. Two years after I left Dunedin we were married. In more ways than one, the Otago experience provided opportunities for me that would not otherwise have been possible.

Kim Alty (executive assistant, MANU AO Academy), Taniya Ward (administrator, MANU AO Academy), Lady Arohia and Sir Mason Durie.

Professional career

Like most students, after leaving university you're pleased to be able to enter the real world and put theory into practice, rather than read about it and follow the words of older experts. I soon learned, however, that to keep up to date, ongoing study was important. But essentially I welcomed becoming a practitioner and spent two years at Palmerston North Hospital as a house surgeon before deciding an area of specialisation. I had developed an interest in psychiatry, though I had little experience of that as a house surgeon. In those days it was not possible to study psychiatry in New Zealand. Most who did specialise in psychiatry had either gone to Sydney or to the Maudsley Hospital in London for specialist training. I was fortunate enough to meet another New Zealander who had studied psychiatry at McGill University in Montréal — a four-year programme with an international flavour. During my secondary and university education the help of scholarships was critical, and when I went to study overseas at McGill University I received a postgraduate Ngārimu Scholarship, which helped me for the first two years. I greatly valued the assistance though realised that there is an obligation that goes with all scholarships for Māori.

Arohia and I went to Montréal in 1966, having before that acted as medical superintendent at the Kimberley Hospital just out of Levin. I was 26 at the time and went there for six months, while waiting to go to Montréal. To my surprise, and with no previous management experience, I was in charge of this 800-bed hospital. It was a premature appointment, but was probably good character building.

One reason for choosing McGill for psychiatric study was its broad and eclectic approach. The course drew on the philosophies and theories coming from the United Kingdom and Europe, as well as those that were developing in the United States. Psychiatry in those days was divided between the organic approach to understanding mental problems and the psychological approach, which was dominated then by psychoanalysis. McGill had a good mix between the two with opportunities for experience across the spectrum. While in Montréal I moved around four different training hospitals. One was a large mental hospital with about 1500 patients where I was introduced to pharmacological treatments for mental disorders. New tranquillisers had only recently become available, and were being used on a trial basis. Then I went to the Royal Victoria Hospital where they had a different approach, emphasising much more psychotherapy and psychoanalysis. I was also introduced to transcultural psychiatry — the study of culture in relationship to health and especially mental health. Later those insights were to shape my own thinking and practice. My third year of training was spent at the Jewish General Hospital where the approach was primarily on community psychiatry and family psychiatry. It was also to shape thinking and practice over the next decades. I spent the final training year in child psychiatry at the Montréal Children's Hospital.

While in Montréal we spent a summer with Whatarangi and Francie Winiata and their children. Whata was involved in post-doctoral research at the University of British Columbia and was undertaking field work in Montréal. Among many other things, Whata discussed the possibility of establishing a Māori university. When he returned to New Zealand he converted the idea into reality by establishing Te Wānanga o Raukawa based in Ōtaki.

For our part, Arohia and I returned to New Zealand in 1970, back to Palmerston North, where a psychiatric unit had just opened. I came in as one of the two psychiatrists, and discovered that the high levels of specialisation in pharmacology or child psychiatry or psychoanalysis were not always appreciated in Palmerston North. It was necessary to be more of an all-rounder. But the interest in cultural perspectives, social and family psychiatry continued and I persuaded the hospital to adopt a more community-focused approach to mental health; to recognise family therapy as a discipline and an important one, and to move away from in-patient treatment as the main treatment option. I became director of psychiatry in 1976. That entailed a clinical role as well as an advisory role, providing advice to the Board on the development of mental health services.

While professional activities demanded time and energy, we were by then living in the family homestead, adjacent to the Aorangi marae. Inevitably Arohia and I both became involved in marae management, community health and education, and iwi development. Professional activities were balanced by participation in the Rangitāne Māori Committee, the Raukawa District

Māori Council and later Te Rūnanga o Raukawa (as chair) and Te Wānanga o Raukawa. I am still secretary to the Aorangi Marae Trustees.

There was also pressure to extend my professional bias towards issues broader than mental health. Psychiatry in some ways was a narrow discipline, but the advent of community psychiatry extended the reach towards a public health model and in that respect my interest increasingly moved to Māori health. At the hospital we started a small Māori health team, six or seven nurses and myself, and decided that what was needed were not just professionals, but community workers who were respected by community and who had sound knowledge of whānau needs. After obtaining a grant from the Department of Health we were able to employ five Māori health community workers in 1983. They were the first Māori health community workers in New Zealand. These five people, untrained, took on the new roles with enthusiasm and courage. We had no idea at the time that the initiative would develop into a major way of delivering services; the five community workers were the forerunners of a much larger movement.

In 1984, the first national health hui in New Zealand since 1907, the Hui Whakaoranga, was held at Hoani Waititi Marae. It was a pivotal hui for defining Māori health as a discipline in its own right. From then on I found myself increasingly being drawn away from clinical practice into other dimensions of health and was asked to participate in a range of boards and committees, including the National Health Committee, the Alcohol Advisory Council and the Mental Health Foundation.

In 1986 I was appointed as a commissioner on the Royal Commission on Social Policy to recommend on social policies across health, education, social services, and employment. I was one of five commissioners who travelled around the country to undertake a comprehensive consultation process. My particular role was to consider the relevance of social policy to Māori development. The application of the Treaty of Waitangi to social policy had not previously been given serious attention; the main focus had been on land and other resources. The commission concluded, however, that the Treaty was as much about people and social policy as it was about physical resources. The Commission's life was cut short, partly because there was friction between David Lange (prime minister), and Roger Douglas (Minister of Finance). Our chairman, Sir Ivor Richardson, decided that we probably ought to move quickly and publish a report even if it were incomplete, because of the major changes occurring on the political front. The interesting point about that was the realisaion that no matter what the level of scholarship, what theories were relevant, what evidence was produced, there was a political level that shaped context and action. In the event we brought our report forward by some ten months. At a personal

Above: Speaking at a Massey University ceremony to honour Māori graduates.

Right: Sir Eddie Taihākurei Durie and Sir Mason Durie at Mason's investiture.

Below: with Te Aute students at the launch of Mason's book *Ngā Tini Whetū: Navigating Māori Futures* (Huia Publishers).

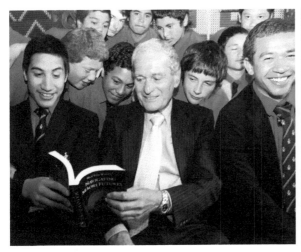

level, the commission experience had been a valuable and rewarding two-year immersion programme in social policy that also touched on economic policy, environmental policy, and Treaty perspectives.

The wide macro-framework was in sharp contrast to working as a clinician in a psychiatric hospital, and after the commission concluded I felt ready for a career change.

Academic work

Hugh Kāwharu had been the first professor of Māori Studies and Social Anthropology at Massey University, and when he returned to Auckland there had been some difficulty getting a replacement. As the commission came to an end, the Vice-Chancellor of Massey, Neil Waters, knew that I had been approached by other Massey staff to apply for the position and asked me to consider it again. His request was supported by a delegation consisting of Pākaka Tāwhai, Taiarahia Black, John Bevan Ford, and Pare Richardson, who also asked me to consider coming to Massey.

Although an academic position had not featured high on my agenda, I had Māori medical colleagues who were making major contributions to Māori health as academics. Professor Eru Pōmare was Dean of the Wellington School of Medicine at the University of Otago and had published extensive data on disparities in health between Māori and non-Māori. Professor Colin Mantell at Auckland University had contributed to research in obstetrics and gynaecology and had also initiated 'Vision 20/20', a programme designed to encourage more Māori to enter medicine. Buoyed by their examples, I decided to accept the invitation to lead Māori Studies at Massey University.

Separating Māori Studies from Anthropology was a first step, and a second was to refocus the academic curriculum to give greater recognition to contemporary Māori realities, including the implications of the Treaty of Waitangi, Māori health and iwi development. Much of my time in Māori Studies was spent embedding a research culture into the school; until then Māori Studies had largely been a teaching programme with very little research emphasis. A significant avenue opened in 1993 when the Health Research Council called for tenders to establish a Māori health research unit. I still had a strong interest in health and although it was unusual for Māori Studies to host a health programme, health research was something that had huge implications for Māori. I made an application from Massey and Eru Pōmare made one from the Otago Medical School. As it happened both were funded and in 1993, the two centres, each named Te Pūmanawa Hauora, were established.

In the same year, we made an application to the Foundation for Research Science and Technology, and were funded for another major project, Te Hoe Nuku Roa, a longitudinal study of Māori households. Both those programmes remain. A third programme was a Māori language development programme and a fourth was the C Company Māori Battalion project, headed by Monty Soutar. So we had four major research projects running in the school. Those programmes boosted the research element and signalled a new dimension for Māori Studies.

Māori scholarship

The research we were doing and the developments at Māori Studies had two elements. One was that it was part of the university context and therefore had to be aware of a range of methodologies and a range of disciplines. To have isolated Māori Studies as if it was somehow totally separate from other university endeavours would have narrowed the focus. But there was also the realisation that conventional university methodologies did not always accommodate Māori world views. Incorporating mātauranga Māori, Māori knowledge, seemed to be a logical step to develop Māori scholarship. So in Te Hoe Nuku Roa, for example, we were largely driven by Māori world views and Māori realities. Similarly in health, I had already formed that opinion, and had presented a paper at the Hui Whakaoranga about 'Whare Tapa Whā' as a model for understanding health. It recognised that health was more than a psychological or biological construct. Building Māori scholarship was about exploring the significance of mātauranga Māori to research, to teaching, to the elaboration of old knowledge and to the creation of new knowledge. Māori scholarship is often referred to as kaupapa Māori, but to me the mātauranga Māori base is what typifies Māori scholarship — it is not a static body of knowledge, but constantly developing.

Academic goals

When first coming to Massey I realised that the Department of Māori Studies was actually quite a small element of the university. If it were going to have impact there would be a requirement on me as the head of the school to make it visible within the wider university. I attempted to do that by volunteering for a wide range of faculty committees and taking a leadership role beyond Māori Studies in what were then the faculties of Humanities and Social Science.

It was also important to give greater clarity about the academic mission of Māori Studies. Because Māori Studies is not a subject area itself, but rather a grouping of a range of subject areas (language, history, political science, health, psychology), the focus of the department sometimes lacked clarity. My goal was to sharpen the focus by identifying Māori Studies as an academic centre committed to developing an integrated body of knowledge built around mātauranga Māori and the contemporary circumstances of Māori people.

My personal goals were to do research and to teach in subjects that interested me, mainly health, Treaty issues and Māori development. But the bigger issue was how to position Māori Studies as a relevant field of study in a modern university. That question deserves further discussion.

Teaching methods

Before coming to Massey I had little formal training in teaching and no real experience as a lecturer. The challenge was how to engage students so that learning became a passion rather than a requirement. In the last five years or so when I was in Māori Studies I would have 200 people in the Treaty of Waitangi class, in the same room. The use of Powerpoint and other technologies helped engagement, as did including topics that were of immediate relevance, but it was often a challenge.

The most significant gain, however, was in postgraduate teaching and supervision. Fostering an interest in advanced studies, including doctoral

Sir Mason and Lady Arohia Durie at the launch of
Te Pou Matakana Whānau Ora Commissioning Agency.

studies, has seen the emergence of a cadre of well qualified and well rounded Māori graduates. Teaching and research at the postgraduate level may become the major contributions that universities can make to Māori education.

In that respect the relationship between Māori Studies and wānanga deserves further attention. While there is an obvious overlap between the two sets of institutions, wānanga are probably better placed to undertake teaching and research that is mainly (if not entirely) built around Māori values, knowledge and perspectives, while universities are better equipped to reflect Māori in a global context, using a range of methods and perspectives.

Academic achievements

Within the university, Māori Studies became better respected and the inclusion of a Māori Knowledge and Development panel within PBRF (performance-based research funding) has given due recognition to Māori methodologies and knowledge. The scope of Māori Studies has also broadened, rather than narrowed. That scope now includes contemporary Māori development and does not relegate Māori Studies to a bygone era. The development of a research culture within Māori Studies and an emphasis on publications in reputable journals has also enabled Māori Studies to be better seen as a significant contributor to the wider university goals.

Māori leadership

Leadership is being able to identify a direction that will be useful to whoever might be following. It is about creating opportunities so that others can flourish. Academic leadership is no different. Leaders must be prepared to lead by example, to have an eye to the future, and to position followers — students or colleagues — to fulfil their own potential so that others can stand in a strong place. At a Hui Taumata Mātauranga I made the observation that Māori education is about living as Māori and as citizens of the world. Academic endeavours — research and teaching — will be more meaningful if they enable Māori to achieve both goals. Teaching for the sake of teaching; learning for the sake of learning; research for the sake of research will be hollow if in the end they do not serve a useful purpose.

I have been fortunate to have been influenced by some great leaders in health, at university, in communities and within iwi. One especially who has had a lasting impression was Hepi Te Heuheu. I had the privilege of serving as secretary of the Māori Congress not long after I came into Māori Studies, and saw first-hand the extent of inspirational leaders among iwi. But Hepi Te Heuheu stood out as one who had an uncanny knack of knowing what an issue was, when to pursue it, and when not to pursue it. I learned a lot from him. I recall when the idea of establishing a national Māori Congress to bring iwi together was first raised. It seemed overly ambitious. Others had tried it in the past but maybe the time was now right, and Hepi had taken the initiative to host the first meeting along with Te Ātairangikaahu, and Te Reo Hura from Rātana. Hepi chaired the hui. He went around the room asking one person from each iwi group to say what they thought about forming a Congress. When all had spoken and expressed support for the concept, he simply said "Well, that's really interesting. I think that's what we should do, but why don't we have lunch before you go." This left everyone feeling pleased on the one hand, but a little disappointed because there had been no opportunity to discuss the detail. I suspect Hepi knew that he had gone as far as he could, and that it was better not to push into an area that was going to be contentious, even difficult, at least not then. I saw him do it on other occasions when he took something to a point, judged that it might be better to hold off further discussion for the time being, and then reconvened when a positive approach was likely to be more certain.

Similarly Te Ātairangikaahu was a hugely impressive person to observe. She also had a skill for timing; when it was time to do something, or time to hold off. At Congress hui when some delegates would say "This is an important issue, we should take it back to our people to see what they think", she would often respond, "If you can't speak for your people, why are you here?" She was a pragmatic person, with great dignity coupled with much common sense.

I have also always been impressed by Whatarangi Winiata's leadership — his ability to look at the detail and the big picture at the same time. Whatarangi can draw attention to the last line of a complicated accounts system and talk about

Vice Chancellor Steve Maharey and Professor Taiarahia Black presenting a taonga to Sir Mason at a university function following his knighthood.

why there's a discrepancy of five dollars, and in the next breath can be talking about the impact of a government policy on Māori. He has a remarkable mind that can go from little things to great things. So he's been a good role model as well.

I like Hugh Kāwharu's approach to scholarship; he was a great scholar. He looked at the evidence. He wrote well and left a remarkable legacy for Māori academics. When I came to Massey he had been my predecessor and his shoes were always difficult to fill.

Balancing work and whānau

I have not always balanced work and whānau well. A combination of academic demands, the demands of marae, iwi, community, health and education interests often meant that family were disadvantaged. But any imbalance has been at least partially overcome by the way in which Arohia and I have been able to share the load. Her position as professor of Māori Education at Massey University inevitably made demands, not unlike those I experienced. But it also enabled us to at least understand the demands and to juggle them so that our children were not unduly displaced or our whānau ever ignored.

Challenges for future Māori academics

Māori academics have two major challenges: to be great academics judged by worldwide standards, and to be relevant to Māori. Being an academic is a means to an end, it's not an end in itself. Knowing there is a bigger picture, and that being an academic enables a contribution to that picture, will be important. Quite often academics get so involved in university business that they think being an academic is about the university.

Teaching, researching and publishing are critical for Māori academics, and in addition, translating academic work into gains for Māori is an equally important goal.

Future aspirations

My aspirations are essentially that the foundations we have built on will have been strengthened by our efforts and that the large cohort of current Māori academics will continue to build the knowledge base so that future generations can stand tall in a world that will be infinitely more complex than we have known.

Linda Tuhiwai Smith

Linda Tuhiwai Smith, of Ngāti Awa and Ngāti Porou, is Professor of Education and Māori Development, Pro Vice-Chancellor Māori and Dean of the School of Māori and Pacific Development at the University of Waikato. She has worked in the field of Māori education and health for many years as an educator and researcher and is well known for her work in Kaupapa Māori research. Professor Smith has published widely in journals and books. Her book *Decolonizing Methodologies: Research and Indigenous Peoples* has sold internationally since its publication in 1998. Linda is married to Māori educationalist Graham Smith of Te Whare Wānanga o Awanuiārangi. They have two children between them and two mokopuna.

Whānau background

My parents were teachers. I'm the oldest of three girls and my father, Hirini Mead, is Ngāti Awa from Te Teko, and my mum is Ngāti Porou from Ruatōria. So I grew up practising bi-culturalism across two iwi. My parents taught in places like Ruātoki in the Bay of Plenty, Minginui in the heart of Urewera, Waimārama in the Hawke's Bay, and Whatawhata near Hamilton. I spent quite a bit of time with my maternal grandmother. I grew up in a family that valued education, reading and ideas.

Although my family valued education, my parents were fairly laid back about it too. My father wanted us to be happy, but he did believe that to be happy, you had to work. My parents never came to teacher-only nights and I asked my mum why they never came, because the teachers always said that the Māori parents didn't attend. My mother said that there was no reason to attend, as they already knew all there was to know about us. My parents assumed that my sisters and I would do well, and that if we weren't happy we would tell them. They taught me to be independent and take responsibility for the choices I was making.

Education

My parents taught me until I was about 11, then I went to Waikato Diocesan in Hamilton for a couple of years. We then went to the United States where my father did his PhD. My friendships were mostly family, because we moved all of the time. Unlike some of my friends whose friendships are all about school, none of my friends were schoolmates. I was pretty good at netball and athletics and those sorts of things, but I mastered the art of coming fourth. One club I started at Auckland Girls' Grammar, where I completed sixth and seventh form, was the politics club. I had to ask the principal whether I could start this club, as we already had a French club and a journal club. The principal asked me how many people would join, and I had to think hard, but we managed to get about twenty girls to join the politics club, which consisted of my mates and other Māori girls at the school at the time. I was interested in politics, but I don't think most of my peer group were interested.

I had great high school teachers. I came to understand that I could think for myself and when I returned home to New Zealand, I went to university in the glory days of the 1970s. My parents went back to Canada and worked there while I stayed here in New Zealand. While at the University of Auckland I joined Ngā Tamatoa. I always say I majored in cafeteria studies for my bachelor's degree. I was quite good at 500 and euchre. I didn't take my studies seriously until a history lecturer asked me how much time I spent on writing my essays. I told my lecturer that I did all the reading, but I would start writing at ten o'clock the night before the essay was due. She replied, "Well, if you started a bit earlier, Linda, you could do some fantastic pieces of work, because you're capable of it." That was the first time someone at university had said that to me, that I was capable of doing good work. Up to that point I thought passing was good enough, let alone getting 'A' grades, and so I gradually cleaned up my act. After university I went teaching and then came back to the University of Auckland and did a master's degree, and it was at that level I became more serious about academic study. I ended up obtaining an MA with first class honours in Education.

My father taught Māori at the University of Auckland, so I avoided that area of study. I was interested in history. Keith Sinclair lectured in New Zealand history, and all the Māori students who took it, hated it. It made us feel that we were invisible in our country's history. I majored in medieval European history, then did a minor in Asian Studies. They were the only subjects available outside of Anthropology and Māori Studies. Those were the only areas that had culture in them. Were my choices rational or sensible? No. I chose classes that were after ten o'clock in the morning and I was quite happy to do late classes, because I preferred them. What I got out of a bachelor's degree was a good general education, and a broad knowledge about the world and Māori.

I made some half-hearted attempts to take law, and in Auckland I ran into David Lange, who was a law lecturer. I told him I wanted to take law, but that I was studying politics, geography and history. He told me that these were perfectly good subjects, and that if I wanted to do law, to return as a graduate

Linda with her sister Aroha, her father Hirini Moko Mead and grandmother Paranihia Emery, taken at Kokohinau Marae, Te Teko.

student. It was sound advice, but by then I had developed a particular view of lawyers, and decided that law wasn't for me either. In hindsight, I would like to have had the opportunity to take some of the options that are available now, but weren't available then. Back then we had limited options and strict regulations. It was hard to swap from one degree to the next. You had to pass everything, to pass that year. It was a different era altogether.

I didn't get serious about my studies or direction until my master's degree. Initially I was encouraged to do a master's in counselling, because I was at that time a counsellor in a secondary school. I was doing psychology and counselling when I started to sit in on sociology classes, which I loved. Halfway through, I transferred from counselling to sociology of education, and that became my ultimate educational pathway. I went on to complete my PhD in Education. It's the multi-disciplinary work that I love, essentially in the sociology of education.

Employment opportunities

I came out of an era where employment was not a problem. We all knew we could get work during the university holidays, so that was never a big driver for my generation. For us it was breaking through those barriers of getting to university that was the crucial thing. Once there, we gravitated towards becoming interested in social issues. For example, in Ngā Tamatoa, it was gaining an understanding of the role we could play as a generation in challenging the status quo, challenging racism, challenging the place of the Treaty, and it seemed a more hopeful, promising time for us during that era.

I went teaching because what I learnt was that I didn't want to be a politician. What I learnt about myself is I wanted to make a difference, and I thought the best difference I could make would be through my skills as an educator. I taught for ten years in intermediate schools in Auckland, then went to a secondary school as a counsellor. Through my counselling I became involved in health research, but I also retained my interest and work in educational research. They weren't planned pathways. I fell into them.

One thing I learned as a school counsellor is that you can stand at the bottom of the cliff and you can put rongoā on people and you can put band-aids on them, but you're going to do that every year unless you can get to the top of the cliff and stop them from falling. Once I understood that at a counselling level, I also understood it politically. Inherently it was all about education: if we are to make a difference in education we can't just work at the bottom of the cliff. We need people at the bottom of the cliff, but if we don't have people throughout the education system working in ways that help our people get to the top of the cliff, our lives are going to be an unending story of falling off the cliff and through the cracks, and that is what has really driven me. It's all about the potential that education has to change our lives and to improve our circumstances and to develop us as a people. I've never lost that belief that education is totally critical to our development.

I didn't choose a political career because politics is, to be polite, full of ego, rhetoric and talk. I wanted practical skills — I knew I was a good communicator from when I was in Ngā Tamatoa. I was talking to school assemblies about the Treaty of Waitangi, but that was insufficient. I wanted to change people's minds, and to do that you have to engage them. You have to find pathways for them so that they can come to that change of mind themselves, and that's the bit that interested me and it still interests me.

Doctoral journey

I loved research. I had been doing research prior to my PhD in the health area and I'd started to publish even before I'd begun the PhD. In the end, the PhD was a way for me to bring together quite significant, but diverse, strands of work. I had been doing research in health, sociology and the politics of education. I had been doing research around curriculum and kura kaupapa Māori, which I was part of, and the PhD allowed me to reflect on what it all means, and why I was doing this work. I often found it hard to explain to my supervisors why I was doing all these different things. In the end, I said to my supervisors that I have a child who I want to grow up speaking te reo, so in the morning, I drive in the opposite direction to my work to take her to kōhanga reo, because I believe in that kaupapa. I spend some time working with the nannies and the whānau at the kōhanga, and then I drive across town to school where I had a job working with naughty adolescent Māori girls. Then I would drive to university in the afternoon, and after that I would drive back to the kōhanga to pick up my child and speak with the whānau and nannies. This was my reality, and it's a reality for a lot of Māori. We're trying to build our culture, reclaim our language, look after our people, develop ourselves and that's what it is like every day. I'm interested in that journey, because it's important. Rather than pretending we don't do that and we can just focus on something narrow, I'd rather be realistic about the fact that it is complicated, intense and we have to work on many fronts simultaneously, and that's what development is about. That's what my PhD covered. I had to theorise that physical and material reality and make sense of it.

When I finished my PhD I was already employed part-time with my husband Graham at the University of Auckland. I finished the PhD one day and carried on working the next. I got my PhD first, and then Graham got his the next year, followed by Margie Hōhepa, Leonie Pīhama, Kuni Jenkins and Trish Johnston. We had a group of colleagues that all worked together. All of us got through our PhDs by working together. As one of us finished, we turned to help the others. The day I finished my PhD I became a supervisor of Margie Hōhepa. When Graham finished his PhD, he supervised Trish Johnston. By working that way we tried to bring through a cohort of doctoral students at Auckland.

Graham and I were doing our PhDs at the same time we were raising a family. We just did it. The challenge is being in an urban setting, where you need strong support. If you don't have whānau support, you need friends and colleagues to help. My daughter would probably say that she grew up in the university. I looked after my niece for a while. We took her bassinet and other things to work, and put her in an office next door to me. That's how you do it.

I had no idea what my PhD would look like at the end but I had already been publishing journal articles, so I was fairly confident as a researcher. I had a lot of experience as a researcher and I had two great supervisors, Professor Stuart McNaughton, who is still at the University

Linda and Graham Smith earlier in their careers.

of Auckland and is a developmental psychologist, and Roger Dyer, who is a sociologist and has now returned to England. Both of them encouraged me to say what I wanted to say. Roger would read a whole chapter and he'd write a question mark, a little red squiggle and then would note "I don't understand this piece", and that would be it. Those three pieces of feedback would drive me for a month, to address the feedback provided. I worked hard on my PhD and on pushing myself, reading things I would not normally read. My supervisors didn't give lots of detailed, technical feedback. Feedback was mostly based on the argument, logic, ideas, and the need for more evidence. I loved doing that kind of work and it's the one thing I don't have time to do any more, where you follow a thread — where you take an idea, think about the history of the idea, and it takes you here and takes you there. That was the kind of thinking I was encouraged to do as a student and I'm not sure PhD students get that sort of supervision any more. A lot of it is much more contained. These days, you conduct a literature review. Well, I didn't have to do a literature review, in the technical sense, because every chapter contained elements of a literature review.

Academic career

Having chosen my academic career, I had goals I wanted to achieve and a vision of the big picture. I wanted to transform education for Māori. I wanted to create capacity for Māori education, where we could run our own education. I wanted to train teachers, researchers, administrators and managers, to build this capability across the whole system of education, so that wherever educational decisions were being made, there were Māori in the room. But more than that, I wanted to help turn education over so that in terms of curriculum, pedagogy and systems, we were at the centre of it, not the remedial group on the side. That hasn't changed.

I probably spent ten years trying to learn how not to be a professor's daughter. I was determined to create my own path, because not only was my father a professor, he was pretty well known. I worked hard to develop my own identity and to be really good at what I was good at. I didn't want people to say that I had achieved what I had because I was Hirini Mead's daughter. I wanted to prove that I was a specialist in my field because I had done the work.

Looking back I had good preparation for my academic career for a number of reasons. I grew up in a home that valued reading, literacy and ideas, but more than that, in our home we had visitors, such as Uncle John Waititi, Nanny Amīria Stirling and others. My whānau interactions and connections were with people who were quite well known in the Māori world, but to me they were nannies, aunties, and uncles. That was an important grounding for me. There were others as well. My grandmother on my mother's side had a profound influence on me. She lived on our farm, up a valley between Tikitiki and Ruatōria. She had a one-eyed view about the world. It was like Ngāti Porou was the centre of the universe. Hikurangi is just behind our farm. You look out from this land, this is who you are, and this is your identity. That's your river, that's your maunga. It's not only about where you are from, but where you stand as a person, and how you look out with those eyes to the world. This is an important part of my life, centring me as an academic, and as a person. When I do all my work, it's with that sense. I'm in a Māori world, looking out.

What's unusual about my career is that it's really half of a career, because Graham is the other half. We were appointed to a joint position in Auckland, and then as Graham developed his specialist areas, and I developed mine, we eventually got one whole position each and worked collaboratively in terms of

Linda Smith at Waipapa Marae in Auckland with her father, Hirini Moko Mead, when she became co-director of Ngā Pae o Te Māramatanga.

what we built at the University of Auckland at that time. I basically did what I thought I needed to do. I enjoyed teaching and I loved supervision, and every now and again an opportunity would come my way. Sometimes you decide to decline an opportunity, and at other times, you decide to give it a go.

I was offered an opportunity to become assistant dean of Arts, and my role was to build the University of Auckland programme at Manukau Institute of Technology. There were no plans or preconceived ideas, and I enjoyed that kind of challenge. It meant building the relationships with Manukau and Auckland, trying to persuade departments to develop a first-year paper, produce the business case, negotiate with the librarians and other special interest groups in the university and the Institute to start a programme, and then teach it. I felt I was successful because we got a programme started and it's strong. I continued as assistant dean of Arts, which expanded to include advising academics. I started to learn more about the university. I was on promotions committees, interview panels, the curriculum review, which was a major task. I was on reviews of departments, and reviewed departments in other universities. I got a broad view of how these institutions work, what makes them effective, how you deal with problems in the system, how you reorganise things, and that's what set me up for what I do now. I have a solid understanding of universities and their processes, and how you can cause change to happen in an institution. I used all of those opportunities to learn and to appreciate its strengths, as well as identify where Māori were missing out.

At the University of Auckland it became clear that you had to get merit across teaching, research and service. You had to be outstanding and well rounded. On reflection, the department I was in was ranked as one of the top five education departments in the world at that time. This meant we had great leadership models, fabulous mentoring, as well as a culture where everyone was performing well and a strong work ethic existed. You could go in to the office on Christmas Eve and there would be staff working, as well as students. One Christmas holidays we abandoned Graham, who stayed home and wrote his PhD, while we holidayed. He complained for years about the baked beans he had for Christmas dinner. It was that sort of culture and dedication that differentiated our department from others. It's what we were mentored to do, to work hard. It's a lifetime investment, not a nine-to-five job.

Being Māori

During that era there were a lot of Māori trying not to be Māori, because they were ashamed of being Māori and were ambivalent about their identity. What my generation did was to say that it's time to be proud of our identity, of where we come from, and not try to diminish or tell jokes about it. This is who we are and it's fantastic. This was a generation who wanted to reclaim our identities, and challenge and disrupt the system that we were in, because we saw no future for ourselves if New Zealand carried on the way it was. If New Zealand ignored the Treaty of Waitangi, if it tried to destroy our identity and language, then there was no future for us. Our generation played an important role in saying that we didn't accept the status quo. We need to acknowledge this and we need to move into a different direction, and it's not that previous generations weren't trying. What we had on our side was critical mass, the ability to mobilise people, a youthful message, and some effective political organisation skills. A lot of Ngā Tamatoa people came out of the University of Auckland and there were other groups at Victoria and Massey that were doing similar work. I would characterise it as a generational thing. For those of us at Auckland, we had all come through kōhanga and had all been part of the development of kōhanga and kura kaupapa Māori in Auckland. What we had in common was a commitment to kaupapa Māori, and you will see it in all our written work — a development of kaupapa Māori as an idea, as a way of understanding not just what happens in school, but what happens in the search.

Māori women in academia

There weren't many women professors or Māori women professors for that matter. When I applied for promotion, one of my Pākehā women colleagues suggested that my application for promotion was premature. It made me think. Two years previous, she had advised me against my community work and service, because it wouldn't help my career. She was in a senior position, but I got a professorship faster than her because in the end, service matters, but not service where you are doing what people expect you to do. It is getting leadership through service, being able to have national and international roles and reputations in that service. It's not about doing more; it's about trying to do the kind of service that makes a big impact.

I got solid career advice. The vice-chancellor at Auckland took me for morning tea and told me to think about applying for promotion. I don't think many staff get a visit from a vice-chancellor advising to do this, so to me, it was a sign that maybe I should be thinking about it, and taking it seriously. Once I decided that's what I was going to do, because you do have to consciously make that decision, then I thought all right, I'm going to go for it, and it's a career choice. I will take on board whatever comes with that position.

My move to Waikato University surprised some people, but for me it was a sensible move. Waikato is a lot more visibly Māori. It's also closer to where I'm from, and for me that was important. I can now drive to Ruatōria in a day — leave in the morning, get there and do what I need to do — whereas from Auckland, it was always psychologically much more difficult to get home to Ruatōria. In that respect it was a good natural step for me. In terms of my position here, I feel that I've got the whole institution that I can work with, and therefore I can influence a whole institution, and that's been challenging and interesting. I have been successful in some areas, and in other areas I am building on the success that's already here. I feel valued by my Māori colleagues as well as the vice-chancellor and the university at large, so it's a nice position that I'm in.

Professional achievements

My greatest achievement as an academic scholar is through my students who have done well. Another is the development of the research institutes that I've been part of initiating in the research world. We are in a bit of a glitch at the moment, but we've got this amazing capacity of Māori scholarship, and I think I've played a good role in that development, and been part of something way bigger than myself. In terms of my own research, I was writing at a time when no one else was writing, and that was a pivotal moment. You can't predict that when you do research what's going to take off internationally and what's not, but clearly my work around indigenous methodologies has found an international voice and has helped to create an international platform. It is a major scholarly contribution. It's what I'm known for internationally, but in New Zealand I'm known more as an educationist. I don't see them as being separate; they are different faces of the same coin. The desired outcome of my work is change and transformation, but what I've learned after years of working in the universities is we think we've made space and gains. However, these are old institutions, and when someone moves on, the spaces close. To keep those spaces open all the time we have to have people that fill them and they've got to be good people. They must do the work, be dedicated, and understand what their role is. One concern I have about the younger generation is, they just cruise in and think they can be like any other international scholar. They tend to overlook some of the critical things that we have had to fight for, which is a place for Māori — for Māori knowledge and Māori language. We can never take that for granted. That's a deliberate, conscious kaupapa we have to wear and if we think our students don't need support because they are smart and they can come in like everybody else, then we're fooling ourselves. We have to provide support for them, we have to support each other and we have to understand that these institutions are ancient ones, and to make a foothold in them, we've got to put in decades of work.

I've had an interesting journey and if I was starting again, things would be different because the world is different. The drivers, context and the options are all different. When I look at some of my generation, they might say well you've ended up where you were going to end up. But that's not the perception that I have of my career because along the line I have made different sorts of choices and I don't regret those. I could have gone straight on from a bachelor's to a master's to a PhD, but teaching urban intermediate-aged kids has taught me many things. There's nothing like teaching 30 smart Māori kids in South Auckland and learning how to engage them in learning. In that space you learn more about teaching than you actually teach. Those experiences last a

lifetime. The other thing is that teaching is rewarding. Someone's eyes sparkle and their face lifts and those sorts of experiences have been important.

Graham and Linda Smith at her investiture as a Companion of the NZ Order of Merit.

Māori scholarship

The state of Māori scholarship is lively at one level. There are more publications than ever. When I did my PhD there was hardly any Māori or indigenous literature I could use, and now many of my students can write a literature review and 80% of the literature is Māori or indigenous. In terms of volume across different disciplines, more work is required. I am interested in some of the quality, intellectual depth, thoughtfulness and robustness of that work.

In different disciplines there are different sorts of capacities being developed, and in some disciplines we have a long way to go before we can break through those disciplines. There is definitely more sense of community within Māori academia. Some of our younger scholars are exciting. I love the fact that you could go to a conference and everyone in the room is talking about mātauranga Māori, assuming a high level of Māori language knowledge, and being able to have a conversation that's respectful and challenging. That wasn't there when I did my PhD at the beginning of my career.

The body of literature has expanded, it's lively, there's a lot of divergence in it. Some of the work is interesting, some of it you ponder about, and then some of it is work in progress. We need to do more. Some of the scholarship varies. When I look at my father's work, I'm miles away from what

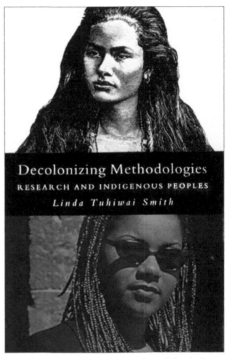

Otago University Press

he's achieved, and he and his generation did that on their own. What Mason Durie has done, and we can go back further to Te Rangi Hīroa and Āpirana Ngata, and the originality and depth of thinking they produced in their era. Our new generation still has to step up. Earlier generations have set a high benchmark for us and we have to work hard to achieve.

It is my hope that *Decolonizing Methodologies* is a useful contribution towards instilling pride and dignity in researchers, whether they be Māori or indigenous peoples all over the world. It demonstrates beyond any questioning that kaupapa Māori research is important for building scholarship about us, and our own culture. It also shows that kaupapa Māori research has a place of its own in today's academia.

Māori academic leadership

My experiences as a Māori academic leader have several dimensions. One is your role in society at large, and that's usually around discipline and strength. There are different ways you can exercise that leadership role, as a support leader or as an active researcher trying to develop knowledge about our system. Being credible out in the world is important. Our research and teaching is what grounds that credibility. Within the institution, if you are successful at leading things then you will get the opportunities to lead. If you stuff up, you're in trouble. My position requires me to pay attention strategically to what's happening in the institution, and to understand both the policy dimension and the people dimension, and trying to read the environment to ensure there are spaces for Māori. It's about knowing how to mount arguments, put up business cases, be proactive, be a good citizen, set a vision and encourage staff to fulfil that vision. It's about having a sense of what you want to achieve in an institution and then going for it and not doing it in a naïve way, but systematically building.

In terms of academic leadership most of my role models weren't Māori, other than my dad. They were people I thought were good people, who achieved things. For many years I have been on committees and I have always learnt from those in chairperson positions. I would have been on committees for twenty years before I chaired a committee, and that's a long apprenticeship. It was a good apprenticeship, because I learnt from some fabulous chairs. There's a level of subtlety in the way you do your work because you always have to be respectful of knowledge and people, and so you've got to figure out how to

Graham and Linda Smith open the Adivasi Institute in India, an educational environment for the study of tribal history, folklore, cultural geography, social dynamics, economy, development studies, medicine, music, arts and theatre.

intervene but still be respectful. That apprenticeship for me has been important. I've had role models but I've also had opportunities where I've learnt.

Many of my relationships with my peers, fellow Māori academics and professionals, have been formed over years, so they are good relationships. We may not communicate much with each other, but when we need each other, an email or a phone call is all that's required. There are some relationships that are formed through people with whom you have commonality. I've got to know people across the institutions. But I also have good connections internationally with indigenous colleagues, as well as good colleagues in education and in health. It's all about relationships and learning that those are important also in the academic world.

In terms of Māori researchers and scholars, I have come to meet and know most of them through Ngā Pae o te Māramatanga (New Zealand's Māori Centre of Research Excellence). The decision by the Government not to continue the funding for Ngā Pae post-2015 was disappointing. A shortsighted decision, it has been met with a lot of confusion and anger within the research community here and abroad. Māori research, and in particular kaupapa Māori research, has a critical role to play in Māori aspirations for wellbeing and development. Many research initiatives have come to fruition and been supported by the innovative approaches taken by Ngā Pae and its researchers over the past decade or so.

What compelled me as a senior Māori academic and 'critic and conscience of society' to become involved and in so doing make public commentaries is that it would be a scandalous waste to dismantle Ngā Pae, that too much hard work will have gone down the drain, that Māori intellectual potential will be squashed, and that it will set Māori research back 30 years. I hadn't spent my whole career studying the institution of research and what it has taken for Māori and indigenous people to engage in that institution just to sit back and watch a key platform dismantled. Many people were asking me what needed to be done. I suggested a range of ideas for those who wanted to show active support, including Māori scholars and our indigenous colleagues overseas to write letters of support for Ngā Pae o te Māramatanga addressed to relevant government ministers like the Minister of Tertiary Education Steven Joyce, and the funder, the Tertiary Education Commission. I encouraged social media experts to use their creative skills. I urged iwi who have engaged in research collaborations to support the cause by writing to Pita Sharples, the Minister of Māori Affairs, and so on. We were fortunate in that eventually the Government showed signs of listening to the protests and backtracked to an extent that it agreed to continue funding Māori research albeit via an open tender process with reduced funding.

Balancing obligations

It's a big assumption that I have balanced my personal, family and community commitments with my academic life. One advantage of having a husband like Graham is that we worked it out between us, and we have also had separate careers for the last two decades, including Graham being away in Canada for six years. How did we balance it? I'm not sure we had a personal life, but we have had a life driven by kaupapa around education. More recently we have started to plan a personal life, a life after university and a life after work, and that's important. It's how you strive for balance and how you value your relationships. It's important to look after your core relationships, because they're your source of support, and not get too carried away with what it means to be well known or to have a flash title. None of those actually matter. What

matters is that you are a good person, and that you are connected to your family. Can you talk with your family, and are you grounded? That's what balance is about. It's about being genuine, down-to-earth and trying to be good at the things you do and practise. In education we talk about whānau all the time, but to me it's hypocritical to be writing about it and not practising it. If it's real, then it's real enough for us to practise it.

Advice for aspiring Māori academics

My advice to aspiring, emerging Māori academics is to broaden your horizons. Part of the challenge that younger ones face is that their thinking is too narrow. They need to broaden their experience. Some romanticise the Māori world and that's dangerous, because it's not romantic, it's hard. Some take the Māori world for granted and don't critically understand that world, and that's another danger. The thing that most frustrates me when I look at some of our students, are those who have got real talent and aren't working it. If you've got talent, you have a duty to work hard at developing that talent, and not to cruise, because in a decade's time the one who didn't have as much talent but did the work will surpass the one with talent. I have seen so many examples of that, and I see these gifted young people and they're not working hard enough. They are too narrow in both what they are studying and also in what they are doing out in the community. Some of them are not politically engaged. You don't have to be in politics to be aware of what's happening in our society, but we owe it to ourselves to know what's going on. We may not be able to change everything, but part of being a good Māori citizen is to know exactly what our society is about and what our role is in that society. Those are the things that concern me about our younger generation. Having said that, I have some fantastic colleagues who have great general knowledge, are grounded in their iwi, are fluent in te reo and doing brilliant research. I hope that they are the ones who, in the next ten years, will be in the positions that I have.

What I most fear is that people will not carry on the work. The next generation have to pick up what the last generation have created, and do more work. There are some people who by nature like to come into places and start writing lots of rules, and I am not that kind of person. They want to impose order, but in the end, it starts to do exactly what colonialism did, and that's a general tendency that some people have. I saw it in the development of kōhanga, of kura kaupapa Māori, and of research institutes. There are those that can open doors and make spaces, and then there are those who want to control and restrict entry to those doorways and spaces. I would want to be known as someone who has opened doors and made spaces, and I would like the next generation to take that seriously. Their job is to keep those spaces open and create new spaces.

Future aspirations

I don't want to stay at Waikato for too long. In the next couple of years I see myself retiring and probably going to Te Whare Wānanga o Awanuiārangi as a retired professor, if they will have me, and putting in more work there at the iwi level. Ruatōria will only be several hours away. I do more work at the moment with my Ngāti Porou side, but I'm always caught between the two iwi and ultimately that's what I want to return to.

GRAHAM HINGANGAROA SMITH

Distinguished Professor Graham Smith is of Ngāti Porou, Kāi Tahu, Ngāti Apa and Ngāti Kahungunu descent. Raised in the Wairarapa by his mother and kuia, he was schooled at St Stephen's, Auckland, and has over forty years of formal involvement in Māori education. His academic field is mostly in Education and other aspects of Māori self-development. During his studies at the University of Auckland, Graham Smith focused much of his attention on the inextricable relationship between education and politics and the subsequent need to reform education and schooling to better deliver Māori social, political, cultural and educational aspirations. He was a key person in the kura kaupapa Māori development, and has been a principal contributor to the debate on Kaupapa Māori theorising. Although his professional career has included teaching and senior management positions within New Zealand schools, Professor Smith has also held senior academic positions at the University of Auckland, the University of British Columbia, and the University of Sydney. He was formerly chief executive for Te Whare Wānanga o Awanuiārangi. Graham and his wife Professor Linda Tuhiwai Smith, have two children between them and two mokopuna.

Whānau and teacher influences

I was probably more interested in sport than schooling in my early years, but at home there was always a strong emphasis and interest in education and schooling. Our mother, who was a single parent raising five kids, was totally interested in education and had made sure that we (at least at home) were doing things that were learning-oriented. At school I was generally interested in everything, but at that early stage the real impact was from our mother's drive and from an intense spirit of competition with my brothers.

The best lesson I learned at school was that I was culturally 'different'. This was an important foundational learning for me. I learned quickly that our cultural nuance needed to be struggled over, given the dominant Pākehā cultural expectations embedded in schooling. We lived in a middle-class area of Masterton. This was very much a Pākehā-dominant neighbourhood and we and a couple of other families were the odd ones out. So in this sense our cultural alienation was both within the school and within the neighbourhood. At various points we were made to feel uncomfortable, but we also managed to have some Pākehā mates and interaction that was positive.

The Wairarapa area has a particular history in terms of its early contact with Pākehā settlers. The Wairarapa was settled very early following initial contact. British settlers under the Wakefield schemes arrived on the Petone foreshore in Wellington and walked over the hills to settle the low-lying lands of Kahungunu in the Wairarapa and Hawke's Bay. This early intrusion by Pākehā facilitated the early loss of culture and language from the Māori who occupied these areas. To put it politely, the subsequent climate of race relations was tense and always high-profile in these parts and overtly played out within schools and other institutional environments. So you learned quickly that you were different, particularly when you went to a Pākehā-dominant school like Landsdowne. This experience hardened me up to understanding quickly which side of the fence I belonged on, and the things that I needed to subsequently organise in terms of my future. It wasn't totally 'black and white' in that sense. There were some excellent teachers that I've encountered at different places within my formal schooling and yet other people who were not very supportive of Māori (and myself). More often I feel that I got great support probably because I was talented at sport. I played rugby and cricket to a high level, not just in schools but also at representative level as well — this all starting at primary school.

Two teachers were influential in my primary schooling, both of whom were immigrants. When I was at primary school, a man came out with the Dutch resettlement programme to New Zealand in the 1950s. His name was Peter Aerts. He was a young teacher, and in his class he treated everybody as equals.

He was interested in culture and difference, and consequently sent positive messages about Māori culture. This made me feel accepted and worthwhile. He was also making an effort to learn Māori language himself and would practise on the class. He was also strongly interested in his own culture and I can still remember Dutch phrases he taught us in the class and I liked that. There was an empathy for the cultural context of my own background and I found it easy to fit in.

Even though we lived in this middle-class area of Masterton, we were still a poor family; there was always that cringe or whakamā associated with this. For example, when I was supposed to pick up a prize at the school assembly I didn't want to go to the prize-giving; I wanted to stay at home, more for social-class elements rather than cultural impediments. I didn't want to go to prize-giving because the only footwear I had was a pair of old gumboots I used to wear to school every day, as I didn't have any real shoes. I didn't want to go up on the stage looking different to all of the other kids who had flash shoes, so I stayed away. But Mr Aerts brought the prize around to our house and knocked on our door. I saw his shadow through the glass door and I ran away down to the back of the house and hid, because I was ashamed he would see inside our house. We had hardly any furniture and things like that. He came around and made sure I got my prize. The fact that he did this sent messages that he understood all of that stuff and yet he believed in me. He was supportive.

Another primary teacher from Landsdowne who helped me was Mervyn Parkinson. He came from Lancashire in England. He also encouraged me a lot with my schooling and sporting development. He kept telling me I was bright and that I should go on to intermediate.

Beyond primary school the one teacher that really influenced me was Evan (Joe) Lewis, the principal at the predominantly Māori boarding school of St Stephen's, at Bombay in Auckland. He was the principal during the time I attended in the mid-'60s. He was an extremely astute educator, and understood the need to develop us young Māori boys strongly in both worlds: Māori and Pākehā. He also understood that we needed to succeed both within and also as a result of the education and schooling system.

He was also concerned to build young Māori men with character. He encouraged within us a strong desire of getting out there — of being challenging but also engaging in the 'doing', yet always maintaining our Māori culture.

Joe Lewis was also a renowned rugby coach. He built schooling success off the back of this strong sporting influence. While I was at St Stephen's we never saw the sporting and educational elements as being independent of each other; rather they, along with kapa haka, were regarded as strong complementary skills. There was also the boarding school context of being kept away for five years with other young Māori students who thought similarly and who were travelling in basically the same direction. Another important element was the compulsory prep, every night for two hours. It was all good, and really formative for the way in which I've carried on things later in life, particularly with my own educational career.

At the age of 12 I was living with my grandmother Te Paea Paku, who was a kuia in the Wairarapa. She was a prominent leader and spoke on the marae. I lived with her for some time while attending the intermediate school in Masterton. I stayed with her because my mother wanted me to attend the intermediate, which had just opened, and at that time we were living out in the country at Ngaumu State Forest. When I started at the intermediate we had bright red jerseys, bright red caps and so on. I had won my way into the top class. It was a huge school and served several primary schools in the Wairarapa. The school was streamed and students allocated to classes according to a selection process conducted at the primary schools. Getting into the top class was significant because I was the only Māori pupil in any of the top three classes. I found the size of the school and heavy Pākehā cultural context difficult and even hostile at times. After about a term, a group of us got into a big scrap in the playground and that switched me off, because the ones who got punished were the Māori and the Cook Islanders. I felt a great sense of injustice as the incident was very much about us being teased as Māori kids by some of the Pākehā. After that happened, I packed in schooling; my grandmother used to send me off to school and I never used to get there. I would divert to Queen Elizabeth Park, which had big beautiful gardens, lots of people and visitors and a hive of other activities going on, including sports, all of this in the centre of town. I dodged school for several weeks until I was found out.

I often tell the story about eating my lunch at intermediate school. My grandmother used to get up early in the morning, and light up the stove to fry bread at about six o'clock. She would butter it, wrap it in newspaper and put it in a flax kit ready for me to take to school. I'd get to school and then at lunchtime we used to sit in an alcove outside the classroom to eat lunch together. My Pākehā classmates would open up their plastic lunch boxes with their 'nice' sandwiches, no crust on their bread, diagonally cut and so on. On the other hand, I would pull out my paper from the kete, and unwrap it, pull out the fried bread with golden syrup smeared over it. But often, when I would pull the fried bread out of the newspaper and go to eat it — it would have words like *Wairarapa Times-Age* printed across it! Of course all the kids would notice, pull faces and make rude comments like — "Oooh, look at his Māori food." In these circumstances, you learn quickly to throw your lunch away on your way to school because of the whakamā, shame. While those types of incidents are all formative experiences, they were hurtful and I still remember them today. In the end, I abandoned school for a while, 'truanted' is probably a more accurate word. I did this until my mother found out about it and then she came in to town and took me away. I then went back to the forestry and caught the country bus every morning to attend Wainuioru Country School. This was far better and more enjoyable. It had a good mix of down-to-earth country kids; farmers' kids, forestry workers' kids, and Māori kids from the marae. We all got on well but at age 12 I would say that I didn't have any aspirations about what I wanted to be. Although some ideas were starting to form, my mind was made up for me in a way because at that stage I won a scholarship to go to St Stephen's in Auckland, all the way from the backblocks of the Wairarapa. That's what turned the corner for me, winning a Pāpāwai Kaikōkirikiri Scholarship. I was being sent to St Stephen's to receive a serious education.

Secondary and tertiary education

I fell into things after being sent off to boarding school. Boarding school was a totally new experience. I was frightened when I began, but after five years and lots of success both on the academic and sporting fronts, I left with my university entrance and seventh form certificate, and a high profile in sport. I went straight from St Stephen's to the University of Auckland, because my father was living in Auckland and he was visiting me at school and had supported me going to boarding school. I got to know Auckland quite well. I'd originally started off studying for a joint BA/LLB degree, but I also early on played rugby for the University of Auckland rugby club and with interesting identities like Graham Henry, Winston Peters, Graeme Thorne, and a bit later on with John Drake, Grant Fox, Sean Fitzpatrick and those guys. Because I was really interested in sport and I was also playing cricket, it distracted me quite a bit from my studies, plus I was heavily involved in the Māori club and other student activities at university. I pulled out of the LLB part and studied for my BA in Anthropology and Māori Studies. I liked Anthropology because it resonated with a lot of my background experiences up to that time. I dropped the LLB part thinking I'd come back to it, but I never did. I stayed at Auckland right through my undergraduate studies and went straight into a master's. Taura Eruera, who at the time was leading Ngā Tamatoa, and myself, were the only Māori master's students in Anthropology. Anthropology was a big department at Auckland. We used to meet at the Māori club, including Ngā Tamatoa members Syd and Hana Jackson, Tame Iti, Donna Awatere and Ngāhuia Te Awekōtuku. Pita Sharples, Bob Mahuta, Hone Kaa, Jim Milroy and Hirini Melbourne were also contemporaries at the time I was at Auckland.

Notable staff members included Bruce Biggs, Pat Hōhepa, Sid Mead and Matiu Te Hau. I came to university with a 'boarding school' view, and as such very much captured within the hegemony of 'it's all about sport'. I was politically conscientised about the differences between Māori and non-Māori at that point, and certainly had a lot of experiences, but you didn't really articulate it within an overt or coherent conscious understanding. Anthropology helped me to understand a little bit more about that. Of course, the politics of Ngā Tamatoa and other things that were going on at the University of Auckland at the time also helped my political understanding. I guess, in a sense, the boarding school environment is so closeted that you come out thinking in a particular way and that the world is 'this big', when in actual fact it's much bigger and far more complex. At university, and living in the big city of Auckland, I learned a lot of things about life in general, about myself, and about understanding that Māori advancement is a political struggle. My subsequent engagement in and through education has been predicated on this understanding that education and schooling are an important site of struggle to enable the transforming of the Māori social, economic, cultural and political condition.

At that time in the University of Auckland, we had a fledging Māori Studies department, which was a sub-department of Anthropology. Bruce Biggs had laid out a vision for a language grammar and a linguistic methodology to formally teach it. We had a large number of Māori staff. Dr Pat Hōhepa had just come back from overseas, as had Dr Sid Mead. They were there as staff members and also provided the benchmark as Māori 'scholars'. Rangi Walker was still in Extension Studies, and wasn't in Māori Studies. Once I had completed my master's in Anthropology I had sought to go straight on to do a PhD at Auckland — but I specifically requested to do my PhD in Māori Studies. Māori Studies at that time did not offer a PhD in its own right, but allowed students to undertake their PhD as part of the Anthropology Department. In making the request to do it in Māori Studies I was trying to get the mana of Māori Studies out from under the colonising umbrella of Anthropology. What I was doing was actually part of a wider political initiative. At the time I applied to do a PhD, a series of meetings were convened by the professors of Anthropology and Māori Studies (Ralph Bulmer, Bruce Biggs and Hugh Kāwharu). My request was that I should do my PhD in Māori Studies, and it should be a doctorate in the Māori Studies arena. In the end they turned me down on the basis that my proposal was too 'ethnographic' and therefore should be done in Anthropology.

At the time, I was beginning to write political papers substantiating my arguments. I wrote a paper called *Propping up the sky: the separation of Ranginui and Papatuanuku*, co-opting the metaphor to express the need for the separation of Māori Studies from Anthropology. I presented the paper at a public seminar at the University of Auckland. It received much support from Māori students and others but not from the staff or the wider university decision-makers.

Because of this lack of change I resolved that I wouldn't be doing a PhD in Māori Studies under the Anthropology Department. However, I would also acknowledge some great people and supportive mentors from within the Anthropology Department, namely my master's supervisors, Professors Anne Salmond and Steven Webster; Drs Garth Rogers, Roger Green, Andy Pawley and others. Māori students were also agitating at the time for the building of the marae, and I was tutoring in Māori Studies. That was an interesting time because I tutored with Wharehuia Milroy. We shared an office, and in the front office was Matt Te Hau. All of these Māori speaking 'icons' of Māoridom I had an opportunity at Auckland to rub shoulders with, and to learn from them — Purewa Biddle, George and Tahi Tait, Brownie Pūriri, Hēmi Pōtatau, Bob Mahuta, Bob Jackson, John Tapiata, John Rangihau — to name a few.

One disappointment of my time at the University of Auckland, and which has influenced the way that I mentor and grow Māori graduate students, was that there wasn't a lot of nurturing of graduate students in my student days. One or two were fortunate because they had other cultural capital, if you like. For example, as in my case, if you played rugby and you were a bit of a star in the Auckland scene you got support, but other than that, there was very little mentoring intentionally aimed at building Māori master's and doctoral student potential. The expectation when I first got to Auckland was that you went overseas to do your doctorate. This was the pathway taken by Sid Mead, Pat Hōhepa, Pare Hopa, Maharaia Winiata, Whata Winiata and others. Doing your doctorate in New Zealand was not the 'done' thing. It was considered to be an inferior pathway and you were encouraged to go overseas to get an international credential. As a result of this lack of mentoring and graduate succession planning, I have put great store on growing the numbers of Māori master's and PhD graduates both in New Zealand and internationally. This growth is not just about the credentials — we also need to create a critical mass of well qualified scholars who have a consciousness about working for the betterment of the people and who are committed to making change happen. Changes not just for themselves as a 'privatised academics', but change as workers for the people, for their iwi, as transforming agents.

Māori scholarship

Māori scholarship is having the intellectual and practical excellence to enable full participation in both Māori and Pākehā worlds. Such an agenda requires all Māori to become transformers, as the status quo situation is not working for too many Māori. This requires 'all hands to the wheel', including our Māori scholars. 'Māori scholarship' requires a critical understanding of the reality of our lives now and where we are up to in respect of our contemporary existence, while simultaneously remembering that Māori still need the knowledge and skills to be Māori citizens. There are still elements of our cultural nuance that need to be supported and I hope that the scholarship element that we produce in Te Whare Wānanga o Awanuiārangi, for example, enables our students to participate equally and fully with excellence in our Māori world and also as citizens of the world — excellence in the world domain and excellence in our Māori domain.

Māori scholarship is not a concept that belongs only in the academic institutional context. It is just as important to recognise our community scholars and their achievements. We need to recognise our organic intellectuals. In this sense, scholarship should not just depend on socially and culturally constructed indicators, such as Performance-Based Research Fund factors. For example, what is the use of having a publication in an obscure international journal with a readership of three people, versus the practical implementation of ideas through a marae development programme that impacts a whole community? The distinction I am making here is that it is one thing to write about what should happen and another thing entirely to make things happen. In other words, don't tell me what you want to do, tell me what you have done — past tense. This is what I mean by the connecting of theory to practice. This is where I have tried to work and what I mean by 'transforming praxis' — the linking of theory to critical practice.

Professional career

I stayed in Auckland after I had completed my degrees and applied to go to teachers' college. I have to admit that my reason for doing this in the first instance was not because I was really interested in teaching kids, but in those days you got paid to train as a teacher and I was broke after doing my master's, so I saw it as a means of getting another qualification and an income at the same time. I went to do the one-year training at the Auckland Teachers' College. When I got there, they didn't have any Māori component in the one-year programme so I ended up teaching that for the rest of the students there. I went through that year, graduated with distinction, went out teaching and loved it. I went to Blockhouse Bay Intermediate and from that first moment of being in the classroom I felt absolutely comfortable and in my niche. I became passionate about it — particularly the opportunity to make a difference in the lives of young kids and I thought it was going to be my career for life.

I did well, and I was supported by the principal and the Auckland inspectorate to go for an early grading. I ended up going for grading around two years early, which had not been done before. They made a special case for me and I ended up with the top grading in that space. I was quickly asked to take up an acting deputy principal role. I was sent in to a school to sort out problems relating to behavioural issues concerning Māori students. This initially took me about a week to do, because the solutions were straightforward. The main issue was that the kids weren't being taken seriously or being meaningfully engaged. So we developed a range of responses. In the classroom we engaged with pedagogical and curriculum issues. In the extra-curricular domain we initiated activities like talent quests, kapa haka, clubs and a full range of sporting activities in lunchtime to occupy the kids.

We also made the teachers get out of the staffroom, walk around the school and participate with the kids. As far as I was concerned, it was a simple set of issues that needed to be addressed. The school righted itself quickly and I enjoyed my time there.

I developed a profile in the teachers' union and among teachers as a counsellor for the union. One of my speciality areas in education at this time was working with children with special abilities. This was an initiative championed by Dave Freeman of the Auckland inspectorate, which shifted away from the narrow focus on the intelligence quotient that was central to the notion of 'gifted children' to emphasising a broader range of talents and skills embraced in the notion of 'children with special abilities'. This notion allowed us to embrace cultural elements and talents, leadership skills and sporting prowess as important learning attributes. In broadening this concept we were able to recognise and include more Māori students as talented and as achievers.

I taught for a little while in schools but didn't last long, not because I didn't like it but because I got invited to take up other opportunities. I was asked to go to the Auckland Secondary Teachers' College to lecture in Education. I taught some generic classes there and I was also asked to contribute to teaching the one-year Ātākura course. This was a special programme developed to attract fluent Māori-speaking individuals into teaching. In this particular course we had people like Irirangi Tiakiawa, Naida Pou, Rotohiko McFarlane, Iti Rangi and so on. These were all well-known kaumātua in their own right. There were twenty-five of them, and I was contributing with Tuki Nepe and Huri Callaghan to teaching that course. It would be more accurate to describe my role as a facilitator as they also taught me a lot, and it would be presumptuous of me to say I was 'teaching' them.

Kura kaupapa Māori

Around this time in 1982, our daughter Kaapua was born. Kaapua's life coincided with the emergence of te kōhanga reo. Linda and I were really interested in the regeneration of Māori language, so our daughter went to kōhanga. She was one of the earliest pupils and at the forefront of the language revitalisation movement in the 1980s. When she was beginning to turn five we became worried about where she would go to school. We, along with other kōhanga reo parents were agitating for the development of a schooling alternative that would carry on the language teaching and learning that had been established in kōhanga. This is actually the beginning of the kura kaupapa Māori movement.

There's been a lot of mystification around the development of kura kaupapa Māori. I want to put the record right here. The key player in the development of kura kaupapa Māori was Tuki (Tuakana) Nepe. The rest of us were supporting acts to her drive and dedication. There is a need to re-centre Tuki in this story as there is a lot of 'amnesia' about her great contribution. Tuki died relatively young, but she gave her life for the language struggle and we should not let her important contribution to kura kaupapa Māori be forgotten. For the record, John Waititi (as Hoani Waititi was known then) and Ruamatā were schools that were already going at that time, but they were not kura kaupapa Māori at that stage. Both of these schools were working with their own communities and were responses developed to service their own kōhanga reo. They were extensions of their existing kōhanga reo, translated into a school. The difference about kura kaupapa Māori development was that it was a political movement deliberately intended to change the *system* of schooling in New Zealand. The movement was begun by two groups of parents who came from Natari Kōhanga Reo and Awhireinga Kōhanga Reo and who were trying to find an appropriate state schooling option that would adequately deal with the language and cultural needs of their children who were to graduate from the respective kōhanga reo. The aim of the kura kaupapa Māori movement was to change the state schooling system and to create an alternative immersion Māori schooling option. The other two schools, Hoani Waititi and Ruamatā, are tuakana in a sense, but they actually joined the political movement later on, after a lot of the political spadework had been done by Tuki and others. This is not to diminish anyone, but I want to tell that story and make clear the differentiations in this history in order to put Tuki Nepe back into the picture because a lot of people have forgotten about her tremendous contribution. She was a significant champion in the revitalisation movement. Let me emphasise that this is not to take away from the other two schools' contributions and efforts, but we should be clear that kura kaupapa Māori began as a political initiative, that's the difference. So I was involved, along with Tuki and others in that, both as a parent and obviously as an educator. I became the first kura kaiako by default really. I was asked to take this task on by the whānau. There was no salary and because Linda and I both had good incomes, I was able to take leave without pay for a year to become the kaiako of the kura kaupapa Māori, which was named Awhireinga. I was supported by Linda, who was the family breadwinner for a year.

This first kura kaupapa Māori was set up at the Auckland College of Education. We had approached the college council to ask for support to run a pilot model of an immersion Māori school. The council agreed to a short-term pilot project and gave us permission to use two classrooms. We set it up right next to the Ātākura Māori language teachers' programme, so we had twenty-five fluent speakers of Māori on call right next door. We had fifteen kids in that first kura. From there it seeded the development of many other schools. The political movement spread and grew, in the early days growing the following kura kaupapa Māori: Waipareira, Māngere, Ōtara, Maungawhau and Maungārongo.

After some years of being at the sharp end of kura kaupapa Māori politics, I deliberately pulled back and picked up a different part of our educational struggle. My thinking then and now is that our political movements need to be owned by the people or the group, not by individuals. I have always thought

Graeme with his father Hingangaroa Smith, daughter Kaapua Smith-Purkis and mokopuna.

that there is a need to avoid creating single leaders or 'gurus' who are hard to replace once they move aside. So once a group of successful kura kaupapa Māori had been established, and we had written Te Aho Matua as part of the 'Tomorrow's Schools' reform, and once the legislation in the Education Act was changed to include kura kaupapa Māori, I decided to move to a different site of the education struggle, namely into wānanga development. This led me into a more formal engagement with the tertiary education system.

I have always wanted to do well personally and to make my mother and whānau proud of my achievements. I had some selfish ambitions as well, in that I wanted to do well with my sport. Once injuries began to take their toll, I focused on doing well in education. I guess I was also motivated a lot by wanting to show people, particularly those Pākehā from the Wairarapa where I had grown up, that even though we weren't given much credence for our potential, Māori could in fact do well and had a positive contribution to make. Once I started on my first degree and was successful, I wanted to continue. In a sense, doing a doctorate seemed to be part of an inevitable progression. My doctorate work looked at the theory and practice of Kaupapa Māori development and connected to the political work that I was engaged in around the establishment of kura kaupapa Māori.

Once the pilot period ran out at the teachers' college, we relocated the Awhireinga Kura to Henderson, to the Kelston School for the Deaf, and there's a history there. We ended up occupying some empty classroom blocks at this site after weeks of trying to find unused education properties to carry on the kura. The movement became more political in the sense of the police coming around wanting to arrest us, because we had occupied empty classrooms to create the new Kura Kaupapa Māori o Waipareira. This set in train a whole lot of other education politics. Once we got that school going (with the help of the Auckland Education Board) we moved on to changing the legislation of the Education Act through the select committee process in Parliament. A group of us went to do that and made submissions, and eventually got the Act changed to include kura kaupapa Māori as a distinctive schooling option. This occurred at a time when the government was changing the legislation to accommodate the Tomorrow Schools policy changes. The creation of a separate section in the Act for kura kaupapa Māori was quite an achievement. Following that, the Ministry of Education made direct funding available for five of the seven kura. One of the powerful stories that needs to be remembered here is about Ruamatā and Cathy Dewes, and her great cultural gesture in stepping back to allow other schools to get the funding even though they were one of the first tuakana schools. This allowed five other schools to pick up the funding. Ruamatā took a hit really, while the rest of the kura got going. Everything positive that accrues to Ruamatā now, including the awarding of an honorary doctorate to Cathy, is fantastic and well deserved because of that rangatira gesture. Ruamatā have been totally fantastic in this, in the tuakana role that they played in this development and gesture that was made. People don't know this story. I try and keep these things in front of people in case they are lost — this includes the work that Tuki Nepe did as well. It is important to remember these nuances of the kura kaupapa Māori struggle, because the gains made here were not easy and lots of people made sacrifices to get the job done.

With respect to my own engagement in this struggle, I quite deliberately changed direction. One of the other factors for this shift was to understand that the development of kura kaupapa Māori needed to be underpinned by an appropriate rationale or logic. This change needed to engage theoretically to make the intellectual 'space' within the taken-for-granted, dominant Pākehā education and schooling system. I recognised that the main site for such theoretical challenge needed to occur within the university. This critical engagement needed to be undertaken in a more formal way through a strategic challenge of the taken-for-granted system. At this point I am positioning not only to help develop alternative schooling models but also to challenge the theoretical capture by the system that preserved and reproduced not just the existing dominant monocultural models but also, simultaneously, undermined

At a Coast Salish welcoming ceremony, University of Victoria, British Columbia, Canada.

In Tiananmen Square, during a visit to Beijing Normal University and Nankai University, 2008.

the validity and legitimacy of Māori knowledge, pedagogies and practice. Again without being whakahīhī I wanted (and still do) to change the education system in many places to positively accommodate Māori aspirations.

Kaupapa Māori theory

I was a good student of the social sciences. I learned sociological methods, mainly qualitative methodologies. My anthropology interest and background developed my ethnographic studies and skills. Basically, I have a reasonably good grounding in both quantitative and qualitative research methods. In general my academic work in the university sector has been around developing 'space' within the academy for Māori language, knowledge and culture. My PhD was about this. It was a challenge to the dominant Pākehā education system with respect to the cultural capture of the institutional learning environments within schools and in other educational institutions. What I was suggesting by adding the word 'theory' to Kaupapa Māori was that the existing taken-for-granted system was both socially and culturally constructed to advance dominant Pākehā interests and to conversely deny, undermine and marginalise the validity of Māori knowledge and ways of knowing. This is of course what we might understand as the processes of colonisation, assimilation and exploitation that remain embedded within our New Zealand education and schooling system.

My interest in challenging 'theory' is that theory is the *raison d'être* of the university. Universities are seen as significant sources for the legitimation of societal knowledge. This is perpetuated through the production and repro-duction of dominant knowledge forms — i.e. what counts as valid knowledge facilitated by means of the narrow social and cultural interpretations that are reinforced within the academy. Universities are subsequently able to 'capture' the meaning of theory. There are a whole range of beliefs that then lend support to this capture; for example, the belief that only 'real and worthwhile' knowledge is underpinned by theory. My view then was that if we were to make progress with Māori language, knowledge and cultural regeneration, we needed to take on the universities and undo their control over the production and reproduction of dominant forms of knowledge. We needed to challenge the taken-for-granted beliefs that legitimated 'selected' knowledge forms and to recognise that theory was actually culturally constructed, politically loaded, and ultimately served the needs of dominant Pākehā interest groups.

My challenge was, why can't we call our Māori cultural logic and Māori cultural rationale 'theory' as well? It has antagonised many people, putting the term 'theory' after the words 'Kaupapa Māori' — including some Māori who still do not get the political challenge here. It does not matter so much today, as its intention has been mostly accomplished. It's raised awareness among Māori about the social, cultural, political and economic construction of knowledge and how this hegemonic control over what counts as knowledge has assisted and enabled our colonisation by Pākehā.

Critical theory and critical theorists have helped to identify, critically analyse and deconstruct the hidden forces which enable dominant interest groups to reproduce their power and privilege over less powerful groups. In the international indigenous arena, what counts as theory and the cultural construction of the academy is under challenge. More and more Māori have come to understand that the university is a site that supports a collection of selected theories; some theories are selected *in* and reinforced, some are selected *out* and marginalised. A great many of our indigenous knowledge forms have been selected *out* of the legitimating context of the academy and consequently there is a need to struggle for their inclusion. This summarises my struggle to legitimate Kaupapa Māori theory. What I have also aimed to do is add some of our own Māori theorising to the walls of the academy; to hang Māori research tools such as Kaupapa Māori theory alongside all the other Western theory tools that are available within the academy. Sometimes the issues that we're working on are Māori issues and the tools that we have available to use in the academy may not quite fit. In these circumstances we should be able to employ culturally appropriate tools that do fit, that is, in such cases be able to draw on research tools, theories and methods that are culturally made for that circumstance. It is not an either/or choice between Western and indigenous knowledges; both are important and both should be respected. What I am concerned to do is to unpack the way in which public education sites, such as universities, have become complicit in the gate-keeping of knowledge, and the building of hierarchies of knowledge that end up excluding and undermining the validity of Māori knowledge and practice.

The one thing I would say of our whare wānanga students is that they are very good theoretically. You can't fully understand Kaupapa Māori theory without first understanding 'theory' more broadly. You've got to know what you're moving away from (what you are rejecting) as well as the space that you're creating for the new theory to occupy. Again it's not either/or in that sense. We need to understand both ends. Some academics dismiss this challenge as being of little importance — not at all. I think you have to be doubly serious to fully engage and understand the challenge of Kaupapa Māori theory.

Having said that, I also note another problem. This relates to a number of Māori scholars who have not done the reading or the depth of study required to understand the overt and submerged issues. Many of these commentators have seemingly engaged in shallow ways with the readings and research on Kaupapa Māori theory and often superficially apply the term Kaupapa Māori theory without actually understanding the theoretical space that's actually been won there. On the other hand, we have growing numbers of Māori scholars who have done the foundational groundwork and who are appropriately interrogating the critical issues, and who are therefore able to contribute to building and adding to the original concept of Kaupapa Māori theorising. For example, Leonie Pīhama's work with the concept of Mana Wahine, Taina Pōhatu's work with Kaupapa Māori as a socialised concept and Wiremu Doherty's work on 'Mātauranga ā Iwi'.

The important point here is that Kaupapa Māori theory is not just about what I have written. It's a more profound concept that's engaged with by other Māori scholars and practitioners. Each of these scholars has changed and added elements to the original notion and that's what good 'theory' should be doing. It's alive, it's being constantly interrogated, it has flexibility and is portable, it has relevance to the community it's purporting to serve. I'm pleased that it has got its own momentum; that Māori scholars are 'into' it and that they see its capacity for opening up 'space' for transforming the Māori condition.

With the Hon Dr Pita Sharples, Minister of Māori Affairs,
during the building of the campus at Te Whare Wānanga o Awanuiārangi.

Academic career

Linda and I started working at the University of Auckland together, where we
jointly applied to share one teaching position. This type of appointment was
new for the University of Auckland. They'd never appointed two people to one
position before, but at the time we were both doing our doctorates and we
thought that it would enable us to do our study and at the same time provide
some income. We went into the job with a clear plan. We wanted to change
the Education Department from one which had few Māori students, to one
which would foster the development of Māori Education as a distinctive field
of educational study. Furthermore, we planned to build a significant graduate
programme — at the time of our arrival there were only two Māori master's
students. After a year we'd moved from two master's students in education
to about thirty; in about two years, we had about sixty master's students, all
Māori, all in education. Basically we were doing two full jobs on one salary.
This was eventually acknowledged and two distinct jobs were created. By year
three I was a senior lecturer, and we were contributing to the foundational Stage
I courses as well. When we first applied for this job, we had said that we would
contribute a certain amount of teaching within other lecturers' courses, to help
build them, but that our primary concern was to build our own Māori-focused

education papers, courses and programmes. In a short time we developed the Māori Education 'Department' within the School of Education. Shortly after this other Schools of Education in some of the other universities followed this model and started to identify Māori Education as a specific area for academic study. I would say that the development of Māori Education as a distinctive discipline within the education arena was a major achievement. We built a big graduate programme inside this — the accent on graduate programming and research was designed to be consistent with the research-led institutional focus of the University of Auckland. Once I completed my doctorate, I turned my interest to making change across the whole of the institution. I also went for an external review and promotion to a full professor of Education, which was successful.

I chaired our internal Māori academic staff group of the University of Auckland, initially formed under the name of Te Wānanga o Waipapa. This group worked to establish the first Pro Vice-Chancellor Māori position. Rangi Walker served I think a full semester in that role, and then I took up the role of Pro Vice-Chancellor Māori at Auckland. I did that for four and a half years, and in that time I would like to think that we established a whole lot of things, including Ngā Pae o te Māramatanga — New Zealand's Māori Centre of Research Excellence, the MAI Programme — which was a Māori doctoral student mentoring programme, changing faculty structures to include senior positions such as assistant dean Māori, to oversee the development of Māori elements inside each of their faculties. Most of these changes were done in

Speaking at Parliament at the Treaty settlement for the wānanga claim.

concert with the vice-chancellor, John Hood, in whose office I was working at the time. He was a good leader who understood the politics of structural change and how to facilitate this. I was not surprised that he went on to become the vice-chancellor of Oxford University. I learned much from my working with him in my senior management role.

After four and a half years as Pro Vice-Chancellor Māori, I decided to accept a position associated with the Universitas 21 group based at the University of British Columbia in Canada, where I worked for five years. Just before I left Auckland, I was floating the idea of the Māori pro vice-chancellors' group, because all the other universities had started to appoint such positions. Toby Curtis and I went to the Vice-Chancellors' Committee to present that case and then thereafter Mason Durie and Piri Sciascia and others have carried on and built that element. But there are a lot of other things internally that we established at Auckland as part of that first Pro Vice-Chancellor role. I have to say I was disappointed in Auckland. When I came back from overseas I was re-offered the position of Pro Vice-Chancellor and I turned it down, because I felt that in the time that I was away that a lot of things had regressed and that there had been a domestication of Māori academic struggle. This is the reason that I decided to move on.

I had been head-hunted in Canada to come back to Te Whare Wānanga o Awanuiārangi because I'd previously been the foundation chair of council for Awanuiārangi. It was a huge challenge that was waiting for me here, but I was always interested in the potential of the wānanga to be an educationally transforming site. For me, I don't care where we're actually based, whether we're inside the conventional institutions or within the wānanga. The point is that *all* Māori academics need to be working for change. I'm very much concerned here at Te Whare Wānanga o Awanuiārangi to ensure that we position ourselves in that role as an innovative educational site for transforming Māori education. Ideally, I would hope that we're just one of a number of institutions dedicated to developing transforming outcomes and working this way. Te Whare Wānanga o Awanuiārangi is a particular type of tertiary offering that may not meet the needs of everyone. We understand that Māori have diverse educational interests and therefore are not necessarily homogenous in terms of their educational aspirations. We at the wānanga don't yet have a medical school or a law school and therefore our job must be to facilitate Māori kids going to the best options that are available to them. We're doing pretty well here now. However, we're still impacted by the current moratorium on student growth and the ceiling put on enrolments. This creates a further struggle for our institution as we attempt to find an appropriate economy of scale. In terms of where we're heading, I'm feeling good about this space that we've got here at Te Whare Wānanga o Awanuiārangi and the innovative opportunities we are providing — and again it's not *either/or*; it's excellence in Māori *and* world knowledge. We need excellent educational options for all of our kids, in a range of different sites perhaps. There are still a great number of inequities that accrue to the wānanga sector and to ourselves here at Awanuiārangi and these will be the subject of further challenge to the Crown. We would like a bit more of the action, but we're still a young institution that is merely twenty years old.

I'm quite happy with where I'm at now and what we as an institution of Māori scholars are contributing in respect of transforming Māori education. My broad experience within education and schooling has prepared me well for this current role at Te Whare Wānanga o Awanuiārangi. I have been hardened and shaped by some of the formative experiences and the lessons I've learnt in life. If your life is too smooth and uneventful then you may be too accepting of the status quo. In this regard, struggle is important. I've often said in my writings that struggle is very formative; it makes you think about what you're *for*, as well as what you're *against*. People often just see what they're against, as opposed to being able to understand what it is they are struggling *for* and to change. Once we understand our struggle from both of these perspectives it can be genuinely transforming.

Māori leadership

Māori leadership must enable the social, cultural, economic and political well-being of Māori. A fundamental premise of good leadership, as Monte Ohia argued in his PhD thesis, is the necessity of a moral and ethical leadership practice. It's also a balance between knowing when to invest in your own expertise, and when to take advice from others and move with the people. Certainly, good leadership is not about getting too far out in front of the group or assuming some hierarchical model with the leader at the top. Leadership should always be striving to develop buy-in from others. At other times, leaders need to be courageous and to lead and challenge in order to make change. A Māori leader should focus on being transforming. This is important because there is also a need to ensure some change outcomes, given that for many Māori the status quo is not working.

Within a lot of my writing I've pulled back from using the word *transformation* to now emphasising the term *transforming*. The distinction here is that transformation is a noun and transforming is a verb. What I am drawing attention to is that transformation is past tense, whereas transforming captures the idea of continuous change, and therefore continuous improvement. Transforming is the enactment of transformation. In this sense, I am making the point that change needs to be constantly engaged with, and we should be continually transforming ourselves and our experiences. This too is an important component of effective Māori leadership.

I'd like to think that good Māori leadership is responsive to the needs of our communities and iwi at large. Māori leadership must engage with social justice and equity outcomes given the unequal power and social relations between dominant Pākehā and subordinate Māori interests. It must aim to improve the underdeveloped circumstances faced by high and disproportionate numbers of Māori. While in general we are making gradual progress and for some, conditions are getting better, in many places large sections of the Māori population remain relatively 'underdeveloped'. I use the term 'underdeveloped' quite deliberately because there are lots of other terms that describe Māori education crises which are too deficit-oriented. That somehow there's something wrong with us. By using the term 'underdeveloped', I also implicate the system as potentially being part of the problem. It's not just about our failings. There is a need to sometimes get the system and the structures of society up to scratch. While I acknowledge that there are some issues that we Māori need to deal with, and that we ourselves might take responsibility for, there are yet other issues that are structural impediments. This kind of thinking is in part what Kaupapa Māori theory is doing. It links the politics of our existence via critical theory, to our cultural struggle and our social and economic well-being.

Working with Arizona students.

I don't think you can have one without the other when you live in a society of unequal power relations. You need the tools to engage with the structures of society that constrain us, and although they're not an end in themselves, they do help make space for self-actualisation, or self-development. They go hand-in-hand and we try and encourage others to think this way. Our struggle is not just cultural. It's not just about our language, knowledge and culture, which are important, but unless you can make the political space and the structural space for their legitimate existence, we will be continually held down and remain 'underdeveloped'.

Sir Hirini Mead is a person who has done it all. He is that model that I'm talking about. He has proven excellence in the Māori knowledge domain academically and as a cultural practitioner. He also has proven excellence in world knowledge and academia. He works in iwi and Māori community contexts. He is an acknowledged leader in both Māori and Pākehā worlds. But most importantly he has also excelled in an area that in my view is the most important of all, and that is, he has enacted his transforming work within major practical projects. He is someone who is able to bring his theorising together with practical outcomes. It's not just simply about being an academic; that is, simply being someone who is expert in describing our potential and/or describing our pathology. He is someone who actually initiates projects to make change. Te Whare Wānanga o Awanuiārangi is an outcome of his academic work and his engagement with the iwi and his practical desire to do something transforming. Although I'm identifying Hirini specifically, it's the typology of an effective Māori academic leader that I am drawing attention to. It's these kinds of people that I admire, those who can translate the academic writing and learning and so on into action; into practical outcomes that are positive and transformative of our condition. At this year's American Educational Research Association Conference, the theme was 'To Know is not Enough' and it's that point that I'm taking up here — it's not enough to describe what's going wrong. It's not enough just to have great credentials. The most important question is 'What have you done?' It's not 'What are you going to do?' Don't tell me about what your intentions are or what your dreams are and so on. Tell me and show me what you have actually achieved. I'd like to think that people we're educating here at Awanuiārangi recognise the limitations of credentials without actions. In this regard a qualification is merely an enabler to make things happen; it's not necessarily a sufficient end in itself.

On a more lighthearted note, when students ask me why they should do a PhD, I often reply that "A PhD is a miracle cure for acute deafness and blindness; once I got my PhD a lot of people who didn't see me before or didn't listen to me, suddenly saw and heard me."

Challenges for future Māori academics

I'm positive about what we're doing, as Māori academics. I've written quite a sharp critique about native intellectuals. It focused on what I call the 'privatised academic' and my criticism is that too many Māori and other indigenous academics are self-serving, engaged simply for their own personal outcomes. It's all about the large salaries they'll get at the end of their study. It's not about a contribution to others, or a sense of collegial struggle, or the sense of responsibilty to the collective. In many instances, I see a co-option of the 'struggle' by many individuals to enhance their own mana. There is an important distinction here, in that a claim to being a Māori academic has to be more than a whakapapa claim. It also has to be what you do, how you act and what you contribute in respect of changing our conditions of underdevelopment. This is an important point. There are heaps of pretenders out there who play up to and exploit the white privilege that is associated with this. I'm pleased with the intention of the MANU AO initiative. It has been nicely done. Hopefully, it has challenged Māori academics about their responsibilities as Māori and as academics. I would have liked for Te Whare Wānanga o Awanuiārangi to have been included in this opportunity, given the large numbers of Māori doctoral students we have enrolled here. I heard there were some preclusions related to the funding, and this is the point about Māori academics being contained and constrained by the system. I don't think we should listen to the way in which funders give us funding. There's a transforming job to be done and we all need to do it. We should have opened up MANU AO more broadly beyond the universities because we have a huge number of doctoral students here who are outside of that. We have some sixty-two doctoral students at Te Whare Wānanga o Awanuiārangi. Not all are Māori, but around 90% are, all of whom are committed to transforming projects. The important project here is to build a critical mass of talented, well credentialed, well trained, culturally competent, collectively focused Māori academics, who will assist the urgent transforming of the Māori social, economic, political and cultural condition.

Māori academics have an important role to play. Credentials are important, as long as they're being used appropriately. They're certainly not an end in themselves. You can go out to some of our marae here and you're still in the kitchen; that's my place at home, and rightly so. I love it. There are other times when my academic skills are needed as well. Māori academics need to position themselves alongside their iwi and communities. They have to guard against the seduction of elitism. An academic credential does not automatically confer leadership status. We also need to recognise our academics who are involved in education as a discipline. Education is an important foundational discipline in our struggle — we will not have a sustainable socio-economic revolution for Māori without a prior or simultaneous education revolution. This is why education is important.

To be a Māori academic, you need to have a critical perspective. We do not exist in a level playing field situation in New Zealand. Pākehā enjoy social, economic, political, cultural, hegemonic, population dominance. Māori, in this sense, are a subordinated people who depend upon the goodwill of the dominant group to share equally and equitably in the democratic promises embedded in the Treaty of Waitangi. The harsh reality is that we exist in a political context of unequal power relations. As a consequence, Māori are often engaged in the politics of distraction, in being captured by reactive politics which distract us from being positive and proactive about our own aspirations. This is part of the colonising process — it distracts us from the real business of developing change by being continually involved in multiple struggles, in multiple sites, often simultaneously. We need to at least understand the field on which we're playing and the rules. If you can understand the rules of the game, then you can get more done in a transparent, honest and appropriate ways. This is why a critical perspective has always been embedded in my work and why the work of Habermas and other critical theorists is important. They provide tools and insights by which we can engage the context of unequal relations and the politics of distraction. The lesson I believe we need to learn is that we need to be critical, to have critical tools and understandings that make our work count. Get beyond the privatised academic sort of behaviour, and have a consciousness about our collectivity and our responsibilities to others. I see more and more of our younger Māori academics who 'get it' and who are out there doing the business. I'd like to think that some of the work that we've done in growing a critical mass of Māori PhD students has contributed to that.

Future aspirations

I'm currently a visiting professor at Sydney University and I'm honoured to have that invitation and recognition, because it's a position built around my skill set. I'm a professor there when I am able to get across and support. I have lots of international work to attend to around the Pacific Rim — in the United States, Canada, Alaska, Hawai'i, India, Micronesia, Australia and so on. A lot of this work extends out of the five years I spent in Canada at the University of British Columbia. I do want to get more into my own international work and to enable our ideas to be translated and transposed into other indigenous contexts. While I want to do some of that international contribution, I also want to maintain my contribution to Te Whare Wānanga o Awanuiārangi. I've heard that as you get older, you are supposed to get wiser, and so that's the very time we need our people to contribute, anyway that's my excuse for staying on. I don't necessarily want to stay on as vice-chancellor/chief executive here, but my expectation is that I'll be contributing as a professor to help mentor others, and to participate where I can in the academic/iwi struggle. I'll be attached to Awanuiārangi and working in various other contexts where I think I can make a contribution. However, I've yet to ask my family about this.

There is an enormous untapped potential within Māoridom, more specifically with respect to the academic contribution that's been made to the indigenous field. I do a lot of work in other countries and contexts, and many of the indigenous populations in these jurisdictions look to Māori for what's happening here, because we're viewed as being at the forefront — at the cutting edge for indigenous education development. That's a responsibility we need to take seriously within Māori academia, and make sure that we have got our moral and ethical positions aligned with our work behaviours so that we can do justice to that grand expectation. We have the talent, experience and innovative ideas that we can share respectfully with others. We can only say that this is where we are up to in our particular struggle here in Aotearoa. There are many things here that are potentially useful for consideration in other indigenous contexts. But that's for them to decide what might be useful — not for us to tell them what they should do.

Irrespective of our indigenous context, we *all* need more indigenous academics who are committed to transforming work, because that's the cutting edge. This is a fundamental prerequisite in the battle to profoundly transform all of our lives.

TAIARAHIA BLACK

He ahorangi a Taiarahia Black ki Te Whare Wānanga o Awanuiārangi
ā, i ahu mai ia i ngā kāwai heke o Tūhoe, o Te Whānau-ā-Apanui me
Ngāti Tūwharetoa. I whānau ia ki Whakatāne, i pakeke, i kuraina ki
ngā kura ō raro o Tāwera, o Ruātoki, me Kawerau. Mai i Kawerau ka
hīkoi atu ia ki Hāto Tīpene kura tuarua. Muri ō Tīpene ka mahi ia ki
te mira ki Kawerau. Mai i Kawerau ka haere ki te Whare Wānanga o
Waikato. Muri tonu iho i Te Whare Wānanga o Waikato ka whakaritea
e Hoani Rangihau kia haere a Taiarahia me tana wahine a Shelley ki
te Te Kunenga ki Pūrehuroa ki Manawatū, ki raro i te maru o Ahorangi
Tā Hugh Kāwharu. I Te Kunenga ki Pūrehuroa ka whāia e Taiarahia
ana tohu mātauranga katoa tatū noa ki te tohu kairangi reo. Ko tana
tuhinga kairangi reo, te kairangi tuatahi i tuhia ki roto i te reo Māori
ki Aotearoa, ki te ao whānui. I roto i ngā tau rua tekau mā rima, toru
tekau ka whakatipu kahatia e Taiarahia te kāpura whakahikahika
o te reo mai i ngā taumata kōkiri takatika akoranga, whakangungu
rangahau, paetahi, paerua, tohu kairangi ki Te Kunenga ki Pūrehuroa.
Ka hīkina ake e ia ana mahi akoranga reo rangahau ki ngā whare
wānanga o te ao whānui. Atu i ngā whare wānanga o Aotearoa me
ngā wānanga Māori, ka horapa ana mahi ki Rānana, ki Cambridge,
ki Dublin, ki Hawai'i, ki Poihākena, ki Kānata, ki Āmerika me ngā

moutere o Te Moana-nui-a Kiwa. I ā ia i Te Kunenga ki Pūrehuroa ka tīmataria e ia te tūru Ahorangi Reo. I roto i ngā tau tekau mā toru ka whakatipuria ngā momo rautaki reo rangahau, reo paetahi, paerua, reo kairangi, reo kauhau, whakahuihui mātanga reo. I te tau 2013 ka hiwā ake te tono a Te Whare Wānanga o Awanuiārangi kia tau mai ia ki Te Mānuka Tūtahi. 2014 ka tīmata ia i te tūranga Ahorangi ki Te Whare Wānanga o Awanuiārangi. I konei ko tana mahi kua whakaritea e ia, he whakatipu i te Ahunga Rautaki Reo mā Te Whare Wānanga o Awanuiārangi hāngai ki ngā hāpori reo o Mātaatua, me te motu. Tuarua ka whakaara ake e ia he Ahunga Rangahau mo te kounga o te reo, tuatoru ka whakaaratia he Ahunga Rautaki Toitū Mata Tuhirae o Mātaatua waka. Ē whā katoa ngā tamariki a Taiarahia rāua ko tana wahine rangatira; ē rua ā rāua mokopuna ātaahua. Hāere ake nei ngā tau ka hīkoi mai anō te huhua o te mokopuna aroha mā rāua.

Ko Ruātoki he kāinga kōrero

Ko te whakaaro nui o te whakapuakitanga o tēnei tuhinga kōrero me tīmata pēnei. Ko Ruātoki he wāhi, he kāinga, he pānga ki ngā hua mana pokapū papatipu whenua, toitū ā-mātauranga tuku iho piripono ki tōku ngākau. He waihanga whakatinana tēnei papatipu whenua a Ruātoki o tōku kāinga, tō mātau kāinga mata-nuku, mata-kerepū, mata-whakatipu i te hinengaro, wairua, tinana, whakaaraara kōrero. Ko tēnei whenua a Ruātoki he kāinga ākonga ihumanea mo ngā mahi katoa i ahau e kōpīpī, rangatahi, taiohi ā, pakeke noa me tōku whānau. He kōhiti kōrero a Ruātoki mō te huinga o te whakaaro nui mo tōku whānau. I roto i te whakaaro nui, ka titiro iho ahau, mātau ki te takoto o tēnei whaitua whenua aroha a Ruātoki. Ko ngā pae maunga e karapoti ana i tēnei whenua a Ruātoki ko Taiarahia, ko Parekohe, ko Hui te Rangiora, ko Te Waipōtiki, ko Te Ika Whenua, ko te kōmata o te rangi, o Te Hikuroa o Te Urewera. Ko ēnei paritū kārangaranga katoa he kura akoranga, he wānanga matapopore, he whare kōrero whakangungu tohu whakatipu, ā-tikanga, ā-whānau, ā-hapu, ā-iwi mo te whakatipu, tātari i te hinengaro. He kupu tohutohu a Ruātoki i ahau, i a mātau katoa ko tōku whānau haere ake nei ngā tau. He kāinga ako i ahau, i a mātau, ki te whakatakoto i te kupu, me te hā o te huatau o te hinengaro kōkoi.

Ko te tipuna awa o Ōhinemataroa e rere kau ana i waenga o Ruātoki, he reo taketake tēnei awa o te oro o tōna reo whakatipu i te hā. He reo hohonu o tōna whakaaro hai whāngai i ngā kokona katoa o taua papatipu whenua, whakaū ngātahi o te hinengaro akoako. Ko ngā puna wai o Ōhinemataroa, he puna ira maiorooro o te whare maire. He huhua ōna tikanga whakaū i te taiao.

Tai at his beloved river, Ōhinemataroa.

He tāheke wai, he kōkōuri wai ka whāngai i ngā kokoru, i ngā tahataha, i ngā tokatoka e noho ai, e tipu ai te hāroterote, whāngai i ngā momo kararehe katoa ki runga ki raro i te wai. Koia rā tēnei tō mātau, tōku whakaruruhau akoranga whakairo i te hinengaro kōrero, whakapakeke i te hinengaro. Kua mōhio nō atu mātau, ahau rā, ahakoa pēhea ko tēnei tipuna awa a Ōhinemataroa, te papatipu whenua o Ruātoki he kāinga whakatipu kōrero mo te pupuri i te awe, i te hā, i te piripono, o te whakaaro nui kia pūmau ki ngā kōrero tuku iho, momo arotūruki ā-hau nui, ā-toi te kupu, ā-toi te mana, ā-toi te whenua, huhua mātauranga o te papatipu whenua.

Ko te kāinga kōrero nui ā-toi te kupu i mau ki taku hinengaro, ki taku ngākau kōroiroi, kōioioi, i taku ngākau hihiko he taumata kōrero ēnei whenua, tēnei tipuna awa hai kākahu haepapa matatautanga, whakanoho kōkōtea kupu mo te hinengaro. Nōku, i roto i te ao kōpīpī, rangatahi haere ake nei. Ka taiohi, ka pakeke noa nei, ka whakaakona ki te kura nui o te papatipu whenua. Ka kuraina i roto i ngā tau i te kekē, i te mōtiwha o te reo kōrero ka tipu te hā, e tōia mai ai ngā tāiaro kōrero tuku iho hai whakapuaki, wherawhera i ngā momo tohu mātauranga me ngā mōhiotanga o te ao Pākehā hai whāngai ki ngā kai māro o te ao whakaawatea kōkōuri o Ruātoki. Taro ake nei i te hurihanga whakaaro, ka tipu ahau ki roto i te rongo o te hau puanui o Te Ōkiwa. Ko tēnei momo hau a Te Ōkiwa he kaiwhiringa whakaaro i te ui mai o te makariri o te takurua.

Te hinengaro mākohi

Ki te pupuhi mai te hau māeneene o Te Ōkiwa mōhio tonu ahau he hau whakahikahika i te kaikaiwaiū o te whatumanawa. He hau hai kāpura i tō matatau ki te takurua e rere whakauta mai ana, kotahi tonu mai ki te taha i te awa tipuna nei a Ōhinemataroa. He hau tiotio, he hau whakaputa whakaaro, he hau hai whakarongo tai, hai koungu ki ngā kaiketekete momo mātauranga ā-toka, ā-hōpua, ā-tāheke. Ko ngā kāinga i whakatipu i taku hinengaro ko Maringiāwai, ko Ōruakōrau, ko Te Tapuae, ko Te Pōhue. Inā tēnei kōrero mo Te Pōhue. Ko Te Pōhue ara mai te whetū nui o te ata, te ura mai o te motu, ko manu kopakopa, ko Ngautoka. Ko Ngautoka, ko Parekohe, ko Toketēhua, ko Te Ana Kaiaraara a Waerore, ko Ōnuiterā, ko Hāmoremore, ko Ōhinenaenae, ko Rangimāhana ka rere tika ki Ōhinemataroa. Whakawhiti ki uta, ko Kawekawe, ko Hui te Rangiora ko Paekoa, ko Te Tawa, ko Te Waipōtiki ko Ōwhakatoro, ka wiri ngā papa pakoko ngā ngutu. Haere tonu atu ki Matahina, ka tau atu ki te kāinga kōrero nei a Te Rewatū. Ko Rewatū te papa tāhuaroa.

Titiro tonu atu ki Te Tawhero, ki Te Pōroa, ko Tātāhoata, ko Ōtere, whakawhiti mai ki Ōtarahīoi ki Tāneatua, ko Te Hūrepo. Ka hiki ki te tumu whakarae o Te Pae o Tūhoe. Ko Te Pūtere-o-Pōtaka ēnei kāinga a Ōwaka, Te Ahitawa, Tāpuewahine, Ōtāpora, Maungawhio, Te Rangaātepihi, Mahihi-o-terangi, Tūtūmanuka Te Māhoe, Te Kiwi, Raorao, Pūkawa, Te Tātua, Mātihetihe, Tunanui, Hukikapea, Te Whāwhā, Te Reiroa, Waikirikiri, Pāraeroa, Maroera, Ōtere, Te Ākau, Hūtieke, Karioi, Te Kauangaroa o Te Rangimōnoa. Koia ēnei ngā papatipu whakawhanake i tōku hinengaro i tōku pakeketanga mai, he whenua, he kāinga tipu, he kāinga aroha. Ko ēnei kāinga, ēnei whenua, he huhua ōna kōrero hai whakatōpū, waihanga i te whakaaro nui no te mea hoki ko mātau ngā tamariki haututū, kōioio, kore taringa, ringa takawaenga o te ringa matatika. Ngā ēnei poraka whenua i whakairo ō mātau hinengaro, kia pākaha, kia piripono ki te whenua. He mana whakaoreore, he mana pāhekeheke kōrero, tohutohu i te kotahitanga o te whakaaro, o te hinengaro. I konei ka rongo ahau, mātau i Te Reo Ahurei o Tūhoe, te reo ōkawa, i te reo ōpaki o ō mātau marae o roto o Ruātoki; Te Poho-o-Tahatū-o-te-Ao te whare, Ōtenuku te marae, Kourakino te whare, Te Papakāinga te marae, Te Puhi-o-Mātaatua te whare, Tōtara te marae, Rongokārae te whare, Tauarau te marae, Toi-kai-Rākau te whare, Waikirikiri te marae, Tāwhaki te whare, Ngāhina te marae, Hui-te-Rangiora te whare, Pane-te-ure te marae, Tā Apirana Turupā Ngata te whare, Ōwhakatoro te marae, Pōtiki te whare, Ōhotu te marae, Kuramihirangi me Rangimōaho ngā whare, Te Rewarewa te marae. I konei anō hoki ka rongo ahau, mātau i te reo raupatu whenua, i te hahani o te mana mo aua whenua aroha. I murua ai, i takahia mai ai e ngā panewhero. I takahia mai ai e ngā pūtu kaiā pakanga, e whai ana i te tautoko, takahi mai a te ture kāwanatanga i aua tau tūkino 1866.

Ka whakaara ake ko ngā mate urutā! Pakaru whenua, pakaru hinengaro, pakaru tangata, pakaru tikanga, pakaru reo, pakaru manawa. I maringi kau ai te toto o ngā whakatipuranga o ngā tīpuna tōmua, tōmuri haere ake nei ngā tau. I ēnei tauheke kōrero, whakaparahako a te Karauna o aua tau tūkino. Ko te mōmona o te whenua i riro, ko te māramatanga i murua. Ko te mōmona, ātaahua o te whenua i tukua ki tētahi atu hai kāinga kōrero mō rātau, hai kāinga whakapiki i a rātau. I konei ka tipu ko rātau atu, ō rātau whānau, ō rātau whakatipuranga katoa i roto i ngā hekenga tau. Ka whai rawa rātau i runga atu i ahau, i a mātau katoa, ka whai ā-mātauranga hoki rātau i runga atu i a mātau. Ka mutu ka tukua, ka tukua e rātau tō rātau reo kōrero ki runga i ō mātau, tātau whenua. Ō rātau ingoa e mau tonu nei i ēnei rā pāhekeheke hai titiro kau mā mātau, mā tātau katoa. Ka whai rawa, ka whai rawa te iwi manene, ka tūpuhi rawa, ka tūpuhi rawa te iwi nō tātau ake nei ēnei whenua, whenua o te rau, o te rau angaanga whakaaro nui, whakatipu hinengaro.

Ka mōrikarika, ka mōrikarika te iwi o Tūhoe o Te Rohe Pōtae ō Tūhoe, ka tukia ki roto i aku mahi rangahau mōteatea, o te muru whenua, o ngā tau ō muri, ō nāianei. I roto i ēnei mōrika, kauheke kōrero ka rongo ahau, mātau i te pakū o ngā pūrepo, ka rongo mātau mo te whakaekenga ki Ōrākau. Ka tika te kōrero a Te Kooti Ārikirangi Te Tūruki 'ngā rākau kōhuru a te Pākehā e takoto nei'. Haere ake nei ēnei momo whakaekenga kōhuru katoa huri i te motu whānui. Ko wai atu te whenua mōmona o aua whenua o te motu, o te whānau, hapū, me te iwi kāre i whakaeketia e te Karauna i aua tau tūkino kia tukua e rātau ki te hunga manene ngā rahinga whenua. Ka rongo anō hoki ahau, mātau mō Maungapōhatu. Ko tō mātau kuia nei ko Ngāpera Black tētahi o ngā wahine, tekau mā tahi a Rua Kēnana o te whare o Hīona ki Maungapōhatu.

He toi mataora katoa ēnei kōrero, hai tuitui i tōku tau whare kōrero hinengaro nui i te putunga o te hinu, o te mātauranga hai whāngai, whakairo i te hinengaro kōioio, hinengaro kōpīpī nei, mo te noho tahi mai o te Karauna ki ana mahi hahani. He kohikohi ēnei kōrero, he kohinga pātaka kōrero o ngā maramara kōrero i mahue iho. He mahinga nui o te kōrero whakaharahara whakaputa whakaaro o te kohinga kāmehameha a ō tātau koroua, kuia o aua rau tau tūkino, i hira ake. Kai roto katoa i ā tātau tuhinga haetara kōrero, i ā tātau kohinga mōteatea e apakura ana, e tau marere ana te kōrero kai roto i ngā hekenga whare whakaū, whakatinana kōrero kā rewatū ake ki te rangi mahea o tōku hinengaro. Ngā pūtake kōrero nei, katoa kai konei o te orokohanga o te mamae. Ka tipu te mamae ki roto i te hinengaro, ka tipu te hōtaka whakaaro, ka whakatangatatia e ahau i roto i ngā tau nei, ka takoto he kōrero tuhituhi te kounga o te hōmiromiro. Te ihoiho o te urupare takatū whakaaro nui ka mau te mātauranga ō koro mā, ō kui mā o te hunga tapu, o te hunga whakaāhua whakatumatuma kupu.

Kai ahau he kura mōu

Ko te Matua Tangata, Te Kooti Ārikirangi Te Tūruki tēnā ka whakatipuria te whawhai nui kia whakaaratia ki roto i te kākānui o te whakatakoto kōrero, ka tipu te karakia, te tipu mai o te hāhi Ringatū, o te hāhi Mihingare ki roto o Ruātoki. I konei ka rongo ahau i ngā rārangi kōrero, whakatau, whakahāngai kōrero. Ka whakaara ake ko te reo karanga, ko te reo whaikōrero, ko te reo mōteatea ki runga i ō mātau marae ō roto o Ruātoki, he kāinga kaitiaki ānewa ki te rangi. Koia tēnei te kura whakaora kōrero mōku, te kura whakatipu kōrero, te kura i uru mai ki roto i ahau, ka tōia ahau ki ngā tai e whā o te hinengaro; taitonga, tairāwhiti, taihauāuru, taitokerau tai timu, tai pari. Ka tipu te hinengaro ka kawea te wairua o te kupu kōrero. I kuraina i whakapūmautia ai ahau e ēnei tai e whā! Ā koia taku ingoa ko Tai ā, ko Taiarahia o ngā Tai whā!

Kāre ahau, mātau i tohutohutia mai, kāre mātau i whakanohoia ka whakangungua i ahau e kōpīpī ana, engari i te kaha o ngā ruanuku, māreikura kuia, ngā tohunga koroua kōrero ka noho ko ā rātau kōrero ki roto i ahau. Te oro o ā rātau kōrero hai pakitara whakangungu rākau i ahau, i a mātau katoa o te hunga kōpīpī, kōioio! Haere ake nei ngā tau ki roto i te wā e kōpīpī ana te hekenga kōrero ā-waha, ā-wairua, ā-hono tātai kōrero ki te karaipiture, ki te whenua ka mau te hinengaro ki ngā taiaro akoako. Koia te tīmata o te whakaeke nui ki ngā whakaaro o te mātauranga taketake, teitei nui. Ka kākahutia te hinengaro ka tipu te whare kōrero, pouāniwa mōku o te hau kāinga, e hau ai te rongo o tēnei momo mātauranga o te kura nui o Ruātoki mai. E paneke whakamua ana ngā kōrero o te ao tuhituhi kia whāngaihia mai ki ahau, ki ō mātau hinengaro ka tipu te whare kōrero. Hau ake ai ngā kōrero o te karaipiture o te Paipera Tapu ka tipu ahau, mātau katoa. Koia hoki tēnei te huarahi e tipu ai te reo o tēnei momo kōrero, 'kai ahau he kura mōu'.

I tipu pēnei mai ahau, mātau. I konei, he hahua ngā whakatauira mo tēnei mea te kōrero, he ahurei, he amorangi, he ngūha o te whakatipu i te momo titiro tata, titiro tawhiti, titiro i te wehi o te whakaaro nui e āpiti atu ai ki ētahi atu momo kōrero. Hora ake nei ka tipu te whakaāriki whakatangatanga o ngā kōrero, pēnei i te whakarongo rua ki te tauparapara, whakataukī, pepeha, o ngā momo hekenga mōteatea, pātere, manawa wera, puha, waiata tangi, haka, tohu whakaū, hāngai ki te papatipu whenua. I roto i ēnei kura katoa ka tīmataria te tipu o te reo wawata, te reo wairua, te reo titiro whakatēmāui, te reo rangahau ki tua o te pae. Kāre i roa ka whakawhāiti mai ngā hau whakariterite whakaaro, ka whakaara ake te rārangi tūhono o te whakaaro ki roto i te hinengaro, he mahi tika tonu tēnei te whakarārangi o te whare kōrero hinengaro. Nōhea rā ēnei kōrero, o te whare kōrero, ā, i ahu mai ēnei kōrero i hea, he aha te mōteatea,

Above: Tai at his graduation with his wife Shelley and their grandson Owaka Black.

Right: Tai and Shelley with their son Otere, who plays for the Hurricanes rugby team and the Junior All Blacks.

he aha te karakia Māori, nōhea te ingoa o tērā papatipu whenua, nōhea tērā hekenga tipuna wai, nōhea te ingoa o tērā tipuna whare.

I roto i ēnei haututū, ka uia te koroua, te kuia māreikura, te whānau, te hapū, te tipuna nāna ia aua kōrero, aua waiata, aua karakia o te hāhi Ringatū, o te hāhi Mihingare. Ka kōrerotia te pūtake o te hāhi, huia ana, i titoa ai ōna takutaku kōrero. Ka hīmenetia, ka pānuitia, ka waiatatia ka mau ki taku hinengaro. Hinengaro kōioio o roto o tō mātau tipuna whare a Poho-taha-tū-ki-te-Ao. Anei tēnei kāinga kōrero i rongo ā-wairua ai mātau, ahau i tīmata ai mātau ki te whakaaro nui o te hekenga kōrero, ka mātua whakatau hoki ki roto i ō mātau whare kōrero ka tipu te ara atu ki te tuhinga mātauranga teitei, te ara atu ki te hōtaka kōrero o te hāhi Ringatū e whai ake nei:

> E te Atua o Āperahama, o Īhaka, o Hākopa, tēnei mātau ka tuku atu i ngā whakamoemiti ki mua i tōu aroaro, i roto i tēnei whare kōrero o mātau, me tēnei huihuinga, me tēnei whakaminenga i tatū mai nei i roto i tēnei rā. Ka tuku whakawhetai atu ki a koe e te Atua, e Te Matua i te Rangi, mo ngā manaakitanga katoa i whakawhiwhia mai e koe kia mātau mai rā anō i ngā rā ka huri, tae noa mai ki tēnei wā. I roto anō hoki i ngā whakaaro i tūmanakotia ai e tō mātau Atua i te rangi, ā, kua tae mai tēnei ki te wā e noho tahi ai mātau, Āmine.

Mutu tonu tēnei karakia ki roto i tō mātau whare kōrero a Poho-taha-tū-ki-te-Ao ka rongo āniwaniwa atu ahau i te ruanuku koroua e hāhaka ana i tana tauparapara. Ko te ngako o te kōrero mo ngā ingoa rangatira, arotakenga o ngā hōtaka whakatipu hinengaro e āhei ai ahau, mātau ki te tipu ki roto i ēnei momo mātauranga, ki te tiaki i ngā taonga tuku iho. Ka tukua mai tēnei tauparapara hai whakamiha i tōku hinengaro, i te nui, i te ātaahua o ngā kōrero e whai ake nei i tēnei tauparapara. Kai roto i tēnei tauparapara i raro nei, ka nanao atu i ngā whakamaunga kōrero o te hinengaro:

> Whakapiki tonu rā ki te tāhūhū a Haokitaha, he au whakaū
> Ko Kōura Kino, ko Poho-taha-tū-ki-te-Ao ka hiki, ka titiro
> Tītia e Te Ngahuru nā meremere mata rua, tai whakarongo
> Ō Ngāti Koura, kiri kawa ki te riri ē, whakarongo rua ki Ōruakōrau
> Ōhinemataroa e rere atu rā, ōpua mai tō whare whakarei tangata
> Ko Toi Matua, te au nei rangi, ko ia takere nuku, ko ia takere rangi,
> Te tipua kokoti kōmata te rongo, ko Toi-kai-Rākau ki Hāmua tonu ko Ngautoka
> Ūiraira Papa ki Te Whaitiri, ko Tāwhaki o te Rangi, o te rangi whakaheke
> Ko Rongokārae kia Ngāti Rongo
> Te uri o Te Urewera, ko Te Whenuanui
> E pupuri tonu nei ki te mauri o Mātaatua Waka
> Ko Hui-te-Rangiora, ko Te Rakuraku a Tāwhaki, ki Kaiti ki a Tāwera
> Ko Hinepūkohurangi, ko Pōtiki ki a Te Whānau-Pani
> Ko Taiarahia ki a Te Māhurehure, ko Kuramihirangi, ko Te Rangimōaho
> Ko Te Pūrewa, e rāngaki nei i ōna mate o te rohe pōtae ō Tūhoe

Hāngai tonu te titiro ki Ōhāua ko Te toko toru a Paewhiti
Ko Rangitihi, ko Koikoi, Ōtūtāwiri, ko Ōtere, ko Puketī
Ko ngā nōhanga ēnei o ngā tīpuna
Ko Ōtarahīoi ki Tāneatua
Ko Te Hūrepo ki ā Ngāi Te Kapo o te Rangi, ko Tītītangiao
Inu manga wai ki Te Rito o te Rangi
Ko Pūkahunui, ko Tamahore ka riro ki te pō, ka riro ki te pō
Tihē … i mauri ora!

Kai ngā waihanga kōrero katoa o tēnei tauparapara, tae atu ki te karakia Ringatū
i takahia mai ai ngā momo hōtaka tāuhu o tōku hinengaro whare kōrero, ka
whakawhiti atu te hinengaro ki te oro o te au nui kōrero e āritarita nei ki roto
i tōku ngākau, ae ka whakairotia tōku hinengaro. I konei ka tipu ngā aronga
nui, ka kohia ahau, mātau katoa ka haria ki te wā o te takatū mata kōrero
o te whenua. Ko te hinengaro ā-mātauranga, ā-whakarongo i te pari mai ki
uta o ngā hautū hekenga kōrero whakaū, ka tipu. He ruruku, he kohinga, kia
kōmira te hinengaro, te arumanga mai o te whakaaro nui. Ka tipu te hā tūmata
iti, tūmata rahi te tūmata o te mauri o te hau tāhengihengi o te whakaaro. Ka
rangona te ihi, ka rangona tōna wehi, tōna wana puta noa ki roto i ahau, kia
mātau katoa ō Ruātoki. Nā ēnei kōrero e rua, te karakia o te karaipiture, o te
hira mai o tēnei tauparapara tōku hinengaro kōioio i whakatipu mai i te wā e
kōpīpī ana. I roto i ēnei kura, whare kōrero ē rua, he mutunga kore, ka kuraina
ahau, mātau ko tōku whānau ki Kawerau, ā, ki Hāto Tīpene kura.

Te kāinga aroha nei a Kawerau

Ko Kawerau he kāinga pākaha ki ahau, ki a mātau ko tō mātau whānau, hāngai
tonu ki tō mātau haere ki Kawerau noho ai ki te whai oranga mo te whānau
ki te mira nui o Kawerau. Ko tēnei kāinga, whenua o Kawerau he puna rau
aroha nui, whakaū i ahau, i a mātau katoa ko tō mātau whānau. Ka hira ake te
tipu nui, te tipu kaha o te ngākau, hinengaro i Kawerau i ngā rerekētanga o te
ao, mai i roto o Ruātoki. I pai ai, he nui ngā uri e noho kau ana ki Kawerau, e
mahi tahi ana i te wāhi kotahi, ki te mira ki Tāhimana i taua wā. Ki taku titiro
i taua wā pau katoa mai ngā iwi katoa o Aotearoa, o tēnei motu e mahi ana ki
Kawerau. Kāre tonu pea he iwi o Aotearoa nei, kāre i whai wāhi, kāre i mahue
ki waho o ngā momo mahi ki te kāinga ātaahua, rangatira nei a Kawerau. Ko
Pūtauaki tōna maunga whakawhiti rā, ko Pūtauaki tōna maunga nui, te tohu
mātauranga tuitui whakaaro. Ko Pūtauaki te whakaawatea, te whakataki o te
oro o te hinengaro ātaahua. Ko te awa o Te Tarawera te whakaata nui o te kupu
whakatipu whakaaro, whakatipu i te pātaka kai. Ko aua maunga kōrero nei ngā
paetara whakaakoako i ahau, i a mātau katoa haere ake nei ngā tau ki Kawerau
ko Pūtauaki, rāua ko tahi Maungawhakamana.

Mai i Kawerau, ki Hāto Tīpene Kura

Ko ngā tohutohu a ngā pakeke o Kawerau, nui atu rātau i whakareri i ahau kia āta noho ki te whakamātautau i te ao, i te ao mātauranga e kaikapakapa mai nei. He nui ā rātau whakahoki tonu i te hau kōtuku o te kōrero, kia mau ki te reo kōrero, kia mau ki te reo whakamārama. Kia mau ki ngā whāinga mo te mana o te reo hai whakaara i tēnei mea te whakanoho haetara rapu i te rautaki, titiro whakamua hai mahere whakatinana i ngā whakawhitinga pae kōrero, akoranga, pae whakakotahi tumu whakarae kaupapa. I roto i ēnei whakataunga kōrero me ngā pae kōrero ō ngā pakeke ō Kawerau taha i aku mātua, tuākana, teina ka tau mai te pae matatau i te huinga mai o ngā kāhui pou whakaara, whakatinana kōrero. Ko ēnei whakaū, haepapa whakatipu kōrero, kia noho ko te reo ā-waha hai kupu whakaako i ahau, i a mātau katoa, hai kupu whakaakoako i te whakangungu tāwera, i te mere tūahiahi o te kupu huatau nui, i konei i Kawerau me tō mātau kura matua a Hāto Tīpene. I Hāto Tīpene ka tino kounga rawatia kia hira ake ahau ki ngā taumata ātaahua e pōpō mai ai ngā whakaaro o te hinengaro, te rauhī mai o te wānanga mo te whakatipu, whakaritorito i te mātauranga tuhi, mātauranga whakarongo, mātauranga wetewete whakaaro ka rarau ake he kāinga whakawhiti ki te arotake kōrero ki roto i ahau, i a mātau katoa ngā tama o Hāto Tīpene.

Koia rā te kaupapa ātaahua i ēnei kura nui a Kawerau rāua tahi ko Hāto Tīpene kura. I konei ka tipu te kāinga kōrero ki roto i ahau. Nui atu ngā momo akoranga i whakatipuria ki tōku hinengaro ki ēnei kāinga karangatanga nui, ka tākina te hinengaro ka whakatūturutia te mahi akoako. He hinengaro, he arero whakatauira kōrero te mutunga iho. Ko te oranga o te māramatanga ko te kupu ātaahua nei, te tūhonotanga. Ko te kupu tūhonotanga he taumata whakamārohi kia tino whakahiwātia te hinengaro poipoi, te hinengaro pōpō. I Kawerau i Hāto Tīpene kura i tukua mai te whakapakari o te kokona hinengaro, kokona manaakitanga, kokona titiro ki ngā taumata whitirere ki te ao whānui. He kāinga rua a Kawerau, a Hāto Tīpene i tukua mai ai te putuputu kōrero, te kupu tikanga ā-whānau, ā-tangata, ā tuākana, ā-teina kia noho tahi, me te hono ki ngā tai e whā. Tama tāne o te ao tūroa e tipu kaha ai ngā kēkete kōrero o te hinengaro e tau ai te māhuri kai mua i ahau mo taku tūranga, whakatipuranga ahorangi ki Te Kunenga ki Pūrehuroa haere ake nei ngā tauhekeheke. He mea whakareri tika ahau e ngā kōrero putuputu nui i te wā e kōpīpī kau ana, mātau tonu te titiro ki Ruātoki, haere ake nei ki Kawerau ki Hāto Tīpene ka ara ake, he tangata. He pae kōrero i tipu, he pae whakakotahi, he mātua titiro ki ngā hinengaro o tēnā whakatipuranga, o tēnā whakatipuranga.

Te Whare Wānanga o Waikato, takahi atu ki Te Kunenga ki Pūrehuroa

He nui ngā kākānui, ngā kārearea, ngā kūaka mārangaranga, ngā toimata whakatipu o te ao ā-mātauranga ō ngā tai ē whā, haere ake nei māua ko taku wahine ātaahua a Shelley ki Te Whare Wānanga o Waikato me Te Kunenga ki Pūrehuroa. Ko ngā haetara whakanoho tonu i te kōrero ki ahau, kia mātau ki Te Whare Wānanga o Waikato ko Hoani Te Rangiāniwaniwa Rangihau. Na tēnei toitū rangatira o te mātauranga ō ngā whare kōrero huhua ahau, mātau o Ruātoki i manaaki, i whakatipu kaha. Ko ana tohutohu he ātaahua, he mahana, he koingo ki te ngākau e hihiko ana. He tangata tau ki te tō mai i te kōrero mai i tōna hinengaro ka horapa ki te katoa. Inā kōrero a Te Rangihau mo te whā hāora ka mau katoa mātau ki ana kōrero i te mea hoki he kōrero whakatipu hinengaro. Mai i Waikato ki Te Kunenga ki Pūrehuroa ko Tā Hugh Kāwharu, ko Te Karauna me Huia Whakamoe, Timi Rāwiri Maatamua Moses me Terehia Moses. Ko Te Āwhina Kōhanga Reo, ko Te Kura Kaupapa Māori o Manawatū. Ko Te Pākaka Tāwhai, ko Hone me Ūnaihi Kamāriera, ko Pare me Pita Richardson. Me aku hoa mahi, aku hoa mahi katoa o Te Pūtahi-ā-Toi o ngā tau ki Te Kunenga ki Pūrehuroa. Ko te tangata nui o ngā tau ki Te Kunenga ki Pūrehuroa, kukume, tākirikiri hinengaro, ko tēnei rangatira nui, rangatira kau kapakapa o te momo whakairo o te kōrero ā-tuhi, ā-waha, ā-titiro whakamua ko Mason Durie. Mīharo ki ahau tēnei tangata, he kākānui o te toitū o te tangata. Ka hiwā ake hoki ēnei kura nui a Hāto Pāora me Turakina kura mo ngā kōtiro Māori, ngā kura ātaahua o ā māua tamariki ko Shelley. I roto i ngā tau ō 1980 haere ake nei ka whakaritea ka pakeke ahau i roto i ngā ātaahua o te kotahitanga o te ao ā-mātauranga heke nui, o te ao mātauranga whakatakoto i te huarahi i runga i te whakaaetanga o te kotahitanga o te hinengaro mākihoi, hinengaro tākina o te kupu kōrero.

Wānanga taketake ā-mātauranga, **te kounga o te reo**

I konei ka whakapūmau ahau ki ngā kaupapa tika, kaupapa ā-whakarongo, kaupapa ā-tātari, kaupapa ā-whakairo rangahau kaha i te hinengaro me ngā tikanga mātauranga ā ēnei momo tāngata e whakahuatia nei ō rātau ingoa i mua atu nei. Ko rātau ngā pūnaha whakahaere me ngā whakatinana o te aro matawai i ahau, e tipu ai ahau. Koia tēnei te huihui mai o aku whakaaro kia pakari te mātauranga taketake, kia pakari te reo kōrero, te reo tuhi ā-Māori, te reo tuhi ā-Pākehā. He puna whakahuihui o ngā mātāpono i puta ai taku hinengaro ki te ao whānui. Ko te whenua, ko te taiao i taunakitia hai tautoko, kia hohou ki ngā tikanga ā-mātauranga a ēnei tāngata me ngā kura nui o Papa-i-ōea, Manawatū. Koia nei ahau, mātau katoa he mea whakatipu, whakatau mai i ngā taonga tuku ā-mātauranga o te ao whakarangatira kōrero. I raro i ēnei tāngata katoa, i ngā kura hoki ka tipu te motuhake o ā rātau tohutohu, ngā āhuatanga mana whakairo i te hinengaro, ā-mātauranga teitei o ngā ao e rua. Ko aua ao ē rua ko ngā mātauranga o te tai whakarongo, te tai whakarongo kōrero tuku iho i te pū o te ihoiho, mata nuku, mata rangi, mata pū kaha tonu hai koko i ngā kaupapa hāngai ki ēnei rā.

I roto i aua tau ki Ngāti Rangitāne ki Te Kunenga ki Pūrehuroa, pakaru mai ana tēnā mea te tohutohu, hōtaka whakatakoto kaupapa. Mahuta mai ana i te pae o ngā momo mātauranga o te hinengaro, whakairo kōrero karapīpiti. Ko te whāinga he rapu tikanga hai whakatinana i aua kaupapa huhua ki ngā momo tohutohu, mārangaranga kia mārama ai. I konei e tautuhi ai ngā taonga kōrero ā-waha, ā-tuhi, ā-taonga tikanga ā-whānau, ā-tirotiro kau, ā-tūhono, he taonga whakairo i tōku hinengaro, rokohanga atu ki ngā parepare mākahu whāia, whāia māta huri waka nui o nāianei. Ko ēnei titiro hai mana kaitiaki i ngā mana tikanga ā-whānau o te ao pū kōrero, ā-wehe i te rangi kōrero, e mārama mai ai te ata ki te tihi, ki te tihi apoapo i te hua wānanga o te kōrero. Kai te pari, kai te pari o te rua te ao whakangungu rākau, mere tūahiahi. I konei i roto i ēnei tohutohu ka whakaara ake te hua o te wānanga, e tau ai te aroha, te tākiri nui e whakarewarua ai te hinengaro tuku kōrero.

Te hua o te wānanga

E mahara ana ahau ki ngā whakatipuranga hekenga kōrero e taea ana e ngā tikanga whakanoho kōrero te whera i ngā pewa o te wānanga i roto i ngā taumata katoa, ka tāwhai mai te rārangi kōrero o ngā kupu, o te huhua o ngā tohutohu wānanga o ngā tau. I konei i roto i ēnei tohutohu ka hāpainga ngā tikanga ō mua kōrero, ō muri kōrero, hai rehurehu i te tūroa whakatakoto, matatika mo te hunga kia kounga te hōhonu, te ātaahua ki te tikanga whakahaere,

whakatau, hokotahi kōrero. He mana whakarewa katoa ēnei i te kakau o te hoe o te tohu teitei mātauranga ka māunu mai te tapuae ā-nuku rongo, tapuae ā-nuku matapopore nui. I konei, i roto i ēnei whakaaro ka whera tonu atu ahau i te whare kōrero tuia ana te puna whakatōtō ka tipu mai ngā tuhinga kōrero paerua reo, ngā tuhinga kōrero kairangi reo te hua o ēnei wānanga ātaahua ka whakatipuria e ahau.

Ko ēnei momo tuhituhi i paenga mai i ngā kaiwaka, whakarauika kōrero o te papatipu whenua, he rauawa whakapae, whakarewa rua i te kōrero. Tautika atu ki ngā wawata, tūmanako whakarārangi, whakatū i te pokapū akoranga. Ko te rangahau, ko te rangahau whakaako i ngā kaupapa ātaahua ēnei o te mātauranga hai hopu i ngā kōrero ātaata, rongo maraeroa, tautuhinga o te whakaaro nui, whakaaro tawhiti. I konei ka mōwai ake taku titiro ki ēnei tautuhinga whakaaro e pā ana ki ngā tikanga me te rapu tonu i te auaha mo ngā mātauranga tuku iho, me ngā mātauranga o ēnei rā. Whāia ka whakahiwā ake, ka tipu kaha mai te hua o te wānanga ki ngā huhua nui o te tuhinga paerua reo, tuhinga kairangi reo.

Ko te kauwhata mai o aua kōrero, aua momo mātauranga i pōpō mai i ngā whakarārangi tohutohu o te huhua tāngata mātauranga o ngā parekawakawa hai taunaki i ngā mātauranga me ngā tikanga tuku iho o te taiao, tai timu, tai pari. Te koko rā tēnei o te whakaaro o te hua o te wānanga. Ko tēnei taiao, tai timu, tai pari kai roto anō hoki i te takoto o te whenua, o te moana, o te ngāherehere. Nō reira mai anō hoki aku tohutohu nui. Mā tēra takotoranga o te whenua ka kite atu i te rū, i te koa, kia rere awatea te kite, te whakarongo ka mau mai ko te hua o te wānanga. He kupu whakatangata katoa ēnei kia ora mai te kōrero, kia ora te pūehu, te pakanga o te whakaaro nui o te hinengaro. Ko te whenua te mataoho papatipu o ngā whakatipuranga o te tino pūtake i roto i ngā tau nei. Koia nei te tūranga taunaki i ngā ahuwhenua whakaaro mōku. Te tū ana o te hua o te wānanga ka pakari ake te pupuri i ngā tikanga ā-whānau, ā-hapū, ā-iwi i roto i ngā tau nei mōku. He ture, tikanga katoa ēnei hai pēhi atu i te aukati a te kūware i tūtū mai ki mua i ahau whakapōrearea ai. Ko tāku he hanga he tikanga o te kōrero hai tiaki, hai pupuri, hai whakaara i ngā taonga, i ngā tikanga reo whakairo i te hinengaro. Me arotake ka tika ki ēnei āhuatanga katoa hai kākahu whakanui, whakaora i ngā kōrero ā-waha me te āhua o te whakanoho i aua kōrero.

Koia te tino whāinga ko te rau whakatū tōtika, me whai mana te whakahiato kōrero. Me whai tikanga ai hoki aua kōrero kia whakaūtia, kia aroturukitia ngā mana aru nunui reo ā-waha, reo ā-whakaaro te ara tuku kōrero mo tēnei momo mātauranga. Ka hua ake te wānanga ki ngā whakatipuranga katoa. I roto i ēnei tirohanga ka tipu mai te hunga tūmatanui, tūmatakākā, tūmata kārangaranga ki roto i aku tauira, akonga o ngā tau maha nei. I konei anō hoki ka haere ake te whakaaro, he kupu āwhina, he kupu whakamanawa, he kupu tiaki nui i te mātauranga e hikahika ai te kōrero, mā aua tauira, akonga hoki. Ko ēnei kōrero katoa i hīkina e ahau ki mua i te aroaro o te tangata i ngā tau nei. Haere ake nei ngā tau. Ko te toi mataora e kōrero nei ahau ko te tuhinga whakapae e rewa mai ai te hanganga, momo rangahau, tātaritanga, te huarahi ki te wānanga, me tuhi ki roto i te reo Māori kā tika. Ko te huarahi hei whai atu he whakatakoto tikanga, whakahuihui whakawhitiwhiti kōrero, o te whakaaro o te wānanga i ngā tikanga hou e whaiwāhi ai ko ngā whakaputanga mai i te ao Māori e kuhua mai ai te momo reo o mua, me te reo o tēnei ao hurihuri, ōna momo whakatakotoranga kōrero. Ko te hua o te wānanga o tētahi tuhinga whakapae ki te reo Māori.

Āe, he nui ngā mātanga whakaruruhau i tū mai, hai taunaki i ngā mahara ka taea te whakaahaere i raro i ngā mātauranga mātanga nui tuku iho, hāngai ki ēnei rā. Ka mātua whakatau hoki ki ngā kaiwhiriwhiri takuhe o ngā momo mātauranga i whakaaratia mai ki mua i ahau. Koia nei ngā papa ātaahua tuitui kia rangona ngā hua ātaahua. Ahakoa anō i konā anō ngā taumata whakapōrearea, pārure, kaikinikini nei. He huarahi tūkino anō i whakaara mai ki mua i ahau. Engari kai te mōhio nei ahau, pakangatia e ahau ēnei pārure i runga i te whakaaro nui, ka mātua tukia ki te horopaki o te ao Māori mātauranga i raro i te whakaaro nui o te reo. Ko ēnei tōmina katoa i hinga atu, ka toitū ko ngā tohutohu a ngā pakeke hōmiromiro. Āe, he kōkiri whakamua te mahi, he whakawhitinga kōrero haepapa matatuanga ki te mātauranga o tāua te Māori, ahakoa ka rū mai te hunga kūware, mahi huna, mahi tinihanga. Ka wai kawa, pūrangiaho, ko ngā taonga nui a tāua te Māori te kākahu whakataratara, taukaikai, ātētē ki te uru pounamu o te mātauranga reo teitei, mātauranga teitei o te ao whānui.

I runga i ngā mahi whakatau, whakaora, whakatinana kāre he pokanoa, ka tipu ko te mātauranga i homai ki taku hinengaro e te rārangi tohunga, rangatira o ngā hau āwhiowhio e whakahuahuatia nei ki roto i te whānuitanga atu o tēnei tuhituhi. I runga i ngā mahi whakatakoto kōrero ka hiwā ake ngā tohutohu o te mātauranga a tāua, tātau te Māori.

E tino whakaae ana ahau he ōrite ēnei momo tāngata katoa ki o rātau maunga, he ōrite o rātau kitenga ki ngā hau o ō rātau wā kāinga e kauhautia ai e rātau te reka o te mātauranga ki ahau ki ngā whakatipuranga katoa haere ake nei ngā tau. He tikanga mīharo i ngā painga ki ngā taumata mātauranga mo ngā tāngata ā-titiro, ā-pukenga, ā-nanaiore katoa rātau o te ao whakairo i te mātauranga o te hinengaro. I runga, i raro ki ngā kokona katoa o ā rātau mahi ka taea ngā taumata mātauranga katoa, ahakoa he aha. Ko rātau he tāngata kauhau whānui i te mātauranga hai tuku i ō rātau mōhio ki ahau, ki te katoa o ngā tāngata e tūtaki ai rātau. Ka whakamoemiti nei ahau mo ēnei tohu ātaahua.

Te rapu huarahi ki waenga taku whānau

Mā ēnei kohinga kōrero katoa, whakatakotoranga o te whakaaro o te reo whakawhiti ki te hinengaro. Ki te whenua, ngā kura o raro, kāinga kōrero katoa hai whakaatu te hāngai o tēnei tuhinga āku ki aku whakaaro ki tōku ake whānau, taku rahi nunui o Tūhoe, me ā māua tamariki ko taku wahine rangatira a Shelley. Kāore i whakanoho wehetia te kōrero mai i te whānau. I haere tahi tonu ngā mahi! I haere tahi katoa te whānau me ngā kaitūruki kōrero pō awatea atu i ngā wā katoa o ēnei tau ki tēnei ao matatū, matahohoro, mata whakatinana o te ao mātauranga. Ko te kōrero ā-waha, ā-whakarongo te whenuanui o te kōrero, me ōna hononga kia tatu ki ngā momo waka kawe i ngā tūmanako, whakaaro, tikanga, hiahia, tohutohu, whakatūpato, wawata, mātauranga, mamae, pōuri mo te āhua o ngā tohutohu, kōrero e whakaaratia ana ki roto i tēnei tuhituhi. Ko te whakapae, ahakoa he aha te kaupapa kai konā tō tātau reo hai whakaatu i ētahi momo kōrero e tipu ai ō whakaaro, ō hiahia ki tō tātau piripono ki ngā taonga kōrero e pā ana kia tātau ake.

Titiro whakamua

He ātamira pupuri i ngā kōrero tuku iho tō whakakoikoi i tō hinengaro hei whakaatu i te auaha, i te rangatira o te whakaaro, o te kōrero hei whakatipu kupu hei whakahau i tō hinengaro kia whakaaro whānuitia te kaupapa, te āhua o te whakanoho kōrero mo ngā tau kai mua i a tātau katoa. He painga whakaataata, he huapai whakatū kai roto i ēnei tau e heke mai nei ki taku whakaaro mo tēnā whakatipuranga, mo tēnā whakatipuranga hei tūhono i ā tātau kōrero kia titiro whakamua, kia titiro whakamuri. Ko te whakaaro he tauira reo hinengaro Māori e taea ai te mōhio, te ako ki te whakatakoto, ki te rangahau i te kupu, i te whakaaro auaha ki roto, ki waho kia mau ai te mātauranga o tāua ake hai reo ā-kōrero, hai reo ā-tuhi. Āe rā, ko te whakapae he taha auaha kai roto i a tātau katoa e pā ana ki ā tātau kōrero whakatipu kaupapa ātaahua, whakatipu hoki i tētahi atu. Koia te kaupapa o tēnei tuhituhi hai whakapuaki i te momo auaha e tipu ai he kupu, he whakaaro ka whakatau iho ēnei taonga kōrero, he tāonga tuku iho pupuri kōrero mā tātau o tēnei whenua.

Ngā rangatira tōitū

He nui ngā hua o tēnei ao i kitea e ahau hai whakatutuki i ngā wawata o tātau o tēnei motu i runga anō i te whakaaro kia manaakitia te reo ka tipu ngā toitū whakatipu i ngā whakatipuranga, kia whakaaratia ngā kōrero ā tātau kōrero ake hei puna kōrero. He ira whakaū ēnei kōrero hai whakahoki i ō tātau mahara ki ngā kaupapa e manakotia ana e te ngākau kia mau ngā kōrero e pā ana kia tātau ake. Ko aua kōrero hoki he momo reo mihi, he momo reo whakatau, he momo reo whakatinana kaupapa. He momo reo whakapakari i ngā whakatipuranga nō hea ake rātau, ā, i ahu mai rātau i hea. He momo reo tēnei i ārahi i ahau hei whakarongo atu ki te reo auaha e ahu mai ana mai i roto, i roto i ngā whare kōrero huhua i rongo, i kite ahau. Ka tika rā he whare whakawhānau whakaaro hou katoa ēnei āhuatanga mo ngā kōrero whakapakari, whakawhānui ake i o wheako whaiaro. I konei tonu ka heipū ake te tūhono i te ao o nanahi ki te ao o nāianei, me āpōpō.

Ko ēnei momo kōrero katoa hai whakatuarā whakaaro kia whakakitea tātau ki ētahi atu kaupapa e manakotia ana, hāngai ki ngā tirohanga. Ko ngā kōrero i whakaaratia ake i te ao mātauranga he whakaatu i te āhua, te tauira pai hei whakatakoto kupu kōrero hāngai ki tō reo kōrero, hai whakaako i a koe i ngā kōrero whakatūāpapa. I te ao Māori kia haere whakamua ai tātau katoa ki roto i te ao whakawhiti kōrero, ki roto i te ao tuhi kōrero, whakairo kōrero o te hinengaro, e mau ai te reo. Whāia tōna tīmatatanga o te whakaaro mo

Family Christmas: Sheridan Bignall (left front) with Shelley, Whitiaua, Hona, Taiarahia, Puhiaurangi and Ōtere Black.

Below: the Jones whānau — Shelley's family.

tētahi kaupapa tae noa atu ki tōna whakamutunga. Ko ia ahau i matatau ai ki ngā tūmomo kōrero whakapakari reo kōrero, reo ā-tuhi, reo ā-wetewete, whakakaupapa i tētahi atu āhuatanga ōrite whakawhanake i tōku hinengaro.

Ipu whakairo

Ka hoki ahau ki ngā hōtaka kōrero katoa, ko ia aku ipu whakairo hai whakatipu i taku titiro i roto i ngā tau nei piki whakarunga tonu. Ko ngā kōrero whakatipu i ahau nā taku hoa rangatira, me wā māua tamariki, mokopuna ātaahua, me ngā kokona katoa o te motu, o te ao whānui i kōrero ai ki ahau. Ko ēnei momo kōrero hoki ngā pakitara kōrero mo te hunga e whai ana i ngā tohu teitei ā-mātauranga hihiko, ātaahua. Ko tāku tohutohu ki ngā whakatipuranga katoa. Kaua, kaua e noho ka titiro ki te kokona kotahi noa iho o tō whare kōrero. Titiro ki ngā kokona katoa o ngā tai e whā o tō whare kōrero, ka tāpiri atu i ngā kōrero o tai timu, o tai pari ki ngā kokona e whā o tō hinengaro. Kai konā ka tipu kaha koe.

NGĀPARE HOPA

When Ngāpare Kaihina Hopa of Waikato-Tainui, Ngāti Tūwharetoa and Ngāti Ruanui graduated from Oxford University she became the first Māori woman to receive a doctorate. Ngāpare trained as a post-primary teacher, working in New Zealand and abroad in the London Comprehensive system and Oxbridge schools. At the tertiary level she has taught at the universities of Auckland and Waikato and in the California State University and community college systems. Her first book, in 1971, was on the art of piupiu making. She has published in the journal of the Association of Social Anthropology, and has recently co-edited a collection of essays *Rere atu, taku manu! – Discovering History, Language & Politics in Māori Language Newspapers* (AUP 2002) and *He Pitopito Kōrero nō te Perehi Māori. Readings from the Māori Language Press* (AUP 2006). Ngāpare's research interests include the intellectual property rights of indigenous people, the theory and practice of kaupapa Māori, mahi toi (Māori arts) including live theatre, urban Māori associations, various Waitangi Tribunal claims and the impact of post-claim settlements on the life of claimant communities.

Growing up on raupatu land at Hukanui

My home was a typical three-generational household (and sometimes four), a common feature — so demographers claim — of pre-war communities, including Māori. Sometimes I felt that our home had expanding walls for the number of visitors and whānau who passed through, some of whom remained (as over-stayers). My mother would take in whāngai and others whom my father called her 'waifs'. I was the eldest of their three children, with one sister and a brother.

Near the end of my primary schooling, in the mid-1940s, an itinerant Anglican missioner suggested to my mother that I should go to Queen Victoria School (QVS), which the Anglicans operated as a girls' boarding school in Auckland. My mother said if I wanted to go to QVS she and my father would support me. It was a defining moment and the start of my personal takarangi — a motif representing progress. My grandfather drew attention to the fact that if I went away to school, I would be the first member of the whānau, indeed of our hapū, to do so.

My father was worried about the costs of my education. Even with a scholarship and our mother's earnings from the hospital laundry where she worked, the budget would still be tight. He was already holding down two jobs, farming the small land block we lived on but which never generated enough to survive on, and working as a linesman for the state hydro. To compound matters, he faced the same problem as countless other Māori landholders, the scourge of land fragmentation created under the imposition of succession to Māori land which led to continuing fragmentation of ownership with each succeeding generation. Later I came to regard our farm and many others like it, as a subsistence plot, not unlike land holdings typical of other colonised third world countries.

I did go to QVS but came home soon afterwards to the tangihanga of first my beloved rūruhi and then the following year, to that of my quietly spoken koro, both steeped in tikanga, especially of the Kīngitanga. Death had deprived us of our prime kaiako, kaimanaaki and kaiwhakaruruhau. Their loss weighed heavily on us all.

I am grateful to the Anglican scholarship, which helped my parents send me to attend QVS in Auckland. My indebtedness to my parents left me hoping still that I have honoured them appropriately during their lives and as they now rest in the bosom of our ancestors.

I came in time to realise that I had some powerful female leaders as role models like Alice Berridge (principal at QVS), Mira Szaszy, whom I wanted to emulate after enrolling at QVS and, very much later still other inspirational and courageous women like Iriaka Rātana, my aunt Rūmātiki Wright, Whina Cooper, Tuaiwa Rickard, Dame Te Ātairangikaahu and many others, including Te Ata's tupuna whaea Te Puea Hērangi whom I remember clearly from my childhood.

I missed my whānau, my home and the institutional supports of the Kīngitanga, their koroneihana and poukai. We were Kingites, and our home a Kīngitanga stronghold. This accounted for the traffic that came through our house, sometimes well into the night, discussing political issues relating to the king movement and wider Māoridom. As kids we didn't understand all the issues except that we were never in doubt over how to behave toward the kāhui ariki (people basking in the prestigious status of an ariki) and to provide for their needs.

At Te Kura o Wikitōria — QVS

As a student at QVS I became exposed to and given the opportunity to engage with the world close by with the church and the universe beyond it. A wide range of educational, social and cultural institutions lay there, and with which I would become involved. I had a great urge, a boundless curiosity and, unrealistic as it may sound, a burning enthusiasm to explore everything QVS had to offer. And, I was privileged to have had an extraordinary band of dedicated and inspirational teachers including Hoani Waititi who a year or so later, joined the staff.

Our classes were small, with the teaching delivered on an almost one-to-one basis. I lapped up all the

Teenagers: with cousin Pareopenui Thompson.

offerings except general science and mathematics. I could not get excited about either of those subjects. They were too esoteric and beyond me to get anything more than a pass. On the other hand I soaked up our principal Miss Berridge's class on human biology and led the team that won three times in a row the St John's Ambulance national competitions. Combined with my performance in human biology, I thought I might become a doctor. It didn't take too long to learn that my parents could never afford my living and accommodation costs at Otago Medical School in Dunedin, nor that I could succeed in passing the chemistry and mathematics entrance papers. I was enthused by Hoani Waititi's personable style of teaching te reo rangatira and the texts he was writing and testing on us. I loved, and passed with flying colours, Mrs Barry's English and history papers and Mrs Helm's geography lessons. Her courses inspired my interest in travel, and in what was to become my defining area of study — anthropology.

I told my parents that I wanted to become a singer, not of my rūruhi's waiata but of the songs I came to learn, arias. I had a passion for music, and dreamed of singing opera one day. I started down that path quite late in my career, however, learning from a world famous teacher of voice, Sister Mary Leo. QVS had quite an early and close relationship with her through our own songbird contralto, Hana Tātana from Taupō. In the end I opted for working for the 'collective', i.e. for our people, who at that time were caught up in the maelstrom of the rural to urban drift.

There were plenty of opportunities to grow the 'voice' in school and further afield. I was a lead singer at school and was a member of St Mary's Cathedral choir that sang for the Queen on one of her visits to Aotearoa and, together with the entire school, sang in every Auckland secondary schools' annual music festival for as long as it was on Auckland's schedule of events.

School was an eventful place — chapel every morning and night was compulsory. With matins and communion there was some choice around attendance but it was compulsory for everyone to go to Sunday evening matins. We could listen to the National Radio programme on a Sunday afternoon and, if I happened to be absent, Sister Maris Clark, our nurse, would send someone to find me, so I would not 'miss a note' as Sister put it. Hosting visitors from various parts of the city, country and world was not only a frequent occurrence, but it also expanded our social and cultural horizons. I began learning the piano before I enrolled at QVS and so continued lessons throughout my time at QVS. My teacher back home was a young woman in the district who took me on and because I did not have a piano, allowed me to use her piano to practise on after school. My parents eventually stretched their budget to buy me a piano. I wonder how they might have reacted to the concert harp I started learning to play when I was in California working at the California State University in Fullerton, and brought home with me in 1986.

Epsom Girls Grammar School

After four years at QVS I went on to Epsom Girls Grammar School (EGGS), to join its 6A class. This was not of my own choosing but the consequence, I believe, of a conversation between the principal of QVS and her counterpart at EGGS. QVS did not have a 6A class at the time and so the principals arranged for me to attend and wear EGGS uniform during the day and the uniform of QVS once I returned there after school. From Monday to Friday during the week I rode the bus from Parnell to Epsom. I was the only Māori in the class but was never made to feel that I was a one-person minority. In fact, it was quite the opposite; I think I was thoroughly indulged. The class was wonderfully eclectic in subject matter and approach and since everyone was preparing to go on to university, I simply tagged along after them.

Auckland University College

I recall my very first day at Auckland University campus when I met a few other Māori who, like me, were working their way through enrolments and other administrative requirements. That encounter led to the formation of a nucleus of Māori students that included Pat Hōhepa, Arapera Kaa, Tūroa Royal, Peter Gordon, John Tapiata, and Taimahinga (Toots) Taua. We have been described as the first wave of Māori students to hit Auckland University, and there is some truth in that claim. We were few in number, studying and hanging out with each other, sharing notes and ideas from lectures and tutorials. We considered ourselves fortunate to have a close relationship with lecturers like Professor Bruce Biggs from the Anthropology Department and Dr Bill Pearson from the English Department. They were our tutors and mentors and were always willing to discuss academic and pastoral problems. We all graduated with BAs, albeit at different times, while two of our company went on to earn doctorates.

Suffice to say it did not take long for the nucleus and whakawhanaungatanga of our group to form a Māori club, with membership open to all including students who were at Auckland Teachers' College, some of whom were part-timers at the university. We ran a version of the university's coffee evening gigs that differed only in the kapa haka we provided as entertainment and in keeping with tikanga, a hākari for the pōhara among us, which were most of us. Some of our men drove taxis at night to make ends meet. I, on the other hand, had taken up the QVS offer of lodgings in exchange for supervising prep nights and taking over the kitchen at weekends.

After completing my post-primary teacher's credentials, I got a job at a brand new school, Lynfield College in Blockhouse Bay. There was a roll of 90 form 3 students only. I taught social studies and other classes in art, music, physical education and girls sports. Notwithstanding my teacher's credentials, I was raw, inexperienced and a little naïve. Especially in handling mixed and single-sex classes of teenagers. When it came to teaching music or more to the point, of teaching six-foot tall teenage boys to sing sea shanties, I had to call on the headmaster or another staff member to be present. Although the boys were rarely disrespectful, they did put me through the hoops. I was also trying to finish my BA degree so it was always a struggle to coach sports after school and then race for the bus to catch a seven o'clock lecture at university.

After two years of working this schedule I was worn out. I won an advertised position as a cadet in the Welfare Division of the Department of Māori Affairs, Auckland. The director at the time was Arapeta Awatere, formerly of the 28th Māori Battalion. I was assigned to work with Mrs Taku Trotman, from whom I would learn a great deal while helping her with her caseload. Some problems could be handled from the office, others required field visits to people's homes in the inner city, the suburbs or wider afield. The work I most enjoyed was helping whānau into homes that they eventually came to own. The department had a scheme for that purpose and once the house was built a welfare officer was assigned to take the whānau shopping with what remained of their savings set aside for essentials like whiteware, lounge suite, table and chairs, and so on. I always included linen and drapes, which I sometimes found myself sewing and hanging up over a weekend with the whānau looking on a lot of the time. Many Māori families I encountered were struggling. This was at the height of government's rural-urban relocation programme.

It was not long before I got thrown to the wolves because the department was too short-staffed to cope with the workload that filled files of extraordinary weight and height, covering issues like poor housing, or the lack of it, stressed-out whānau, neglected or abandoned children, domestic violence linked to over-indulgence in alcohol. And among other things, dealing with Pākehā complaints about all-night Māori parties. To compound my situation, I was assigned to South Auckland, a huge area that included Papatoetoe, Pukekohe, Tuakau, Waiuku and Port Waikato, settlements that are barely recognisable today as they have become part of an almost continuous metropolitan Auckland. I lasted barely a year in the job. The stress, deep feelings of helplessness and disenchantment undid me and the effects worried my parents. They turned up on my doorstep one night determined to take me away — 'far from the madding crowd'.

Auckland Girls' Grammar School and Hoani Waititi

My former reo teacher Hoani Waititi came to visit me after he had heard that I had resigned from the Department of Māori Affairs. On behalf of the headmistress of Auckland Girls' Grammar School, Miss Rua Gardner, he offered me a position as Māori language teacher and kaitakawaenga between hostel and school. I jumped at the offer because I had also made up my mind to go on my big OE once I had finished my BA. The headmistress and I worked side by side to make the hostel work as a friendly place away from home and hopefully create an environment that was more conducive to study. Georgina Te Heuheu was in my upper sixth reo and tikanga class, along with a number of girls from Ngāpuhi-nui-tonu. I enjoyed my three years at Auckland Girls' for the support and camaraderie of the staff and because I was able to pursue my passion to study voice with Sister Mary Leo along with Hana Tātana, Kiri Te Kanawa and Donna Awatere.

Encountering the University of New Zealand

Recalling my first days on campus, we Māori hit a major hurdle. The language requirement for the BA did not include te reo, which was taught merely as an adjunct to anthropology, not as an academic discipline in its own right. When we arrived on campus, Bruce Biggs was continuing with the task begun by Tā Āpirana Ngata to challenge the University of New Zealand ruling that was still in place. To compound matters, the Auckland BA required a foreign language unit which most of us could not meet for lack of knowledge or facility in a foreign language. Māori did not qualify so we were required to shop around looking for a foreign language we thought we could handle. Pat Hōhepa, as I recall, began learning Italian. I tried German. Taimahinga Taua was fortunate in that she had studied French at Epsom Girls Grammar and so needed only to refresh herself. Halfway through the year we learned that Dr Biggs had succeeded in having the rules on Māori language changed. It was good news to know that te reo was a language worthy in its own right, worthy of academic study and able to meet the language requirement of the BA degree. Imagine the celebrations we had that day! (I don't think I have read a German sentence since). Although the teaching of Māori was now acceptable and thus a major step forward, it was then confined only to Auckland University College.

London's calling

I had a travel package which provided me a passage to Britain and a week's accommodation in London. Once there I needed somewhere to live and somewhere to work. I found a flat with three Australian girls I met on board ship, and got a job as a substitute primary teacher. In conversation with a Kiwi expat I was told that anyone with a first degree could be considered for a place at Oxford University. Later I enquired at the Oxford Institute of Anthropology and, after being interviewed, was lucky enough to be accepted.

My next big challenge was finding the money to cover tuition costs, accommodation and numerous other student charges. I was determined to give it my best shot, however, and so wrote home for help from Ngāti Tūwharetoa Trust Board on my mother's side and, on my father's side, to the Tainui Māori Trust Board. It took some time before I heard but eventually both boards agreed to support me for two years. I was euphoric but also fearful. Having come this far, did I have the roro and stamina to stay the course, to be worthy of the tautoko? I didn't agonise for too long. The opportunity would not come again.

During term breaks when students are expected to go home, I would search locally for substitute teaching to help my budget. My third year was particularly difficult as the scholarship had run out and, except from my immediate whānau, all my efforts to seek more funding from sources back home proved depressingly fruitless. Eventually my supervisor secured a modest grant from within the university that augmented the help I had from whānau and carried me over the last hump.

With whānau on the eve of her departure overseas: Ernest Ngahina, her mother Ngamora Elsie and father Aperahama Tea, Reimana, Taurima Lillian, Ngāpare and Desmond Manuwhiri.

At Oxford, tutorials were the critical component of teaching and the one-on-one learning experience. Many were informal meetings with my tutor, or group meetings with the tutors and groups of students in the local pubs. The group might be entertained by the retelling of a tutor's field work venture or discussions about the freshly won independencies of African nations like Kenya in 1963, Tanzania in 1961 and Uganda in 1962.

If I had any worries about making it through the exams in Trinity term, they were dispelled when my tutor assured me that no one failed the diploma because the viva (orals) allowed a student to defend his or her performance. Everyone in our class passed the diploma, which then allowed each one to decide whether or not to go on to do the Bachelor of Letters (B Litt) degree or to skip it and go directly into the doctoral programme.

With the diploma under my belt I did the B Litt, which required a thesis based on archival research or field work, a written examination and a viva. I had chosen to research the status and role of the rangatira in traditional Māori society. It took me two years. The archive was far more extensive than I had anticipated. And to compound matters, I had run out of scholarship money.

A class of international scholars

When I joined the institute I became a member of an extraordinary community of international scholars. They had come to study at Oxford because of the academic reputation of Africanists among its senior staff, the dons. They included the head of the institute, Professor Evans-Pritchard, and Professors John Beattie, Rodney Needham and Godfrey Lienhardt. The latter would in time become my doctoral supervisor. Most of my student contemporaries had only recently been freed from 'empire' — from imperialist restraints imposed by Britain, France, Belgium, and others recently emancipated from colonies to independent states.

My scholarly friends were to make an extraordinary impact on me as we talked, debated, and decided the future of the homelands of Africa during the latter part of the 20th century. Similarly at my hall of residence (Queen Elizabeth House) there was another cohort of international scholars studying in different disciplines, but from all around the world's recently decolonised African and Asia societies. In my intake alone were students from Ghana, Nigeria, Tanzania, Uganda, Kenya, Sierra Leone to name a few. I came to value and enjoy the intellectual stimulus and camaraderie of these students. There were other colleagues attached elsewhere in the university, including Jesuits taking time out from their pastoral duties in places like Malawi, Ghana, and Japan. Outstanding among us all was Joseph, a seven-foot-tall Nuer studying mathematics, who joked that he had to resort to Professor Evans-Pritchard's study of the Nuer to bone up on their customs and practices. I wasn't sure whether he was being serious or just joking but wondered whether that might be occurring among my own people back home. Then there was a Ghanaian, Father Peter Sapong who had degrees as long as my arm and who besides his own Tiwi language was fluent in several European languages. He jested one day, that I was his "wife from the South Pacific". Another Jesuit priest studying PPE (philosophy, politics and economics) was Father Stephan Kachmankoi from the Belgian Congo. He often had his studies interrupted by duties in the United Nations Office in Geneva. Once, on returning from Geneva, he confided in me that he could not serve his country from within the Roman Catholic church and fought a long battle to be released from Holy Orders. I was thus surrounded by intelligent elites who were likely to become the movers and shakers in their newly independent countries. They were conscious of the 1960 'Wind of Change' speech delivered in Cape Town, South Africa, by UK prime minister Harold Macmillan. He announced that the time was right for Britain to grant independence to all its colonies. It met with resistance from the European settlers in many colonies but with jubilation from African nationalists. France followed Macmillan's path soon afterwards and granted independence to its extensive African colonial empire.

My tutors and fellow students followed every twist and turn in these developments; often debating vigorously their general or specific components. While I participated in these discussions, my thoughts usually turned homeward to pondering whether ngā hau e whā were also blowing back home, challenging the British assimilationist policies and practices the colonial power had imposed since 1840.

Homeward bound

In 1966, with a Diploma in Anthropology and a Bachelor of Letters, I returned home to Aotearoa to a position with the Department of Continuing Education at Auckland University. My time was divided between teaching anthropology on and off campus and accompanying Matiu Te Hau in serving rural Māori communities from Te Hāpua in the North to Rangitukia on the East Coast. I loved the off-campus work most of all because it took me out among our people.

The best example of this occurred at Rangitukia marae where Matt and I ran mahi toi classes for both Māori and Pākehā under the tutorship of the inimitable tohunga whakairo and storyteller, Pine Taiapa. Kuia who were experts in whāriki, kete, pōtae and tukutuku made possible not only the exchange of knowledge but also for a lot of fun, laughter and fellowship. I have happy memories of students sitting on the floor of the dining room, which was our classroom, stripping flax under the watchful eyes of the kuia, who would then with deft hands show how a whole piece might be fashioned. I have the same recall of the males listening intently and watching Pine at work on a slab of tōtara. The evenings were given over to Pine telling stories, jokes and lessons in tikanga, whaikōrero, waiata and so on. On one occasion he invited me 'ki te ruku wai' which I thought meant being taken down to the beach near the Tikitiki shops a short distance from the marae there to be cleansed or baptised! As I was soon to discover, it was a baptism of sorts, if joining the regulars at the bar of the local pub could be regarded as a baptism. Thinking back, it may be that the germ of sodalities, the subject that became my doctoral thesis some years later, was sown in this context or in many other contexts old or modern where whanaungatanga is paramount. It was interesting how these wānanga became 'social events' not only for the locals but also for whānau who lived in the cities and came home to learn.

These wānanga ushered in the revival and renaissance in mahi toi that has flourished ever since. As the Te Māori Exhibition testified, Māori creativity was placed on the world stage. I was working in America at the time Te Māori opened in New York and had been invited to join the kaikaranga group who would act on behalf of the Metropolitan Museum as tangata whenua. I met up with the Aotearoa contingent when they broke their journey in California where I lived. I needed to touch base with kaumātua from home, with the kāhui ariki Tūmate Mahuta and koro Hēnare Tūwhāngai from whom my invitation had come. The opening of the exhibition followed tikanga in taking place at dawn as the kaitiaki intoned karakia of old while the bulk of New York slept, though not wholly. There were early morning joggers who paused for a moment or two as the manuhiri approached the entrance. It was a moving, almost mystical experience, as one emotional young New Zealander living in New York put it. She had not experienced anything like it back home. I held back from commenting that museums rarely, if ever, bring the artisans and the products of their creativity together in one place or time. Te Māori was an exception and since then such action seems more commonplace. Te Māori achieved widespread media coverage, not only in America but also in a number of international art publications. I still have the newspaper and magazine cuttings covering the event.

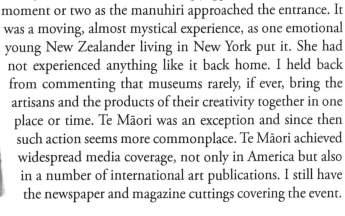

Ngāpare's first book was published in 1971.

145

To California

In the fall of 1969 I took off to California to take up a position at California State University in Fullerton, as an assistant professor in the Department of Anthropology. I got the job with the help of colleagues in Continuing Education after canvassing over a dozen and more Californian colleges. Some colleges were interested but Dr Hans Leder, head of anthropology at Cal State Fullerton was the only one who moved quickly. He was looking for someone to teach a new offering on peoples of the Pacific.

That appointment marked the beginning of my residence in California for the next eighteen years, broken up however by frequent trips home over summer and Christmas breaks. All Californian colleges offer two summer sessions. I always taught in the first, saving my earnings to come home in the second. I used this time back home to reconnect with the haukāinga and to bone up on issues and developments affecting our people and our country in my absence. While I tripped back and forth, the idea of doing a doctorate began to germinate and to take shape in the mid-1970s as the 'winds of change' elsewhere in the world began to rattle the rafters of empire and to push open the doors to decolonisation.

The wind of change

My move to California coincided with a period of great unrest across America. There was a cluster of underlying and defining issues afoot, including widespread opposition on most campuses and elsewhere, to America's involvement in Vietnam, the emergence of Black Power, the increasing public awareness of Latino/Chicano peoples long taken for granted. The seeds of the feminist and gay liberation movements were also beginning to sprout in the fertile soil of discontent and social unrest that at different times served to enthrall, challenge and even frighten me.

An example of student unrest occurred on my campus and was the closest I ever got to witnessing student outrage. Compared with other campuses, California State at Fullerton was relatively quiet until the Governor of California, former actor and later president Ronald Reagan, took umbrage over the heckling he sustained at an anti-Vietnam rally held only a short distance from our campus. Some of our students attended the rally and were identified among the hecklers. Reagan took them and others to court and arranged for the hearing to be held in our Humanities Building. It was cordoned off by armed police in protective gear. The scene was ominous. The atmosphere was tense. I felt threatened. The nerves of the faculty and student supporters who had assembled outside the Humanities stood poised in expectation. The slightest attempt to break through the cordon could trigger a riot. Fortunately, the quick thinking of the chair of our department saved the day by turning the assembly into an outdoor teach-in, allowing public debate to take place. Disaffected staff and students expressed their frustrations, pain and angst over America's involvement in Vietnam.

The Black Power movement had gathered momentum when I arrived at Fullerton. A Department of Ethnic Studies had been established there which incorporated Black, Chicano (Mexican) and American-Indian studies. The head of the department was Dr Wacira Gethaiga, a Kikuyu from Kenya who had been educated in America. Like myself, he was a recent appointee, and he was tasked with getting ethnic studies off the ground. His was not an easy assignment, as the tensions between the 'ethnicities' subsumed under the rubric of Ethnic Studies proved. Wacira and I had a great deal in common. We were both products of British-ruled colonies, even though the decolonisation of Kenya had occurred by this time and their independence won in 1963.

We became staunch friends and have remained so to this day. I learned a great deal about the Black Power movement and its range of political goals, from defence against racial oppression to the establishment of social institutions and a self-sufficient economy. I helped him organise a visit to CSF of the Black Power firebrand Angela Davis. Our campus gym was full to capacity that night.

Not long after arriving at CSF I got an invitation from a Pueblo Indian chief Joe Sandos to attend the First Convocation of American Indians at Princeton University in New Jersey. He was from the Hermez Pueblo in New Mexico and had been a member of a group of American Indian chiefs who visited Aotearoa when I was working for Continuing Education in Auckland. The department hosted them when they were there. Before departing they left contact numbers and invitations to visit their reservations. I touched base with Joe not long after settling at CSF, and his invitation arrived a few weeks later. I flew to Princeton to an auditorium filled to capacity by representatives of most American peoples. I cannot remember how many communities or tribes were there, but as my host pointed out, the seating arrangements made the tribal identities or reservations clear. The Navajos sat together and so too did the Apaches, Sioux, Paiutes and so on. The issues on the agenda reflected those from back home in Aotearoa. I reconnected with activist and Sioux scholar Dr Beatrice Medicine and met her cousin, lawyer, political activist and commentator on Indian affairs Vine Deloria who wrote *Custer Died for Your Sins* and a number of other critiques on the relationship between American Indians and the colonising dominant society. The parallels between the policies and management of the Bureau of Indian Affairs and those of our own Department of Māori Affairs shook me to the core.

Later, and in between my teaching duties, I worked for a San Francisco-based group of consultants who had been tasked by Southern California Edison (SCE) — a utility company — to report on how American Indian reservation communities would respond to a project for transmitting electricity from Phoenix in Arizona to Baha California, that might impact on their reservations. In some respects the task resembled the resource consent policy and practice the New Zealand Government requires of developers today to ensure that cultural artefacts and kōiwi are not damaged in the process.

I was assigned to visit and talk with people in the San Manuel reservation within the San Bernadino mountains and further south to the Morongo and Soboba reservations. In a nutshell, each community saw no value in accommodating SCE's plans. As the shaman on San Manuel reservation remarked, "We have been waiting 600 years for our concerns to be acknowledged, besides you are a 'first nation person' and will understand our position." I decided to leave the project that day — not, however, without sharing the shaman's view with the leader of the project. Notwithstanding he did share with me an example of what had occurred on his watch involving the Chemueve people of Nevada whose reservation bordered the Colorado river. SCE's original plan was to take the transmission lines directly over their sacred mountain. This deeply offended and alarmed the Chemueve. They sent their objections to SCE, who were forced to change their plans to go around rather than over the top of Chemueve's sacred mountain, at some additional cost.

My interest in sodalities

By mid-1973 my interest in a doctorate at Oxford had firmed up, after journeying back and forth across the Pacific to re-connect with the puna wairua of home, do some research and to inform whānau of my intentions, including spending one year in residence. This meant that I would have to take sabbatical leave from my job at Cal State Fullerton to meet the residential requirement and to work closely with an old friend and mentor, Dr Godfrey Lienhardt. My interest in doing a doctorate got a boost from my reading of Robert Lowie's study on sodalities — a term from the Latin *sodalitas* meaning 'fellowship' or comradeship. I concluded that I could adopt Lowie's title and concept for thinking about the human need for fellowship as a paramount value and also for considering the wide range of forms and ways for expressing and implementing it. What is more, I could draw on my own people to make the point and to theorise that some sodalities were predominantly instrumental in aiming to achieve political goals, and others were predominantly expressive of cultural needs and aims. I was thinking about the University of Auckland Māori Club and the Māori Women's Welfare League branches I helped set up when I was a cadet Māori Welfare Officer in Auckland. Eventually I realised that even the marae and poukai committees on my home turf would qualify as sodalities. I could also call on my own experiences of working with iwi-based groupings and observing activist groups such as Te Reo Māori Society, Te Rōpū Wahine Māori Toko i te Ora and Ngā Tamatoa among others. My doctoral thesis was entitled *Urban Māori Sodalities — A Study in Social Change* was submitted and examined in Trinity term in 1978. It seems that I was the first Māori woman to graduate from Oxford University, or anywhere, with a doctorate. It was the culmination of a career begun in 1966 following a defining remark from friends that opened another door of opportunity and set me on a trajectory that continues to influence my life and thinking today.

In her Oxford doctoral robe.

The Claims Environment [Leadership]

I returned home in 1986. I was impressed to see that those winds of change were blowing here too. Māori had become overwhelmingly urban and marae had ceased to be the centre of our lives. The Treaty of Waitangi was approaching centre stage. Iwi were soon to be able to lodge retrospective claims to as far back as 1840. We had our first Māori Governor General (Archbishop Pāora Reeves). Kōhanga reo were springing up all over the place. Chief Judge Eddie Taihākurei Durie had altered the *modus operandi* of the Waitangi Tribunal, making proceedings more comfortable for all parties. The Tribunal was leading the charge which could lead to reconciliation and eventual unity. Most Pākehā didn't like it. They were not ready to board the bus, it seemed.

I wasn't home long before I was approached by Robert Mahuta, who asked me to join Waikato University's Centre for Māori Studies and Research (CMSR) as a senior research fellow. Action research was said to be the kaupapa of CMSR but it was neither discussed nor defined to my satisfaction. I became deeply involved in the real kaupapa of CMSR; pursuing the Waikato-Tainui raupatu claim.

I riro whenua atu, me hoki whenua mai.
As land was taken so should it be returned.

That was the real and overriding objective of the raupatu claim and the work of CMSR, and was the passion of Robert Mahuta. My preference in looking at Māori inquiry, leadership and research, was through a generational cadre, but it soon became clear that this could create more heat than light. If I concentrated on an individual academic I would give insufficient credit to traditional leaders; too many males and I miss the significant and abiding contribution of females; too much focus on one tribe means insufficient focus on others.

I had to compromise because leaders and leadership are idiosyncratic and although they achieve all or many of their objectives, they do so in ways that vary greatly. I could relate to the action-research kaupapa the CMSR pursued, based on what I had learned from working with the Soboba people in Southern California. Their thriving cattle industry collapsed when the state government built the California canal to carry water from northern to southern California. No consultation with the Soboba community took place, nor was any compensation offered for the loss incurred by the community in the construction of the canal.

As Paul Diamond notes in *A Fire in Your Belly*, the Waahi community could have had a similar experience, had Mahuta not challenged the construction of the Huntly power station, which raised the risk of increased flooding and the eventual destruction of Waahi. The community dug its toes in and refused to leave their homes, which they had occupied for decades. An agreement was eventually brokered between the Huntly power station and with the sanction of kaumātua and Waahi community at large. It led to the pumping of a massive amount of sand from the riverbed to raise the marae surface some six to ten feet above flood level. Mahuta cut his teeth on this issue, preparing him for the next equally contentious battle with the Crown: the confiscation of Waikato lands last century.

Part of my working brief at the CMSR was to attend Waitangi Tribunal hearings, the quality of which depended on the research preparedness of both the claimants and the Crown. Meanwhile I would gain some experience from attending and observing, and later on accompanying Mahuta and other CMSR staff in contributing to the Muriwhenua claim on fish, and the first hearings on the Ngāi Tahu claim. Around that time I was appointed to the Waitangi Tribunal to sit on the Te Rōroa claim in Te Tai Tokerau. Those hearings took me out of circulation in a sense because they were so multi-faceted and included the loss (possible theft) of some hauntingly beautiful waka tupapaku (carved coffins) taken from a cave in Te Rōroa territory. But there was more to the claim than that. It embraced the loss of a wide range of resources including the Waipoua forest, land obtained through deceit of government surveys, the pollution of the Waipoua river and destruction of the fish stock it once supported. It was a huge claim spread over three years of hearings since neither the Crown nor claimants could be totally relied on to set dates for hearings. Eventual settlement took a further seven years before it was reached because the claimants and the Crown defence were often behind with the required research.

Our team spent a long time thinking about how to report our findings, how to structure and frame them. In the end we decided that the report would best fit the traditional structure of whaikōrero (tauparapara, kaupapa-take, whakarāpopoto). Some years passed before the report was ready to be presented to Te Rōroa at Waikara marae, Kaihū. The claimants invoked their tikanga by insisting that their report was their taonga and would not be acceptable under the korowai of the Waitangi Tribunal, which was a Crown entity. For that reason the report did not have the usual tribunal cover motif depicting Hongi and Hobson intricately entwined. It remains under a plain cover today and may well be why the Crown has not bound the report. When the report was presented, the land holdings of two of the main protagonists, Allan Titford and Don Harrison, were already on the market. With that in mind we proposed that the Crown should enter the market as a purchaser since the mechanism was already in place. The Crown's response was to amend the principal Act to stop future tribunals from making any recommendations on general land. This was because government was fearful of creating a precedent they could not control. Te Rōroa tikanga stands as an enduring tribute to the kaumātua of the iwi who suffered the loss of mana, patrimony, and resources throughout their lives and to my fellow members of the tribunal whose honour and integrity never wavered.

Setting coal alight

When Lange's Labour government embarked on its plan for the privatisation of assets, we at the CMSR knew we had a problem for among the assets were extensive coal deposits being mined within the boundaries of the lands that had been confiscated in the second half of the 19th century.

Coal became literally and metaphorically a hot and burning issue for Robert Mahuta. Like many others, including some of my own nephews, he had worked in the mines. For myself and my CMSR colleagues, the government's privatisation scheme set us alight, and energised us as we set about gathering the evidence upon which to challenge the government's privatisation scheme that threatened the chance to resolve the long-unresolved raupatu issue. The

Ngāpare enjoys
playing the harp.

lights often burned late into the night as we dug deep into the archive and digested documents like the 1983 Tainui report which was written while I was away in California, but which touched me deeply for the revelations it contained. It showed how poorly educated and poverty stricken we were. As I read I got all 'shook up'. It also set me to thinking that perhaps these were the issues the old people who visited my home when I was a child were thinking and talking about.

At the CMSR we set about mounting evidence to take the Crown to court. We worked under Mahuta's guidance. He was experienced working with Crown agencies like the Advisory Board of Māori Affairs among other government bodies. His was the responsibility of organising the legal team which helped organise the defence and its presentation to the Court of Appeal. I wrote the research affidavit for the case. The rest of our CMSR staff helped prepare our people for attending the case, including arranging for the Tainui express (train) to take our people down to Wellington to hear the case in the highest court in the land at the time — the Court of Appeal. Our people went well prepared for understanding the issue, having been schooled at wānanga leading up to the hearing.

How could I forget the scene with my mokopuna leading the procession to the court, carrying bunting appropriately worded and with kaumātua to the fore. Portions of the research affidavit for the case were read out by the Appeal Court judge stating that Waikato iwi had a property right to coal. Waikato won their case on those grounds, but before leaving the Court we were treated to a kauhau (oral presentation) from the judge on the need for the Crown and its Treaty partner to enter into genuine negotiations to find a way forward. This case was the catalyst that prepared Tainui for its long haul that followed. The mamae that generations of our people have endured were never forgotten and for many of us are yet to be forgiven.

In *A Fire in Your Belly* Paul Diamond records Mahuta's view of the Coalcorp case as "the catalyst to the raupatu settlement because, by winning the Coalcorp case, the Court demanded that the Crown sit down and negotiate with us. That had nothing to do with the Treaty. It was a straight legal argument. This was ours, you took it and that's fundamentally wrong." I feared that an in-depth history would not be written to match the volumes of other iwi affected by the Crown's machinations. To date, I hear no discussion on that score, a state of affairs that deeply saddens me but ought to be a prime project for the once-upon-a-time Waikato-Tainui endowed college, now called the Waikato College of Research and Development.

Moving on

I moved out of the CMSR shortly after the Court of Appeal case, down the corridor so to speak, into the Department of Sociology and Anthropology at the University of Waikato as an associate professor. I was back into a familiar stride. I presented a graduate seminar called 'Reinventing Tradition', using the Kīngitanga as a case study. Robert Mahuta sent someone to spy on me and report in detail on my presentation. I believed that he did not trust me to keep to the official line promulgated by the kāhui ariki and that might spell trouble for him. I needed space, and when it was suggested that I might consider moving to the University of Auckland and head up the Department of Māori Studies shortly to be vacated by Professor Ranginui Walker, I thought hard before deciding to return to familiar territory and the site of my student days. Professor Walker was a hard act to follow. He had a high public profile as a scholar, teacher and critic and was widely published. University politics, fiscal restructuring and staff tensions within the department compounded my situation. When the university offered an early retirement incentive, I knew that I still needed space and decided to go back home again. On reflection, the most important innovations I can claim for my short time were the emphasis on pedagogy that improved student oral and fluency skills, a paper that critiqued Māori and the media and a graduate paper on urban Māori sodalities. I had become increasingly disillusioned with the competitive university environment. 'Publish or perish' was almost universal as a catchphrase. Much of the cutthroat competitiveness I blame on a long tradition of government parsimony and increased emphasis on 'practical' degrees at the expense of wider education for its own sake.

Te Wānanga o Aotearoa

At home I wondered what to do next and how my background and my passion for education could help our people. I wanted to focus on rangatahi, especially those seeking stimulating and productive lives. I didn't have to wait long. Rongo Wētere came to invite me to join Te Wānanga o Aotearoa (TWOA). I was interested in the approach to education he and his colleague the artist Buck Nin had adopted in educating young people through creative arts. This approach to our young, especially those without skills, education, or money interested me. I believed in hands-on learning. I had a concern that too many people fell through the cracks in our education system. Rongo and Buck seemed to have found a gap that they could fill and did so. I accepted Rongo's invitation and went to work for him at the Te Awamutu campus of TWOA. I had the freedom to develop my and Rongo's interest in setting up a research centre. I implemented a programme for the long neglected kaumātua and kuia which was built around their stories — the telling, expression and recording of them in their own way(s). The course proved popular and fun as some members of the class proved to be 'hard cases' or natural comedians. The course had huge potential but I had to leave that to someone else to grow. I got pulled away to fill another position in the firmament, to lead Rongo's new venture at the Aotearoa Business School (ABS). I had a Massey University Master's in Business Administration which Rongo needed before he could launch the ABS. Besides, there was a School of [Business] Management Studies at the University of Waikato and another at the Waikato Institute of Technology that were already well established. The difference was TWOA's orientation and commitment to servicing the less financially able in the community.

The ABS attracted a rainbow student population and a highly qualified group of lecturers, among whom were three with overseas qualifications. We did well at first with our cultural and ethnic mix of students, even as their command of and understanding of English varied greatly. That was a challenge but not insurmountable. Sadly, however, for the innovation, for the staff, for the students, for its supporters and for myself, a government edict put paid to the ABS project at TWOA. The ABS was forced to shut down. I went home once again.

The next opportunity came from the Tainui Endowed College (TEC) at Hopuhopu. The college was part of the raupatu claim settlement. Soon

Ngāpare Hopa
with her husband
Isaac Kuila and
two mokopuna.

afterwards, Dame Te Ātairangikaahu took me aside and personally asked me to look after the college then being built. She opened it in 2001 and it stood underutilised until October 2007 when representatives of the kauhanganui asked me to accept an appointment as director of the TEC and to write a long-term strategy. I agreed, provided I could name Te Kohu Douglas as assistant director. In ten months we researched all the documentation that had accumulated over the previous six years of debate and produced a 25-year strategic plan — *A 21st Century Strategy for a 21st Century Iwi* —after further legal wrangling and turmoil. In the report we recommended that the iwi would build and ring-fence an endowment fund which would ensure that the director and council would not have to go cap-in-hand to the iwi for everything.

Māori scholarship and leadership

My time as a scholar was memorable. Scholarship of any kind demands curiosity, and the desire to think deeply in and through the traditions or values, because in the end it is values that drive our curiosity or our desire to see how these are expressed in action.

Scholarship has to be very much in-depth and ethical, and the reason I say that is, being trained in anthropology, the discipline has received a lot of criticism in terms of being objective. But scholarship must not only be ethical, it has to be the basis for action. That's why I've researched. We need the research, which is part of being scholarly but the research must have an impact for changing things, for changing attitudes. It must be practical. We don't have enough research at the grassroots and about grassroots. We've got major issues, how can we as scholars produce in-depth research. We talk about the wellbeing of our people. I don't see it expressed. We need more of that, that's what scholarship means for me.

There are certain leadership qualities that one must possess. One is vision and by that I mean foresight. One is to know that whatever one might plan, you're not going to satisfy everybody. That's the nature of human beings. To stand up and follow your dream, the dream has to be realistic. It's nice to have visionaries and so on, but how is that going to translate on the ground? That is the key, even though you are not going to meet everybody's satisfaction. A large part of leadership is personality. Other people might say this is charisma and that's linked to how you inspire people, to inspire hope. You have to be physical and physically able. I look at some of the leaders today and the hours that they put in, so there are these qualities that make up a good leader. There's a saying: 'Contrary to popular opinion, leadership is not about deciding where people should go, it's about finding out where they want to go and then helping them get there'. That's from an unknown scribe, and in a way that sums up what I think. You also have to be a person that people can trust. Leadership has to be ethical and from ethics you have to cultivate real trust in people. Nowadays that's not too evident to me.

That's the other thing about leadership, whether it's academic or otherwise, you have to be open and accessible to those who are in need, whatever, kua pōhara, ahakoa ngā raruraru. You have to be giving of yourself. That means that often you don't have much time for yourself.

Research by Māori scholars writing from a Kaupapa Māori perspective is not new as the work of early scholars like Tā Āpirana Ngata, Te Rangihīroa, Pei Te Hurinui Jones and Professor Bruce Biggs make clear. In my day these works were standard texts for first-year university students like myself. In 1999, Linda Smith published *Decolonising Methodologies,* a penetrating critique of indigenous issues. Its thesis was about the power of the imperialists over indigenous peoples here and overseas. Smith rejected the superior position occupied by Pākehā in their general conceptions of apparently inferior indigenous peoples and indigenous issues. This scholarly work has earned both national and international acclaim from autochthonous peoples and has set a pattern of enquiry and critique for the whole academic sphere of indigenous studies because it captures the very essence and struggles of indigeneity. I salute her and her colleagues at the core of one of the most important scholarly works of our time.

Things in universities are vastly different today. In the last decade of the 20th century Graham and Linda Smith of the Department of Education at the University of Auckland launched MAI, a Māori and indigenous post-graduate student support programme. Through regular mentoring sessions, seminars and tutorials the academic advancement and the research capability of post-graduate students spread to other universities and in 2002, was restructured by Linda Smith under the auspices of Ngā Pae o te Māramatanga, the Centre for Māori Research Excellence. At the same time, Graham Smith, an integral part of this awakening, moved from Auckland to be tumuaki of Te Wānanga o Awanuiārangi in Ngāti Awa's tribal area. This was soon to become the third Māori tertiary institution in Aotearoa to award higher degrees. The MAI network operates in ten tertiary institutions to support and enhance Māori and indigenous post-graduate student research capacity. Within five years the MAI programme contributed to the education of in excess of 500 Māori PhDs awarded or under way. In five years the measures in place have been outstanding. In another 25 years the benefits to our nation and beyond will be incalculable.

I have had a long, interesting, varied and enjoyable career, but there are many tasks still to tackle and battles to win. I try to maintain my scholarly interests in 19th-century newspapers and correspondence among Māori and between Māori and settlers; in my concern at failing education systems which produce high levels of illiteracy among Māori and other indigenous peoples. What continues to fascinate me still is the nature and power of whakapapa in the way that our tūpuna ordered and understood their world. Perhaps they could see that there is a pattern of relationships that could produce a theory of everything, just like the definitive thesis of Stephen Hawkins.

WALLY PENETITO

Professor Wally Penetito belongs to the Tainui iwi of Ngāti Haua, Ngāti Raukawa and Ngāti Tamaterā. Recently retired from Te Kura Māori in the Faculty of Education at Victoria University, Wally supervised master's and doctoral students engaged in various domains of Māori education, such as curriculum, pedagogy, assessment, leadership, change management, history and research. His academic interests are in the area of educational sociology and research, including teacher education and developments in Māori education. He is often called upon to provide advice on Māori education to government agencies such as the Ministry of Education, Te Puni Kōkiri, the Ministry of Māori Development, the Education Review Office, the New Zealand Qualifications Authority, Skill New Zealand, and the Ministry of Social Development.

Whānau and teacher influences

I don't know what I wanted to be when I was a 12-year-old. Part of my up-bringing was on farms with aunties and uncles and a grandmother. We had horses, dogs and cows, geese, turkeys and hens, swamps to play in, big sand banks, drains with tuna and watercress. It seemed like we had everything. In those days it was a utopian lifestyle for young people, especially those on a farm, and there was even a time when I thought I wanted to be a jockey. It didn't take too long before I discovered that wasn't going to happen, but riding horses was something I loved with a passion. I never thought I might want to be a farmer.

However, I wasn't only brought up on a farm. I was also brought up in a small town where my father and mother lived with the rest of my family, and my dad worked in a butter factory. I worked in the butter factory in my late years of school. I knew what I didn't want to be. I knew that there were easier ways of getting through life than having to follow in my father's footsteps; he was a labourer and worked his guts out. He worked hard all the time. My mother did exactly the same, worked hard, so I learned a work ethic from them. I learned how important a work ethic is, and that is still with me to this very day. I'm grateful to my parents for that. They also taught me the value of family and caring for each other.

On the other hand, I also knew that there were people out there who were enjoying life a lot more than my parents were. We couldn't do the things I knew other people did and took for granted, like having birthday parties, getting presents and going on holidays. I knew those things as words; I didn't know them as realities because we didn't really do that. I'm the second eldest of eleven siblings, therefore I don't have any misunderstandings about that, it was the way it was, and if you wanted something you had to work for it. Because I was so passionate about sport I thought there might be a career in there somewhere, maybe a sports commentator or writer. This was prior to the days of professionalism; the only professionals would be coaches or people who worked in the media. I thought at least I'd be doing something I liked and I knew about.

I was taught to read by my infant teacher, who had warm feelings toward me, which was obvious by the way she responded to me when I was in the classroom. In those days, you had the infant teachers for a couple of years at least at primary school level. I had another teacher that I knew when I was in the standards who I really liked as well. He was an energetic young person to start with and spoke to the kids like they were all his mates. He was easy to get on with. He was a good teacher as far as I was concerned because we were doing things that we wanted to do, not because he got us to do them, but because he made you feel like you wanted to do them. At intermediate I had a teacher who was good with me and again, probably more than anything else, she encouraged my reading. I must have been pretty good at reading because I was often asked to read to the class. It was something I didn't like doing because when you do that you're so focused on production that you don't even get to hear the story yourself. By the time I'd finished the story I'd be wanting to know from my mates what I'd been reading about. It was strange but that was quite often the case. I had another teacher there who also took notice of me and treated me and others well. She respected us but she also made us work hard.

Primary and secondary schooling

I went to a school in the middle of the Waikato, a little school where the Māori population was about twenty percent, which is probably around the national average, but most of the kids there were Pākehā. I learned very early in the piece that being Māori in a school like that was an uphill battle. It was hard to recognise yourself in there. It was difficult to understand some things that went on. One lesson was when a teacher asked us Māori kids to get up and go outside while the nurse came and checked us out. What's astonishing is that it never happened to others, and the teacher never acted as though this was something unusual. Nor did the other Pākehā kids in the room ever question why that happened. This was one of those things where Māori get singled out, but nobody saw that as a privilege and nobody spoke about it. That always stuck with me: why are they doing this to us, singling us out, not for any reason that might make you feel good about yourself? As the kids began returning to the classroom, they'd had their heads checked for kutu and things like that. Nobody took any notice or asked questions like "Where have you been? What happened?" Every time another pupil would come back into the classroom, everybody knew because they smelt of this strong stuff the nurses put on their hair. We were always embarrassed.

Why is it taken for granted that it's okay to be like this, when I know that every Māori kid in the room feels, in the vernacular of the day, 'stink' about what was happening to them? All of those teachers were Pākehā, and lots of them I really liked. One or two of them who taught me how to read in my infant classrooms, I loved. I thought my teacher was a brilliant and lovely person. But for it to be accepted that Māori kids be singled out, to be discriminated against, screwed me a bit, it got into my belly as something that was not right; that can't be right, no matter what the reasons.

Secondary school was a little more difficult to comprehend. It's not just a cliché, it's a reality that switches from students to subjects and I never switched on to any subject in particular. I wish I had done, but I don't think I did. It was the time when students were blatantly streamed but in hindsight, streaming was a strange idea. We were situated in the middle of the Waikato, in a farming community, and our secondary school had three streams for boys: professional, industrial, and agricultural. Well you can guess who was in the agricultural classes, which is weird given the whole Waikato is about agriculture, about farming and yet the lower stream in the school was the agricultural stream. The industrial stream was mainly for people who wanted to do carpentry and things like that, but professional was considered the academic stream. I ended up in the academic stream. I think it was as a result of my brother who was ahead of me, my tuakana, and he was in the A stream through intermediate and I rode on that ticket. We had to do another language subject in preparation for senior school and I did French. I did French for three years. Māori wasn't offered; no other language was offered in fact. I did French, not that I can speak French or anything else like that. It was one of those stupid things we did, to learn by rote and never get to use it. So we were being taught by New Zealanders speaking French. Well, these teachers were probably as good at speaking French as they were at speaking Māori, which was zilch. Māori mispronunciation was happening, so it occurred to me that probably the French was as well. Being streamed in that way was a big plus, because you actually worked with students who were bright, and the teachers pushed them. I got pushed and pulled along with "You can do better", and "Do it again".

I'm grateful today for this, because it doesn't happen enough with Māori students. That's my experience. You're going to be a better person for what you do by working with people who are better than you are at academic work. If you're going to go ahead further in your academic work you need somebody who knows more about what you know of the subject that you're involved in. Doesn't matter what it is. It's having that idea there of somebody setting a standard for you, pushing you through it and pulling you along into it. That has played an important role many years later for where I am now, not that I ever knew that was the case at the time. I was mainly at secondary school to play rugby, to play sport, like so many other Māori kids. The only thing I knew, however, is that the longer I stayed at school, fewer Māori students were in my class. I don't think that would be too much different today actually. I often wondered why that was the case because some of the Māori kids I was in primary and intermediate school with were sharp, had good brains and knew how to use them, but a lot of them ended up in lower streams and left school as soon as they turned fifteen.

A couple of years before I left school my father had already told me I was old enough to work, and I needed to start bringing money into the family. Another Māori mate of mine was in the same position as me. We said we wanted to go back to school; to do that we needed to make enough money. Both of us went to Auckland and got a job in the freezing works, at Hellaby's. We got a job in the sausage-making department and worked six weeks solid. We came out like we were millionaires. We had money to buy our uniforms, to pay school fees, to pay for everything we wanted, so our fathers had no say about us going back to school. We did that for the following year as well. We did this horrible job but always did enough hours for six weeks holiday and leaving knowing we were going to be rich. We were going to have all this money to be able to look after ourselves. In my last year at school my brother went to teachers' college. He told me about how good that was, how they played senior rugby in the Counties competition, about the large number of girls who were there, and about how good teaching was. I was an 18-year-old, testosterone flowing, eager to get out in the world. So going teaching sounded like a pretty good career.

The major thing about my schooling years was how important sport was. I've always been able to get through school, but sport was something that was challenging and something that I got a lot out of. Leaving school and getting into teaching was an incredible privilege. Learning at higher academic levels brought a new dimension to my life, but it came much later for me. My first ten years of teaching outside university study were incredibly important for me. It provided me with a particular kind of base. Other academics I work with in education who have gone from school to university, got degrees and then went into teachers' college and teaching have a very different approach to learning and teaching than I have. I know about the education system and how it works and what it feels like, not just what goes on there. The process I went through provided me with an empirical base to everything else that's happened since. Putting history to it and studying it makes it a lot better in the sense that I am now less subjective about the whole thing, although that subjective element is critical.

Tertiary education

Because I'm the second oldest of eleven, I knew a lot about kids. I spent a lot of time bringing up my own brothers and sisters younger than me. That was something I always knew I was good at, so teaching wasn't such a big step. It wasn't until I went to teachers' college and actually got in front of a classroom for the first time that I was sold. I loved it. Even hearing my voice for the first time was freaky. I was saying "Is that what I sound like?" but it was enough to get me excited, and I worked hard in my time at college. I worked hard to be the best teacher I could be and got recognition for it as in those early years.

That was my career. I'm still a teacher at heart. I might be a university one, but I'm a teacher. I didn't have qualifications to go to university when I left school, so I went teaching, because in those days you could get into primary teaching. I didn't even think about wanting to do university studies either. "I'm doing what I want to do," I said to myself. I liked it. I knew that there was a career there and I could spend a lot of time there. I taught for ten years before I went to university to do my first paper and that was only because my brother had done that. He would say I was lazy, because I didn't go and do university studies. I didn't have time to do these other things, I argued, but he kept at me to do extramural studies at Massey University.

After ten years of teaching I eventually did enrol. The first time I turned up at a lecture theatre with what seemed like about 500 other students and listening to this lecturer talking about Plato and Aristotle, I was thinking what the hell are they talking about? Why are they talking about those guys, Greeks most of them, who had died a long time ago? But I got caught up in it because I had read some of that philosophy. I found that I got excited about it. I got motivated and it never stopped really. University study really got me and I don't even know why, except I wanted to keep doing it.

By this time I was running a two-teacher school full-time with my wife, a Māori school in the Eastern Bay of Plenty, and my wife was doing exactly the same thing. We were having kids as well. Doing extramural study was a long-term plan, and the years go by slowly and next thing you know, you only have Stage III papers to complete and you've got your degree.

I don't mean for it to sound accidental, but it's just about as accidental as that. But the whole time I was studying, I was getting more and more involved in it. Particular fields of study, like the sociology of education, were capturing my imagination as part of what I was doing. I was teaching at a Māori school and because I wasn't a native speaker of Māori, I went off to learn Māori at the same university. I never ever wanted to go to university to study school subjects like English, maths and science. I've never ever been interested in doing that. I wanted to know about things like philosophy and sociology. Why are there things that go on in education like this? Even those earlier questions about my primary school: Why is it Māori kids have difficulty in primary schools and Pākehā kids take it for granted that they're going to succeed?

That's how it seemed. I thought no, this can't be right and I never ever let that thought go. It was the motivating force behind trying to learn about what was going on there. University provided an opportunity, and like a lot of other people, I did extramural study and attained my bachelor's degree in education and sociology. I went on to do a master's degree at Massey too. I studied in a university overseas for a while, and had an extraordinary experience working internationally at university level — a phenomenal experience at the Institute of Education at the University of London. It was mind-boggling for me. I was able to build on everything that I ever learnt before, and that also helped me, because of the separation of distance, to bring a different level of objectivity into my thinking to what was happening at home.

Māori scholarship

Scholarship is something which is a generic idea but it is what people bring to it that makes it different. If you're a Scottish academic scholar, you're not the same as an English academic scholar. The same thing applies to Māori. You bring a wealth of stuff with you to the scholarship field and the scholarship field is about learning about the world we live in, and why it operates the way it does. It requires from us to be systematic about that, and not haphazard; to be thoughtful about it, and not jump in to the deep end straight off; to rely on your background experience, but to explore other ideas and thoughts. That's what is important for me about scholarship. It asks you to pull back on your views about things and to consider different approaches and different views. Māori bring a particular brand of scholarship. I can't even say that I understand too much about what it is, except I've no doubt that there is one. There is a Māori scholarship.

Now reading about Ngata and Buck, and then modern times Pat Hōhepa, Ranginui Walker and Whatarangi Winiata — they do bring something, but it's hard to say what it is that they do. The one thing that's important is that they do provide a challenge to the status quo, particularly where the status quo is taken for granted. People in the Pākehā, Western world will write about scholarship, and it comes from the point of view of academia in their culture. In the Māori world it is the same, except it has different bases. Those bases may include the work of tohunga, they may be the work of kaumātua, the work by kuia and koroua, and what they bring with them into the modern world.

In modern Māori terms, you are forced to provide a barrier between the two things in order to go from one to the other. I don't doubt there is such a thing as a Māori scholarship. There are Māori ways of doing things. Sometimes people can get excited about their fields and next minute they're talking about 'the Māori way' as though this is it. I say no, there is no such thing as 'the Māori way' but there are definitely lots of Māori ways. If there is a Māori way, I don't know what it is and I don't know anybody who can tell me what it is. That's the sort of scholarship that you learn in the Pākehā world too, a scepticism about things, but I've seen kaumātua take the same sceptical line too. They might not understand that in the same way, but they ask different kinds of questions about things that people are talking about.

One thing I like about Western academia is how important the whole idea of scepticism is. I try to apply it to my work and the Māori contribution to the work that I do too. We are good at saying what's wrong with the Pākehā world and what they do to us. We're not too good at talking about our own world and what we do to it. Well, if you're going to be critical about things, sceptical about things, you have to apply it to both sides. You probably have to apply it unevenly in the world we live in, because Pākehā dominate culturally, economically, politically, in every way possible. They dominate and that means they actually disadvantage us; but what we must be careful of is that we don't disadvantage ourselves. The question about Māori scholarship, what is that? The easy way out is just to say it's what Māori scholars do, and we're learning a lot more about that today. Books are being written about Ranginui Walker and Āpirana Ngata; things are coming out now to help us better understand the idea of the Māori scholar. The work that is being done as part of MANU AO Academy and talking with someone like Mason Durie — no question at all that he is a Māori scholar that can hack it with any scholar anywhere, at any time.

Professional career

I worked in the public service for years. I worked in the Māori Advisory Service and then I came to university for the first time. After I came back from London University I did a six-month stint at Waikato. That was my first university teaching. Then I left there and went into the public service again. Came out of there and was offered a job at Victoria University in 1994 part-time, to relieve another person who was teaching Māori education. I've been a full-time academic only since 1998. My goals were to work in Māori education. Māori teacher education and Māori education has been in difficulty for so long, and it doesn't look as if it's getting any better. There are a whole lot of things going on, and I wanted to make a contribution to that field. I never thought I had the answer to all these things, but I definitely knew I had a contribution to make, and my contribution was one which I felt was weak within education, and that's to do with critical analysis, critical theory, critical perspectives. In the simplest terms, I mean challenging the status quo, back to my primary school years, asking questions such as "Why is this like this? Why does this hurt for some people and not others? Why is it taken for granted? What can you do about it?" Those are the critical questions we still have to ask and find ways to answer. You soon find out that people don't actually like you asking those questions. Some people would rather you didn't have to do any thinking about it; you just learn how to do it — technique, practise, do those things and everything will turn out sweet. Well, that's how things stay the same. We have to learn how to challenge. It's a lesson in itself, learning how to challenge the system, because I know how powerful the system is. In some ways it's arrogance, but I never back off. I'm about challenging the way the workplace works and that's at every level, including the academic world. Because it has a history of elitism; there's this 'you can't touch it' attitude. University systems have propositions built into them but the education system will have to challenge itself. Universities are supposed to be the critic and conscience of society. Let's be that. Instead of talking about it, let's be it because we don't do enough of that.

I started teaching in Mangakino. It was a huge settlement at one time. When I first got sent there I thought I was being punished for something. In fact, I loved it there. It had a huge Māori population who were there to build dams, the hydro works. The single men outnumbered everybody else, so sport was important there. There was a huge school and I was part of that. I did two-and-a-half years there before work on the dams closed down and everyone had to shift. Whole streets disappeared overnight. I had a look around for a job, and got one in Ōtara. Here I was, a Māori boy in a big city. I stayed with a cousin of mine and taught at Ōtara. I loved it there too. I spent five years teaching there, and it was hard. This is in the early 1960s. People from the Pacific came in large numbers to Ōtara. Māori from rural communities came to Ōtara; families with new homes, mortgaged up to their eyeballs, husband and wife both working, kids running rampant. It was an extraordinary experience and I never would have stayed five years if it wasn't working for me. I learned to teach there. You had no choice. If you're going to survive you had to learn how to work with these kids and I did. I've always been eternally grateful that I taught there. After five years I got married and we started to have children, and I thought it was about time I got out of the city; I was looking for a Māori school. My wife is a Scot, and our first child was very fair-skinned. I thought we needed to do something about this, because I wanted my kids to grow up knowing what it means to be Māori. I didn't want to go back to the Waikato, because I thought my relations were too grumpy, too psychologically disturbed about all sorts of things, such as hangovers from the land wars, like raupatu. The point, of course, is that Waikato-Tainui like many other iwi thoroughly deserve to be grumpy and that's an understatement.

Eventually I got a job in a school in the Eastern Bay of Plenty and went there. It was designated as a Māori school with a Māori community; a marae down the hill, while the major religion in the community was Ringatū. I thought this is where my kids are going to grow up, I'm going to learn to be Māori myself, as well as my kids and my wife. My wife had to trust me and my judgement; she didn't know what she was in for but neither did I really. Like me and our kids, she learned to love it. We came to enjoy the place and got in with the community and we had eight years there so that says something about it. While we were there I started university study. I went teaching on exchange in Britain for a year with my wife and three kids and then came back to our little country school. Eventually we had to move out of there because I had pressure on me from the inspectors to get out of the school, and go and do something else in a bigger school; I'd been there too long in their minds. I would have been happy to stay there.

After eight years in the Eastern Bay of Plenty I went to Whanganui and Taranaki, and the Māori Advisory Service which was again an eye-opener for me. I was thrown in the deep end regarding Māori education in two parts of the country I knew nothing about. I knew nothing about the Māori people there; I found them totally different to Māori I knew before. It was good, really neat. From my early teaching, my studying and starting at university, working in the university degree, now I'm into the Māori Advisory Service, into Māori communities on a broader context. I'd been working on all the things I'd accumulated all those years, putting it into practice in my work with teachers. It was tremendous because in the Māori Advisory Service you worked with teachers in a school, then you'd pack up and go to another school. It was great to see lots of other teachers and lots of other schools. I was working with a team of people, with other Māori people in education. People like Himiona Hunia, Rose Pere, Huirangi Waikerepuru, Akuhata and Cassidy Tangaere, Hape Potae, Anita Moke, John Matthews, Pera Riki, Sonny Mikaere, Mi'i Pamatatau, Jim Leabourn and others. They are my mates. It was a fantastic time for me. I had something like seven or eight years working in that group.

While I was there I went to London on a scholarship. I was getting into a master's degree and they sent me to London for a year. That was cool. I learnt a whole lot of things in London, about black Afro-Caribbean and Indian sub-continent communities. They were far more radical than us Māori when it comes to what's going on in the community. It was really politicised. I loved that too. It was a new era of scholarship for me, reading anti-racism, multicultural education and global education. After a year, I came back to New Zealand and worked in the Department of Education in Auckland. As a public servant, I accepted the things that I learned about working with government, but I can't ever say I really enjoyed it. I spent a fair bit of time working in the Department of Education, then in the Education Review Office, and then in the Ministry of Education. I have always been deeply impressed by the professionalism of the public servants in those departments but in my opinion most of them had too much influence on decisions in Māori education that was not justified. They didn't know how to listen to Māori, and most didn't want to learn either.

Academic career

I started teaching in 1960, and I'm still here. That's been a big achievement for me. I didn't progress from secondary school to university because I went to university later in life, after I had a family. I did it extramurally, and that came with its own difficulties. When you are working full-time, when do you do your assignments, your readings? I became a late-night worker, and it's become a habit for me now. When you're doing extramural study, you have to do all the peer review and discussions by yourself, in your head or with your books or with your papers. I'm thankful that I've been a good reader, that I've enjoyed reading because that's helped me. But I've never learnt all those other things which come with academic life. I've only learnt them in the last few years. I'm still learning them now, such as how to collaborate with other people in research projects or writing articles for publication with other people. I've never known how to do that. It's the little things that have been a handicap for me. I'll deal with what I've got, and do my best. But I do know that some of the problems I've had are linked to not really being socialised into academia. You have to do that. You need to sit with other people, other colleagues and hear yourself talking about what you do and let them challenge you, because if you can't get past that, well go and find another job. That's what you have to learn to be able to do, and it is tough. You put yourself out there in the academic world so you need to be on your guard. You need to do the best you can with it. From the time I completed the BA degree, I've gone to conferences and seminars by the score, and I go out and I talk to public groups and I write papers. Some papers have been slipshod studies, because I didn't know enough, but they are good hallmarks for me. I speak at conferences more than I publish. One reason is because I found writing hard. I like reading and talking, but writing is another thing. It's taken me a long time, but I've got a few publications coming out now. I tell my students that they have to learn to publish earlier. Don't follow my example. If you want to be an academic, that's what you have to learn to do and to be able to do that, you have to put it out there for other people to look at and read and critique and that can be very painful.

Māori leadership

I've never considered myself a leader in the sense of being out the front and saying, "Come on everybody, follow me." I've been a leader from behind, almost by default. All I wanted to do was to contribute. Now most wouldn't count that as being really about leadership, so part of my leadership is as a result of longevity. I've been in the system for this amount of time and when people ask me to do things some of them are looking at me sideways, thinking, he's a teacher, an academic and a public servant. That's true, I've done those things and they are important for me to have done them. But I wouldn't advise other people to follow my example.

There have always been Māori leaders. They are the people who are out front saying "Follow me." They are of warrior breed. They are the ones who are challenging themselves in the status quo. The little village that I come from, Waharoa, was named for Te Waharoa Tarapīpipi, and he was a warrior chief. Ngāti Haua was never as powerful as when he was alive. His son was Wiremu Tamihana, who became the kingmaker, the peacemaker. They were totally different people in a sense, but both extravagant leaders in their own fields. I'm probably more like Wiremu Tamihana than his father, because he was someone who was keen on writing and reading and dealing with politicians. I'm not saying I'm like Wiremu Tamihana, I'm just me. I don't really look to other people as models for me. I don't know who my models are. I don't have any. There are many people who have done magnificent things. There's a guy that I knew as a teacher called Jim Laughton. He used to be principal of Richmond Road School in Ponsonby, and he was Māori. He was the most fantastic educator I'd ever met. His father was Reverend Laughton, who was a missionary among Ngāi Tūhoe. His mother was Māori, Ngāti Kahungunu and Ngāti Porou. He was a leader because he was visionary. I walk around on the ground and I like to pace it with somebody. I like to look them in the eye and talk about things.

Professional links

I've just come from a secondary school conference; they invited me as a guest speaker. I'm willing to talk to teachers all the time, not just Māori teachers, but to all teachers. However, I like to talk to Māori teachers because they're the ones who are going to make the biggest difference for our kids. I'm not sure that's even true, but that's who I'm most keen to work alongside. I nurture them. My links with professionals include the public service. Even though I'm critical of the Ministry of Education, they bring me in to advise on different things. It could be because they know I might highlight some things that they haven't thought about. I've worked for the Education Review Office and the New Zealand Qualifications Authority. If they send me things to read, I'll read it, and if they want me to turn up, I'll turn up. I pride myself on doing those things. I think about my dad. He was a labourer but he never missed a day's work. He prided himself on it. He thought it was wonderful if he could work on Saturday as well. The professionals are just the people who are getting paid to do the same thing, in some ways. The most important ones for me are teachers, because I'm in education. But like all educators, we all have to learn how to work better with community and with whānau. I take that as one of those things for granted that we need to be able to do.

Connections with iwi

It's one of those things as Māori you don't have a choice about, you get on with it and do the best you can with it. No use saying "I can't do it because I'm too busy" or "Nobody cares about that from home." I'm involved with my iwi. I go back to Tainui and I go back to my Ngāti Haua roots and I work with them on their Treaty claims. I don't do this as much as I'd like but certainly as much as I can fit in. There are some things I find extremely difficult. I'm one of the people on the working group with our Treaty claims. Sometimes they ring me on Friday night and say there's a meeting on Saturday. I live in Wellington. There's nothing special about that. I could think of so many people where this is the case. It's a bit of madness, but I try to get a balance. I like living in Wellington. Every time I go home, our kuia will say, "When are you coming home?" They don't stop either. And I am thinking to myself, don't you know by now I'm not. I'm not in a hurry to do that, but one of the reasons is that this distance is important to me. I intend going home but I'm dedicated to my academic work at present. I don't want to put myself under unnecessary pressure to be involved in iwi, because I'm Māori. I'll do it once I've thought about it, I've got time to do it and I want to do it. At the same time I'm saying it's a hell of a position that we're in as Māori. I hate to think how many Māori die on the roads because of travelling long distances to tangi, weddings and other hui. On the other hand I know I've got to do so many things. I love going back to Waikato but I don't want to live there.

Challenges for future Māori academics

There's a lot of work still to be done in the academic world. There have been mighty efforts to indigenise the universities and we're probably doing better than other indigenous peoples, but we still have a lot to do. I've been asked to write a report for Australia. They're looking at the participation of Aboriginal and Torres Islanders in universities in Australia, and they asked me to write a paper about the New Zealand context — what New Zealand have done for Māori, and what Māori have done in New Zealand to indigenise the universities. I thought that sounds like a pretty good topic to work on, so I wrote a report on some very practical reasons why we are where we are. If someone said we couldn't be in universities, then that was more reason for us to be there. It's happening around the country now, not just at universities. Māori are in the media, in business, in medical professions, in law, in politics, in education, in health. I'm glad I'm alive now because it's happening now. This is a real revolution. Pākehā New Zealanders are getting the idea now too. They are picking up on Māori things and making them as part of theirs as well. That is one of the indicators. It's not all about what Māori are doing for society but what Pākehā are doing about things Māori. That's where the future lies in our work. Our contributions have to be in there as much as anybody else's. Academics are feared as people who are in privileged positions and I underline that for me, it has been an absolute privilege to work in the university.

Wally (centre left) and his wife Sheena (centre). Their daughter Kim and her husband Joe are in back row with their three tamariki Paretapu, Darrio and Manihera. Their oldest son Grant is next to Wally, with his wife Susan with their two daughters, Cara (on Susan's knee) and Frances (held by Sheena). Their youngest son Dougal and his wife Kirsty are front right; they have since had three tamariki: Tallulah, Romeo and Willow. The photo was taken in 2007 at Taupō at a celebration birthday for Sheena.

Future aspirations

I've got to spend a lot more time with my mokopuna and my whānau. I love it, and this generation of mokopuna are fantastic. That's part of my future. I still want to write, actually. I have written a book, based on my doctoral thesis. It has ten chapters. Nine chapters are a critique of the system and the last chapter challenges us to think about where we are going next. I want to turn that last chapter into a whole book, and while I'm doing that, a book about my family should also keep me out of mischief for a while.

MARGIE MAAKA

Professor Margaret Maaka has spent nearly 30 years at the University of Hawai'i at Mānoa, formerly as a PhD student and currently as a professor of Education. Her strong teaching background was gained in New Zealand schools, particularly Mt Maunganui College. Her areas of interest include educational psychology/indigenous educational psychology, educational policy, indigenous leadership, language and cognitive development, and indigenous development and advancement. Margie's iwi affiliations are Ngāti Kahungunu, Ngāti Awa and Ngāi Tahu.

I was born in Napier and raised in a small community, Te Hāroto, along the Napier–Taupō Road. My father worked in the timber milling industry. I attended Te Hāroto Māori School, which was one of the early native schools in New Zealand. I had an idyllic upbringing, which, with the wisdom of hindsight, I took for granted. I had very few cares in the world. I started school at Te Hāroto when I was four, and went on to standard four. I have great memories of the school, but not such great memories of the Pākehā teachers who were intent on socialising us into wider society at the expense of our own Māoritanga. Corporal punishment was a daily spectacle. But there were great memories nonetheless. The two best teachers were Māori and while they were strict, they were also very caring. When revisiting the community as an adult, I was struck by the disenfranchisement of the people of that place, Ngāti Hineuru. As children, we were not aware of it at the time. Te Hāroto was a mixture of an awesome place to be raised, but there were great hardships for the people too. In some ways I'm saddened by the fact that, as a child, I didn't have a greater social knowledge or conscience in terms of the hardships faced by Ngāti Hineuru. I know the iwi is currently negotiating its Treaty settlement and it must be supported in its efforts to restore its health and wellbeing through the return of its lands and through other avenues of financial redress.

I come from a family that has always appreciated the value of education, my mother particularly so. On my father's side education was valued too. My father is Ngāti Kahungunu and Ngāi Tahu. He was number nine in the family and so the first couple of children had the benefits of private education, but as more children were born, finances became more and more scarce, which meant the younger ones attended public schools. My father went to good public schools — Hastings Boys' High School and Dannevirke High School — where he was a good scholar and an outstanding sportsman. It took many years for someone to come along and eventually break his records in swimming and athletics. My mother is Ngāti Awa, but was raised in a very Pākehā context. She went to Epsom Girls Grammar in Auckland and then went on to teachers' college in Dunedin. She was a physical education teacher. At one time she considered

Te Hāroto Māori School junior class, 1958; Margie is fourth from the left in the middle row.

the possibility of undertaking graduate study at UCLA but this was curbed by the outbreak of World War II. I was fortunate to have two parents who had enjoyed the fruits of good educations. From both of them I learned to place a strong value on getting a good education and applying that knowledge.

From the beginning, both my parents instilled strong values in my brother and me. For example, there was no question about me graduating from high school, or obtaining University Entrance, or entering a profession — which is what I did. That notion of achievement came from my parents, but the importance of a good education was evident in the wider family. On the Maaka side, several of my cousins were very good at school and so there was this growing tradition on both sides of the family that attaining a good education would be a given, and it was just a natural path for me to take.

My uncle Golan Maaka was a well respected general practitioner in Whakatāne for many years. He had an influence on my decision to pursue a career in education. I can't remember him sitting me down and telling me what to do, but the fact that he was one of the few Māori doctors of that time made me realise that I could also achieve well in education if I really wanted to. There was nothing stopping me. Uncle Golan was somebody in the family who had already achieved that goal, and that's what inspired me. I went to Colenso High School, and I was one of those kids who started at the top of the class in the third form and gradually worked my way to the bottom by the end of my school career. I barely got my University Entrance and my parents weren't quite sure what I was going to do because I was coasting academically. On the other hand, my social and sporting life at high school was flourishing. But after I did my overseas experience in Australia, I came back and it was a natural decision for me to go to university. I think my parents were relieved.

Tertiary education

I applied to go to Hamilton Teachers' College. My primary focus was to become a teacher and when I arrived there, I found out that I could do my bachelor's degree at the University of Waikato as well. So while at teachers' college doing my teacher education courses, I started studying for my Bachelor of Education degree at Waikato. I completed my B Ed and then my master's degree also at Waikato before I embarked on a teaching career. At university, education was my major, but I also undertook papers in English literature. My areas of specialisation were 19th-century British poets, Shakespeare and 20th-century American literature. I still love the arts and literature. My art background was mainly cultivated during my time at teachers' college. I was particularly interested in graphic design too.

While at teachers' college and university, I can't remember anybody telling me that I couldn't do things. But there was an expectation that Māori were not good in some disciplines, especially statistics and maths. I didn't adhere to that kōrero. I actually felt that I had a good education at Waikato because I was able to do what I wanted to do and not be dictated to by what others thought I should do. However, there weren't very many Māori role models, as the university was very Western. There were a lot of American educators on exchange programmes and Waikato University was a very new institution as well. I felt that I pretty much carved out my own career there. I decided what I wanted to do. I went on and did my degrees and felt that the education there provided a strong foundation for my future.

My peers were mainly friends and my husband at the time too. He and I both started at the same time. My peer group were mainly my friends who had gone to Colenso High School and Hastings Boys' High School. There was a group of about six of us that decided to go to the University of Waikato and Hamilton Teachers' College. Syd Jackson's youngest brother Phillip (Jacko) is one of our mates who joined us. He ended up being a principal in Napier. We have iwi connections. Syd Jackson was in Auckland at the time with Ngā Tamatoa, but we were very much younger of course. I remember staying the weekend with Syd and Hana once and being in awe of their politics. Their activism was instrumental in making me think about the plight of the Māori people and my responsibilities as an educator. I do remember Dun Mihaka coming to Waikato and yelling through his megaphone that we needed to get off our arses and get involved in Māori activism. It was all very new and raw but very gutsy at the same time.

There was an absence of Māori role models at Waikato University when I went there. We looked after ourselves. I think it is reasonable to say that we became our own role models. We hung out with each other and formed a group of people, both Māori and Pākehā, who were confident in each other's company. We socialised together, studied together, grew up together.

Teaching experiences

I've been lucky to have lots of different opportunities to be able to choose a career path that I enjoy. I taught at Maeroa Intermediate in Hamilton, and there were a lot of Māori kids there. Then I went to Tauranga Intermediate, not very many Māori there. I then spent the greater part of my teaching career at Mt Maunganui College, where there was a large population of Māori kids. I gravitated to that population or, perhaps, they gravitated to me. I was really into sports. I had played representative netball in Hawke's Bay, and enjoyed tennis, basketball, volleyball, horse riding, anything. I was associated with the surfing world as well, and so a lot of the kids who I had things to do with were also interested in those sports. A lot of Māori kids played basketball and surfed, and through those connections I had some association with the local Māori community. But mainly my association was with the children. I dabbled fleetingly with graphic design because at Mt Maunganui College I taught English literature, graphic arts and art history. If anything, I never ventured down the art path as much as I would have liked too, but I don't have any regrets.

At that stage in my life I was becoming more aware of the fact that if opportunities weren't made available for Māori kids then they would have no options once they left school. I became aware early on at Mt Maunganui College that a number of children belonged to families that had generationally received the unemployment benefit, and that there were few prospects for them once they finished school. Because of this, I worked a lot with Māori kids who looked like they had some potential. I am happy to say that some became managers of companies and some went to university. One of the reasons why I returned to university was because I realised that each year, I was only able to help one or two Māori kids make significant and positive life changes. I felt that if I went to university and became involved in teacher preparation, I could prepare more teachers who would then help more kids, as opposed to me helping two or three students a year. That's one of the main reasons why I went to university to do my PhD and to pursue a career in education.

When I look back at my teaching career, what stands out for me is the fact that I love working with kids. That was one thing I missed when I went into higher education. I liked working at Mt Maunganui College. The kids were just outrageously naughty and unruly yet wonderful at the same time. They were great and their potential for success was amazing. One student in my art history class told me that her dream was to travel to Paris and visit the Louvre. Several years later she did. I thought this was awesome. Not all kids reached that success, but they tried hard notwithstanding the pressures and challenges of life.

Doctoral study

In 1984 I spent my sabbatical leave in the United States and it was something very different. I ended up in Utah and spent the summer and the following winter there. I went to the University of Utah and studied graphic design for a year. I liked the whole idea of studying again and the environment was conducive to bringing out the best in me. After my time in Utah, I returned to New Zealand and I taught for another 18 months. I then decided that I wanted to do my PhD (in educational psychology) in a context other than New Zealand. That wasn't because I thought that New Zealand was a lesser option, it was because I wanted to have a different experience and so I applied to lots of different universities, including UCLA, Santa Barbara and so on. When the University of Hawai'i came up, I decided to go with that option because it had a reasonably good College of Education at that stage, although not as reputable as UCLA or Santa Barbara. I also chose Hawai'i because of its proximity to home in New Zealand and because of the possibility that I might be able to work with Hawaiians. My parents were happy with my decision to study at UH too. While they supported my career decisions one hundred percent, they were happy that I was not too far away. It was important that I could go home at the drop of a hat if necessary.

My doctoral dissertation is in the area of psycholinguistics. I was interested in looking at the cognitive and linguistic development of young children. I conducted my research in Hawke's Bay at schools in Napier, Waipukurau and Takapau. I never published my dissertation only because I got a job immediately after graduating and had to hit the ground running, but I'd quite like to revisit my research sometime.

It was an interesting experience doing my PhD at UH-Mānoa. The Department of Educational Psychology was a quirky place. Looking back, I had a good education there because I was somewhat independent and older. I was able to navigate some of the stumbling blocks that were part of the College of Education and there were a few. I had some professors there who were not entirely sympathetic to other cultures. At that time there were only two native Hawaiian faculty members in the college. There were something like 70 faculty members, so it was a very white experience. Regardless, I still think that I had a good education. Naturally, there were things that could have been better but I don't have any regrets. The college was far more academically rigorous in those days and the quality of teachers graduated was much higher. In part this has to do with the stranglehold of state and national mandates, such as the No Child Left Behind Act and the National Council for Accreditation of Teacher Education. Sadly, the college has become a cookie-cutting teacher preparation factory in many ways. My colleague David Sherrill was a significant influence on my approach to teacher education because he always emphasised the importance of putting student wellbeing at the centre of everything. Nowadays, politics are at the centre of everything. I am hoping that the pendulum will swing back to good teacher preparation practices with a stronger administration.

Graduation Day, University of
Hawai'i at Mānoa, 1992.

Academic career

An academic career was always on the cards for me even back when I decided
to go to Hamilton Teachers' College. In the intake, I was one of a smaller
group who decided to study for the Bachelor of Education degree. That was
when I made a conscious decision that academia was for me. After completing
my B Ed, I went on to do my master's degree, which confirmed that a life in
academia was where I intended to be. I remember the first day at teachers'
college well. There must have been a couple of hundred of us sitting in a big
amphitheatre and the instructor in charge of our intake told us that so many
would graduate with teaching diplomas, a smaller number would graduate with
bachelor's degrees and an even smaller number would graduate with master's
degrees. He finished up by telling us that only two or three would graduate
with doctoral degrees. At that point, everyone started looking at each other
wondering who the two or three might be. I thought to myself, "Yep, one of
them is going to be me!"

I've always been interested in teaching and that was probably from my
mother who was also a teacher. During my time at high school, my parents
didn't think that I was university material because I didn't have my act together.

Even though I goofed off at high school I knew I wanted to go to university at some stage. However, I attended high school at a time when women were not thought of as university material. I graduated from high school in 1970 and most of my female peers went nursing, became secretaries or went teaching. The thought of going to university to study for a degree was not high on the cards for most females.

I've always been single-minded in terms of what I have wanted to achieve. I probably got that from my maternal grandmother. Even when others thought that I was not headed in the right direction, I knew I was. I was just taking a route that was a little bit more fun. When I went back to university I was actually quite scholarly. I had a determination that I was going to do well and I worked hard at teachers' college. I graduated with distinction, so I invested a lot of time and effort into the work I did. I was quite fanatical about completing my work on time and doing a good job at it, which was very different from my experiences at high school. I am not sure why this was so. I liked the university environment, the subjects that I was studying, and the friends I was making.

Once I completed my PhD at the University of Hawai'i, I was given a two-year professional development opportunity. After that, a position came up in the College of Education and I applied for it. That's where I've been ever since. In terms of my professional progress at university, I applied, and won an assistant professor tenure track position. After the required period of time I acquired tenure and was promoted to associate professor. Later, I applied for full professor, which is the position I have now.

There are lots of things in a career that can be hallmarks. Academically

the different stages of acquiring degrees are typical hallmarks — bachelor's, master's and doctoral degrees. I enjoy my relationships with scholars: junior, mid-career and senior scholars in the research arena. I have a long association with the American Educational Research Association (AERA) and that has become the mecca for me. A lot of researchers from around the world, including Māori, go to that conference. We have a group of Māori and Hawaiian scholars that get together a lot, and AERA becomes the gathering place for us. I enjoy going into those arenas and meeting with Māori researchers like Linda

Margie at the American Educational Research Association conference, 1994.

Smith, Graham Smith, Huia Jahnke, Trish Johnston, and Marilyn Brewin and Hawaiian researchers like Kapā Oliveira and Laiana Wong. I also have many Alaska Native, First Nations, and American Indian colleagues and consider all of them great friends. I work a lot with Bryan Brayboy, who is at Arizona State University.

I like working with young scholars, new researchers. I particularly like mentoring at the doctoral level. I now have a lot of doctoral students, but then I've worked in pre-service teacher education as well. Mentoring people in their careers, mentoring people who are going to become teachers and who are able to elevate educational opportunities for others is also something I'm interested in.

Māori scholarship

The Western institution's definition of Māori scholarship is about how many publications a professor has in obscure refereed journals with low acceptance rates that nobody ever reads. For me, scholarship — in terms of indigenous or Māori — is about working with the communities we should be serving. It's about looking at ways in which we can include community members in research projects that are about them. I do a lot of work with native Hawaiian community members. I do a lot of co-mentoring. Māori or indigenous scholarship is about how we maximise a research space to bring about the greater good for indigenous people, and this quite often doesn't translate into publications in journals and books. I don't think that Māori and indigenous scholarship is given the credibility that is merited mainly because racism in Western institutions has a strong foothold. Racism at the University of Hawai'i is alive and well; it used to be blatant but now that everyone is politically correct it has gone underground which is even worse. The university hires a lot of Pākehā professors and administrators from the mainland and they are generally clueless about any worldview other than their own.

Graham Smith talks about the danger of Māori and other indigenous peoples who work within institutions becoming 'privatised academics'. There's a huge danger of that. At the University of Hawai'i at Mānoa, for example, there are many who are privatised academics. As far as I am concerned, if a person does not have an active working relationship with the community then she or he is a privatised academic. And this working relationship has to be on the community's terms, not on the university's terms or our terms. That is not just my opinion, this is also the opinion of the community I work with. Indigenous academics can become too comfortable. We can have good lives at an institution of higher learning. We can go to work and do our research, and we don't necessarily need to come out of our offices. But for me, there's no satisfaction in this. I mean this would be easy. I could belt out copious journal articles and have a much higher publication record, but there would be no satisfaction. I like going out to the community. Most of the time, I sit with elders, eat with them, laugh and joke with them, try to find out what their needs are and how we can work together, and plan and conduct research. At the recent World Indigenous Peoples Conference on Education I co-presented our research with my community elders. The oldest was nearly 90! And they were awesome. They brought a measure of wisdom to the conference that was needed. That's scholarship as far as I'm concerned. It may not have the deliverables that an institution values, but that is the institution's problem.

Recently, a lot of my research has been on indigenous self-determination and education, leadership, working with institutional structures, and politics. I've written a lot in this area. I'm particularly interested in what constitutes good mentoring. I'm interested in looking at education for indigenous peoples within a democratic state, so I'm working on a paper at the moment that looks at whether democracy, by its very nature, is a good fit with indigenous self-determination, especially considering we are on the outside of the common core. If we exist within a democratic state that has a different culture or different worldview, then we are always going to be on the outside. I'm interested in the whole notion of whether indigenous people can function within a democracy.

Being Māori, away from home

I often think about the benefit of being Māori and being outside of New Zealand within another indigenous culture like Hawai'i. I have been outside of the Māori world for nearly 30 years, and I'm very careful. I'm very careful about not coming back as an authority on what's current in the Māori world and things that are Māori. I'm Māori and I consider that I have a right to work with Māori communities, but I'm also very careful about how I do this. I work instead with colleagues mainly at Massey, Auckland, Waikato, Ngā Pae o te Māramatanga and Awanuiārangi. Through them I connect with communities. We have multiple projects that I contribute to. One project is helping to make space for Māori scholars in an international arena, because our research has a lot to offer other groups, not just indigenous groups. I'm always cognisant of the fact that although indigenous, this does not give me automatic rights within a Hawaiian context either. As I mentioned, I have partnered with a local native Hawaiian community and I work at their invitation. When they tell me that my work is no longer needed then I'll move on, but while they ask me to work with them and they think that there are things that I can bring to their community, I'll continue to do that. I try not to do anything with language or cultural revitalisation. I'm very careful about the roles that I take on. I prefer to work with community leadership but I will work with others as well. I'm interested in anything to do with education and anything that I develop is usually in partnership with the community. I have a leadership role; it's part of that negotiation with the community.

As for my work in Hawai'i, the disconnect between the institution and the community is a huge concern at times. Sometimes it is hard to instil in folk the idea of the importance of a commitment to their own Hawaiian community. Sadly, I have had the experience of spending hours and hours mentoring folk into leadership roles, only to find that their own self-interests have taken precedence over the interests of their own community. They have gone on to be the 'privatised academics' that I'm talking about. One hardship is mentoring people into leadership roles and finding out too late that they do not have the 'essence' to become great leaders. Some of this essence has to do with personal qualities and upbringing in a community. There are things as a mentor that I can't bring to people. There are qualities that should be in place to start with, and in some cases they aren't. I have wasted time on these people.

Māori leadership

Māori leadership is about for Māori, by Māori, and ultimately, in Māori. I strongly believe in 'for Māori, by Māori' but it's also about the enhancement of the people, not about individual enhancement. To mentor people into people leadership roles, it is important for the mentor to have to a certain degree of mana in the first place. Māori and indigenous leadership is about the work being done and how leaders are preparing the next generation of leaders to accommodate the needs of our people. You can't be an effective leader if you don't work with the community or understand them and their world.

Balancing work and whānau commitments

It's important to be able to balance your life as a person, as an academic, and as a community citizen. I don't know whether it's because I am older and I am advantaged by hindsight, but I would say that I have placed great priority on my career and on my academic life. I've had a good family life, but my life has been geared too much at times towards my career and my profession. More recently, family has become much more important, and if I have any regrets, I probably should have had more of a balance between my career and my personal life. I regret not spending more time with my parents, who were extremely supportive and extremely proud of the things that I did. But once your parents and your family have gone, there's no taking any of that time back. I have a better balance now. I don't let my work at the university take up as much time as it has in the past. I'm also separating the demands of the university from the work that I do with the community. I've transferred a lot of my focus from the institution to a focus on the community, and that's the work I like doing. I look at the university now as being the vehicle that allows me to work in indigenous education, which includes working with my native Hawaiian community partners. Sadly, in recent years, the University of Hawai'i has lost its way under the current administration. I don't think it is a healthy place for anyone at present. I've got this balance now with family, with a smaller focus on the institution, and then a gradual but deliberate shift to community service.

Community engagement

Most of my role models have been Māori, even in the context of Hawai'i. I have role models like my family, especially my parents, and even some of my younger colleagues. I consider them role models because they do things that I think are important. The community partnerships I work with are primarily elders — our matriarch, Aunty Aggie, has just turned 90. She is amazing. I consider my community partners my extended family. They're my role models too. Awesome folk like Kamaki Kanahele, Myron Brumaghim and Mike Kahikina. They like to get things done. The community developments are extremely impressive and forward-moving. Our work has its detractors (mainly people who complain and do nothing) and it has its supporters as well. Our partnership has been involved in building a Boys & Girls' club, a community comprehensive health centre that includes a traditional healing centre and a low-income housing community. Next on the plans is a community learning centre and a huge commercial centre. They've done significant things, but the most important thing for me is that there's a trust and a loyalty within our group that I haven't found at the university. I have a community that supports me 100 percent. In small groups at the university I have trust, particularly with the immediate colleagues I work with now, but within the broader context I haven't found that trust and camaraderie at the institution.

My role in the native Hawaiian community has changed over time. When I first started working with the community nearly 20 years ago, it took me five or six years before I had any credibility. The community was used to people from the university coming out and using them as research projects and then taking off, never to be seen again. As such, when I first went out there, I was viewed with a sceptical eye. I had to prove myself. The community initially appealed to the university for help and I was one of a few who responded. When we arrived, the community leaders told us that they had no money or resources, and at that stage everyone else departed. I remained. The fact that I continued to work with the community for nothing, and that I financed everything I did, showed them that I was not there for my own benefit, but was genuinely there to help them and to work with them.

I love working with the Hawaiian community. My partners are upfront. They'll say to me things like, "Our people have told us they want a doctoral programme. Can you make that happen?" I'll sit down with them and discuss their ideas, and come up with solutions. I would like them to know that if they have important initiatives, they only need ask and I will use the university as a vehicle to make things happen. Most of the work that I do with them is rolling up the sleeves and getting the job done. This has been a good reality check because I don't want to become part of the university ivory tower mentality. It's very easy to work on a campus, develop a programme and go out to the community and say, "Look what I've done for you." The community I work for will not accept that approach. They want people to visit them, sit at their table, and have conversations. We put something in place together, and then I work on the logistics. Finally, we all come together with everything in place, and that's truly a collective achievement, accomplishment or initiative.

Indigenous scholar engagement

As an academic, my relationship with other Māori and indigenous academics has been close and rewarding. As mentioned, I have close relationships with senior Māori academics at Massey University, the University of Waikato, Te Whare Wānanga o Awanuiārangi, and the University of Auckland. My relationship with colleagues at Ngā Pae o te Māramatanga has evolved over ten years. To be honest, these senior Māori academics are my inspiration. When I become totally frustrated with the University of Hawai'i, they are the people I turn to. I've been away for 30 years, but there's a hotline to at least half a dozen scholars in New Zealand, and we're always on the phone talking to each other about projects, challenges, family, etc. If we have challenges or problems, we talk about them. We joke that this is our therapy line. I don't have that support at Mānoa with senior scholars but I do at home, which is interesting. There's that mutual therapy, inspiration, and shared interest in projects. We are all related, and that kinship is important too. The role I play is interesting. I think I am the safe person who can give some frank feedback without the baggage they have, and without personality and politics getting in the way. Perhaps

Margie with Professor
Sir Hirini Moko Mead,
Te Whare Wānanga o
Awanuiārangi.

I see things clearly and more objectively. I'm not steeped in the politics of a particular institution. When it is my turn to seek counsel, my colleagues or my friends fulfil that role for me too.

The sad thing for me is that life opportunities for Māori have diminished in recent years. There was a time in the 1980s and 1990s when we were making gains, especially relating to footholds in institutions, but over the last ten years or so we've regressed. In terms of research, the mainstay has been Ngā Pae o te Māramatanga, and real gains have been made there. The recent appalling decision to cease funding for a Māori Centre of Research Excellence is probably a good illustration of what's happening to Māori research and Māori researchers. There is a lack of understanding about how critical Māori researchers and Māori research are. Māori research doesn't benefit only Māori; it benefits New Zealand as a whole. In the absence of that research and those structures, everybody loses.

I have managed to navigate the system fairly well. Unfortunately, a lot of Māori students are unable to navigate the system and they get chewed up pretty fast. Nowadays, there are Māori supports and Māori mentors within institutions to support students, but if the current anti-Māori trend continues, these supports are in danger of eroding.

Future aspirations

In the future I would like work with scholars and colleagues in Hawai'i who are interested in the things that I think are important. I'm tired of mentoring people who turn out to have questionable integrity, but then it behoves me to be more discerning about who I choose to work. It is important that people have their own goals and values, but my interest is uplifting indigenous people and their communities. I don't want to work with people who don't have that as a primary goal. I'd like to work outside of the institution to a certain extent, and to have the funding to be able to do so. I don't want to be bound by the constraints or the whims of administrators who are not supportive of the work that I am doing. That's what I would like to do here. I'd like to have much stronger ties to home, to continue to build the connections that I have, and to work within institutions on a part-time basis. I am not sure how that would work, but if there are projects happening at Massey, Te Whare Wānanga o Awanuiārangi, Waikato or Ngā Pae, I'd like to continue those connections so that we advance the health and wellbeing of Māori and other indigenous people.

The legacy I would like to leave is to have it known that my efforts, in collaboration with many others, were designed to uplift Māori, Hawaiian and other indigenous peoples. I have managed to open some doors that allow people to take on leadership and research roles. It is hoped that the people who I've mentored will continue to do good things, and they will mentor other people who will do good things too. That is essentially what my work has been about, and that's what I would like to be remembered for.

I want to be known for being a good friend to my peers, and that the things that they valued were the things that I valued. Together we have worked on a lot of projects, and if we haven't moved a mountain, then we have certainly moved a hill here and there for Māori. These are the things that are important to me. I would like the people who I value to say that I helped them in some way. For me, if the community I'm working with feels that I have made contributions to their community, then that is a great legacy.

Working within other institutional structures

We have an interesting situation in Hawai'i regarding the university and local government. The university is meant to be autonomous from the legislature, but the legislature controls the purse strings. According to law, it's autonomous. According to common sense, it's not. I work with a community that's politically connected. Aunty Aggie has strong connections to the governor, several senators,

US congressman and so on. These bonds have been cemented over the years because of her active leadership in community and Hawaiian development. She is highly respected for the work she has done and continues to do, even at 90. Her son Kamaki is also actively involved in this work. In partnership with legislators, we've managed to achieve things that the university has not been able to achieve. If we have money appropriated to our initiatives, then that develops a very strong jealousy from within the institution. It is seen as 'taking away' from the university's efforts to acquire legislative funding.

There's a great deal of animosity on the part of some university administrators because the community received an appropriation some time ago to advance educational opportunities for Hawaiians. This sent a strong message to those administrators that the legislature did not see them as capable of fulfilling the needs of the community. My relationship with the Hawaiian community in terms of the political arena has therefore made my life very difficult in the university. But such is life.

My allegiance has been called into question by UH administrators. I have been accused of having an ethical conflict because I support the community. But you have to remember that the UH is a land grant institution. It sits on land that was stolen during the illegal overthrow of the Hawaiian monarchy. UH has used these lands for 107 years and has not paid one cent of rent to the Hawaiian people. The university is required to accommodate the needs and interests of the populace of Hawai'i and it doesn't do that. I look at my work as just fulfilling the mission of the institution. Most of our administrators at Mānoa are Pākehā who come from the mainland and who have not one clue about the Hawaiian community, neither are they interested in the Hawaiian community. It appals me that they have very little investment in the university and community as a whole, and they don't see the university as needing to have the same commitment to the community that I do.

Not being an insider here in Hawai'i is a disadvantage, but being an outsider has advantages too. I can play a role on the outside effectively. I don't have a lot of the familial ties that might restrict people. But not having some of those ties can also work as a disadvantage. Working with my Hawaiian colleagues helps address this. My partner, Laiana Wong, and I work together on a lot of projects too. It is right that he takes the lead. My rights, when I work with the community, come from the rights that they wish to accord me at certain times. I work with the community and respect their wishes and I'm very careful not to overstep the bounds. I do not do things that are without their blessing or guidance.

Reflections

One thing I had to give up when I came here to Hawai'i was horse riding. I'm an avid horsewoman. I miss this pastime. What else would I do differently? I'd be much more discerning regarding the people I mentor. Unfortunately, it is not possible to gauge a person's true character until a lot of time and energy has been invested in mentoring. I am regretful that I put too much effort into mentoring people who do not have integrity or mana. I am regretful because this time could have been spent mentoring somebody else who could make huge differences. But I am very happy about those folk who I have mentored who have integrity, mana, intelligence and who will go on to make great opportunities for our indigenous peoples.

If I balance my community work with my academic work, I've had a rewarding career to date. I've enjoyed my career. I probably have another ten years left, but I know that's going to go fast. I'd like to accomplish a lot in this next ten years. If I have any regrets, it would be that I have been away from New Zealand for so long and missed my family life. Both my parents have passed away since I've been here. I miss them and would like to recapture some of that time. I've missed out on having my feet on the ground, within a New Zealand institution and contributing more directly to the advancement of Māori on the home front. That's probably my biggest regret, but I made the choice. I miss home. This feeling has become stronger as I have grown older. I said to someone the other day, I need to fly home, put my feet on Aotearoa soil, and then I'm going to feel fine. I love it in Hawai'i, but New Zealand is home, and I've been away for far too long.

Atholl at Te Papa. 2015.
Norman Heke

ATHOLL ANDERSON

Emeritus Professor Atholl Anderson was born in Hāwera, raised in Dunedin and Nelson, and has iwi affiliations to Ngāi Tahu Whānui through descent from Rakiura Māori. Educated at Canterbury, Otago and Cambridge universities, he was for 17 years on the staff of Otago University, eventually as professor and head of the Anthropology Department. During that time he directed numerous archaeological excavations and published a major work on moa hunting, and other books on the archaeology and early history of southern New Zealand. From 1993 to 2008 Atholl was the professor of Prehistory in the Institute of Advanced Studies at Australian National University, Canberra, where he researched the prehistoric colonisation of the Pacific and Indian Ocean islands. He is a Fellow of the Royal Society of New Zealand, the Australian Academy of the Humanities, and the Society of Antiquaries, London.

Being Māori and Ngāi Tahu

I was born in Hāwera, Taranaki, my mother's home town. Her father's family were early settlers there. Her mother's family were of Ngāi Tahu and Ngāti Māmoe descent from Rakiura, in fact from Whenua Hou, the small island designated by Ngāi Tahu chiefs, sometime before 1820, as a settlement for Pākehā sealers and their Māori families. One of my tūpuna, Wharetutu, lived there in the 1820s, and then her daughter married a Pākehā farmer, and they moved north about 1882 to Taranaki. The place they went to was Parihaka. At that time, Pākehā settlers were seeking Māori land for farming, and she being Māori tried to integrate with the Māori women there. Because she was Ngāi Tahu and married to a Pākehā, she didn't have a great deal of success. Unfortunately, from that point, our connections with Ngāi Tahu were severed. I was born a couple of generations later, and we moved to Dunedin when I was four years old, in the late 1940s. Occasionally we visited several old aunties out at Warrington whom I understood were Māori and related to us, but otherwise we had no contact with Ngāi Tahu that I can recall. To the extent that I have a sense of being Māori it is as an adult rather than as a child.

It was only after I went back to Otago University in 1978 that I began to get in touch with my relatives at Ōtākou. The other things that helped to generate my sense of being Māori were involvement with the Waihopai Māori Committee, the Te Māori Exhibition, and then the Ngāi Tahu claim of 1986 onwards, in which I was deeply involved. It was then that I became fully integrated back into Ngāi Tahu.

Education

I went to Pinehill School, on the outskirts of Dunedin, and then to Dunedin North Intermediate around 1953. I was never particularly interested in hard sciences and maths. History, social studies and biology were the things that interested me particularly. Quite early on I became very interested in dinosaurs. At that time, there was little information available to children about dinosaurs, but there were a number of books written by Roy Chapman Andrews, the director of the New York Museum of Natural History. He was an explorer who went to Mongolia in the 1930s, with open-top Chevy cars driving across the Gobi Desert being chased by bandits, digging up dinosaur bones. I thought that that is what I would like to do.

I was aged eight or nine then, and those experiences influenced the subjects I took an interest in over the years. It certainly helped to crystallise my interests both in history and in biology, which became my best subjects at Nelson College. From Nelson College I went to Canterbury University and did a BA and then an MA, in geography. I wasn't interested in an academic career, but I enjoyed the social aspects of university life. After I graduated I went school teaching for three years, first on the West Coast for two years at Karamea and then for a year in Dunedin. I went back to Dunedin because I'd decided then I did want to have an academic career in archaeology. Those very early interests were starting to come through again.

My change of outlook was triggered, oddly enough, by the absence of a library in Karamea. I was teaching in the district high school, and although I had some books with me, the only person I could get books through otherwise was the local vicar. He travelled to Westport fairly often and offered to get some books for me. I told him my preference was archaeology, and he got me three or four books that spurred my interest to leave school teaching and do something with my life in archaeology.

When I entered Otago University, I started at the Stage III level in anthropology, and after that I did an MA in archaeology. I then was awarded a Commonwealth Scholarship to Cambridge University to do my doctorate. This was a wonderful opportunity. I went to Cambridge for three years, 1973–76. My PhD was about prehistoric economic change in northern Sweden, the region occupied in late prehistory and partly today by the Saami reindeer-herding people. I wrote the first PhD dissertation on the archaeology of this area. In it, I explored the utility of biological competition theory and the ecological notion of edge effect in explaining the transformation of sub-polar economic patterns. It was a very interesting topic, but I did have to learn enough Swedish to read

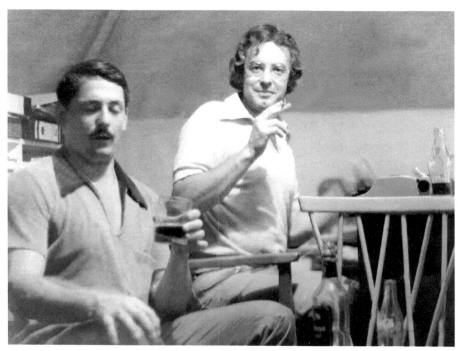

"Trying to type my PhD thesis while smoking and drinking rum with Foss Leach, Cambridge, 1976."

the academic literature and do fieldwork with Saami and others in the region. At the time I was an associate in the British Academy Major Research Project into the early history of agriculture, based in Cambridge. My contemporaries were working in temperate Europe and the Mediterranean, but I chose to go to the margins of agricultural expansion to get a different perspective on the topic. I can see, in retrospect, that this attraction towards the boundaries and margins of things is characteristic of much of my academic working style.

I appreciated the intellectual atmosphere at Cambridge, although it was quite unusual in some ways. There were 75 of us PhD students in archaeology, and this created a certain amount of worry because you were never sure whether somebody else was doing the same topic. Cambridge is famous for people not talking to each other. But that aside, I made valuable contacts through laboratory work and seminars. The famed tutorial system of Cambridge and Oxford didn't exist for PhD students in theory, but something like it operated in practice. My PhD supervisor died during the first year I was at Cambridge, however, and my department neglected to appoint a replacement. I did not remind them because I enjoyed the freedom of working on my own. To preserve the formalities, a new supervisor was appointed after I handed in my dissertation. I graduated PhD in 1977 and in 2002, on the basis of my publications, I was awarded an ScD at Cambridge.

Academic career

After Cambridge, I taught one year as a senior tutor at Auckland University. It was only a temporary position. I was then offered a lectureship in anthropology at Otago University and was there for 17 years, working my way through the ranks up to a personal chair as professor. We had a very big teaching department in those days. In Stage I anthropology there were up to 650 students. This was at least partly because anthropology was one of those topics recommended as an extra subject that could be taken by dental and medical students, among others. We would get 100–150 students per year from the medical school alone taking anthropology Stage I. The numbers dropped tremendously at Stage II, down to about 80, and then down to quite a small department at the post-graduate level.

I enjoyed teaching anthropology because I was interested in intellectual questions that lie somewhere between history and biology; they were interests I was probably always going to pursue in one form or another. I didn't prepare myself for this career during my first degrees at all, 1962–66. I did history to Stage II but I didn't do any biology, for example, and I had no sense of vocation at that time, which is a bit alarming in retrospect. How you can get all the way through to a master's degree without knowing why you're doing it seems astonishing now. But a number of us in those years were a little directionless. We were at university, but we were there because our schools told us that we were to go to university. We went, but we didn't have any particular path we wanted to pursue. The 1960s was very easy in New Zealand in many ways. There was full employment and few thought about the kinds of problems that people have to think about today. University was practically free to attend. In fact, I remember our annoyance when university annual fees went from $15 to $45. University was also very flexible about term work. There was very little internal assessment and going to lectures was effectively optional. We were being given a marvellous opportunity to pursue our own interests, at our own pace, an opportunity which has been progressively removed from tertiary education ever since, more's the pity.

During and after that time I did a lot of casual work, as we all did in those days. I worked on the wharves and in factories and freezing works, drove tractors, worked on the rubbish trucks and so on. I liked labouring and the blokes I worked with, many of them Māori, of course. But the nature of work, and the nature of a career are somewhat different. When I went to training college in 1967 and began teaching I realised that I didn't enjoy its heavily prescribed working patterns. I liked teaching as such, but I preferred it to be within the more flexible arrangements of the university, with its additional opportunities for research.

At Otago University, in 1970, I had the good fortune to be involved in a major archaeological project in Palliser Bay. Foss and Helen Leach, both young lecturers in the department, ran it and allowed me to join. It was a new project, in the sense of archaeological work being conducted by a team of people, doing different things and working in different specialisations on the same set of sites, but towards the same general objectives. This was a common approach overseas, but archaeology in New Zealand had tended to be an individual pursuit, or at least rather narrowly conceived. The Palliser Bay and later projects of a similar kind were interested in new models and theories of archaeology that were coming through from the late 1960s to the 1980s. It was a time of ferment generally in the social sciences. Archaeology, like geography, was adopting explicitly quantitative methods, and systemic theoretical orientations. History was changing too. Many of the humanities and social sciences were undergoing major rethinking about their theoretical stances and perspectives. Cambridge archaeologist Charles Higham was appointed to the first chair in archaeology at the University of Otago in 1968, and he brought the influential palaeo-economics approach, a welcome departure from prevailing culture history.

Involvement with Ngāi Tahu

In 1979 I sought to do salvage excavations of a newly discovered archaeological site on Lee Island in Lake Te Anau. This brought me into contact with the Waihopai Māori Committee, who opposed the proposal. Once it became known that I had southern Māori connections, I was invited to a meeting at George Te Au's house in Invercargill where the committee began by quizzing me in detail about whakapapa, my first experience of this. It was soon apparent that George and I were of the same family, and that my great-grandmother, who was born on Ruapuke Island, had been a relative of the tūpuna of many others on the Committee. They did not approve my proposal, at least not then, but we had a wonderful meal of roasted tītī stuffed with saffron rice, and thereafter remained in close contact. The main opponent of the Lee Island work was Naina Russell. She never relented (even though the committee eventually agreed to the work proceeding) but she became a good friend and once took me on a tour of the old kāika on Ruapuke Island.

From 1987 onward I had to do a lot of research for Waitangi Tribunal claims. There were many people in Ngāi Tahu who wanted to be involved in this research. Normally I would have just gone off by myself to the library and started doing the research on my own. It was obvious very early on that I couldn't do it that way, and we had to do it in what you might call a Māori way. We set up a meeting every Wednesday night in one of the big meeting rooms in the university, and everybody came along and contributed what they had, and we discussed who could do what for the following week. For instance, somebody would go to the Hocken Library and look up this and that; somebody else would visit their relations up the coast to obtain information on fishing history. There were books kept in families about landmarks that showed where fishing grounds were located out to sea. These books were held by Māori families, going back generations, and their data

Atholl at the Shag River Mouth excavations, North Otago, in 1988, holding a large archaic adze. The archaeological work has enhanced understanding of how Māori in the moa-hunting period lived.

were obviously secret. Nevertheless, much of these were released as evidence of deep-sea fishing extending well back into the past. There were many things like that, and they brought a sense of communal enterprise which I found fascinating and quite thrilling. Some of the people I worked with then were youngsters who went on to flourish in the tribe, people like Tahu Pōtiki for example, grandson of Emma Grooby. Emma was working with us on mahinga kai research and one night she came along and spoke about her 15-year-old grandson who had been in a bit of trouble. He had brains and ability, and he got into the claims research. Similarly, Rick Tau brought his son, Te Maire, into claims research. Te Maire later received his doctorate and is now pursuing an academic career at Canterbury University.

It was a marvellous time. Quite apart from the sense of how important it was that the Ngāi Tahu claim should be put together properly and that it should have the best chance of success, there was also this feeling of the iwi coming together and embracing everyone, not just those who had maintained that sense of connection with the rūnanga and whānau, but also those of us who had drifted along aimlessly, far away from it. We were brought back in and embraced within the kaupapa of the claim. Few of us could speak much Māori and I am still learning, as a student at Te Wānanga o Aotearoa, at the age of 72.

My role in Ngāi Tahu's claim was handling the mahinga kai part of the claim. This included all of the places where foods were sourced, by fishing, birding, eeling and gathering. A lot of information had been recorded when Ngāi Tahu chiefs addressed the Smith-Nairn Commission in 1879. Before that, there were observations by Europeans, particularly of Māori activities such as mutton birding, eeling, or catching barracouta. Whatever the activity, there was also abundant archaeological evidence from midden sites and places where settlements had existed, and of how people back then used the land.

One of the big issues for us Ngāi Tahu was to demonstrate, as it was easy enough to do, that Māori had not been just a coastal people; that there were many sites and resources in the interior of Central Otago, the Mackenzie Country, and the back country of Canterbury, which were traditionally used by the tribe. The whole of the landscape was not just owned, but frequently traversed and used by the people. There was a tendency for the Crown to argue that Māori only used the lands that they cultivated, and of course that was never true for Ngāi Tahu or our predecessors. We were never properly compensated for losing the South Island interior, the so-called 'hole in the middle', and that injustice still rankles.

Tīpene O'Regan's leadership of the claim impressed me particularly. As he was also a historian, he understood the nature of dealing with evidence from two perspectives — the historical and legal perspective, and also the Māori community perspective — and of how both views had to be integrated in a way that did not reduce the importance of either side. Faced by professional experts of all kinds, the Waitangi Tribunal would say quite rightly, where are the people? Where is the voice of the people? Where is the voice of your kaumātua? Tīpene O'Regan, Rick Tau, the Ellisons in Otago, and many others came to the fore when required. The claims process was an incubator for leadership.

The benefit of the Waitangi Tribunal claims far outweighed the financial return. For Ngāi Tahu, and I'm sure for other iwi too, being able to pull the people together, to reform the iwi, and to show where it had come from and where it is now was important. Ngāi Tahu operated through each of the papatipu rūnanga marae, so that when working on the claim you were involved with this smaller group to which you had the closest ancestral ties. To that extent it had a whānau feeling about it all.

Te Māori Exhibition and Māori Committee

Te Māori was another significant event in my understanding of Māori perspectives. I'd always been fascinated by material culture, but from an archaeological point of view rather than seeing that these things had a wider significance for people. They may be beautiful, and they are certainly informative of place and time, but the key to the impact of the Te Māori Exhibition, both overseas and when it came back to New Zealand, was that the objects were invested with emotional and spiritual significance. They are not merely museum pieces. They belong to us in several senses and we, in a way, belong to them, particularly historically. I began to understand this first, about 1978, when Tīpene O'Regan came out to a little excavation we were doing at Pūrākaunui. When we found an adze, he picked it up and started talking about it as if it was something that had mauri, a sense of life and kinship which embraced not just people but all the other things that are in our cultural landscape, the places, the houses, the land, and so on.

I wasn't directly involved in the exhibition. I came back to New Zealand in 1987 after a year away on fellowships at Cambridge and Tokyo universities. That was when Te Māori Exhibition was being put together, and I had a little bit to do with talking about it, because I was on the Board of the Historic Places Trust and its Māori committee. There were a number of people deeply involved in it, Cliff Whiting for example, Māui Pōmare, Tīpene O'Regan, John Hippolite, John Klaricich, Lena Manuel and many others. They were a great group of people, and they educated me in things Māori, in ways of being and behaving as Māori. We would stay on marae, which were up for classification by the Historic Places Trust, and talk with whānau. I would certainly have been too shy to go and do that on my own, besides which I didn't have a particular purpose for doing it. However, with this committee, we had our purposes and I could go with people who were at home in these situations. Te Aue Davis was another who was tremendously influential. Te Aue could be quite acerbic, and would tell you off, so you learnt fairly quickly what you should and shouldn't do, but you also sensed her intuitive understanding of Māori culture and how things are operating, and of the dynamics of inter-personal relationships on the marae.

Ōtākou Rūnanga

These experiences helped me build a Māori identity. I became a member of the Ōtākou Māori Committee and the Māori representative on the Otago Museum Board and the Otago University Council. The Māori committee was transformed in the 1980s into the Ōtākou Rūnanga, a process in which we had each to show how we were related together. This was my first opportunity to say that I'm here by some right of ancestry. It was good to know that I hadn't just gone there to talk to them, but that I had some right to stand there on the marae, through whakapapa connections. Of course, with that right came a reciprocal responsibility to work for the whānau. I could do things that were easier for me than for many of the other people on the rūnanga. For example, when we required research into historical matters, my office was near the Hocken Library, and I had the skills and ability in my work environment to go there and do what was required. I could take that responsibility on behalf of the marae and the rūnanga. Once all the rūnanga were set up, everybody in the wider community developed reasons why they had to go to the marae. There was also the Resource Management Act that required people to come to the marae to ask permission or to seek authority, and that put a tremendous burden on rūnanga. Once a month we would spend the whole of a Sunday afternoon dealing with these letters from the City Council, from the Department of Conservation, from schools, or whoever. Each of them was asking us to do something, so everybody had to pull their weight. That was the reality.

Managing rūnanga and Māori community obligations with my academic responsibilities was not too difficult. That's because I didn't have anywhere near the workload in the rūnanga that most of the people had, such as Kuao Langsbury, Edward Ellison, Tātene Wesley, the Russell sisters (Eleanor, Raewyn and Khyla) and others. I was doing some things but the real burden fell on them for organising hui and so on. Equally it fell on those who had grown up closest to the marae, who were used to dealing with the kai, the pōwhiri and all of those things. I certainly wasn't as involved as they were; however, I integrated my interests in Māori into my academic work with projects (for example, on intermarriage), the Waitangi Tribunal claims, and then with my writings on the history of southern Ngāi Tahu, from the traditional iwi period up to the mid-19th century.

Relocating abroad

After 17 years in Dunedin I was offered a research chair at the Australian National University in Canberra. I left Otago and went to Australia for a number of reasons. One of them was that El Niño ensured that we had almost no summer in the early 1990s for three years in a row. A more serious reason was an inability to proceed with a project on Wairau Bar that I was negotiating with Rangitāne. In the end Rangitāne refused the project, and one of the reasons they did so was that some members of their rūnanga did not want me to be involved, because I was Ngāi Tahu. I thought — is this the future of archaeology in New Zealand? Where you can only work in your own iwi district? I felt quite alarmed at that. I don't think that has turned out to be the case, although I do note that my fellow Māori archaeologists tend to work within their own rohe. The third reason was the opportunity to pursue interests that I was beginning to develop in the Indo-Pacific, including oceanic colonisation by Austronesian speaking peoples. I could do that better in Australia from a dedicated research position. I had no teaching commitments, and I was able to conduct fieldwork for months at a time. Normally you would have to wait for a sabbatical to do that. I had only PhD students and I could build a large project on the colonisation of the Pacific islands, which involved fieldwork in French Polynesia, Fiji, Niue, New Caledonia, Palau, and the Line, Batanes, Galapagos and Juan Fernandez islands. For the last five or six years I've been working on the colonisation of islands in the Indian Ocean including Madagascar, the Seychelles, and the Chagos group.

Māori and Western scholarship

For any Māori academic, the nature and practice of scholarship need to be considered especially carefully, because there is a perception that Māori should practise Māori scholarship. But what is that? I think of Māori scholarship simply as being often by Māori, although not just by Māori, but particularly as scholarship about Māori. I don't think there is a paradigm of Māori scholarship in any more profound sense, and I don't think that there could be. Others disagree and the conundrum between Western scholarship and what are perceived as Māori ways of thinking and acting in an academic context is still unresolved.

Working on ethnographic notes with
Rosine Oitokaia on Rapa Island,
French Polynesia, 2002.

Māori scholars can approach Māori topics in rather different ways. There was genuine scholarship in pre-European traditional thinking, and in the meaning of traditions and customs as exemplifying Māori religious and ritual practices and beliefs. Somebody brought up in that way of thinking, within a paradigm of Māori cosmology and culture, could make sense of it as philosophy and codes of practice. Some Māori today try to emulate a perceived traditional way of thinking, and base their conclusions upon that authority. However, the penetration of Christianity, literacy, and all the other intellectual cargo that accompanied European settlement, make modern attempts to revive Māori scholarship in this way appear contrived. I have had debates, mostly amicably, with Māori colleagues over this kind of issue from time to time. Some express views that seem quite unrealistic. One colleague demanded recently that the archaeology we had agreed to had to be integrated with his idiosyncratic sense of a pre-European worldview, a perspective that also enjoined my accepting it as a prerequisite. This is an extreme case, but I just don't think that adopting the underlying principle is possible. What survives of pre-European Māori cosmology, culture, custom and material remains can be studied from a Western scholarly perspective. Archaeological or other scientific approaches to the past can be considered from a derived sense of traditional knowledge or attitudes. But we can't put those two approaches into one methodological basket and mix them up. They are fern root and kūmara.

Archaeology and things related to it, such as radiocarbon dating, genetics of people and birds, etc, are part of an academic scholarly tradition, which has its own ways of dealing with the creation and critique of knowledge. It is scholarship that has to be open to scrutiny at all levels and it has to be testable in the sense of demonstrating how a result or conclusion could be shown as valid or invalid. The quality of scholarship does not depend on who is doing it or upon received authority, but only upon methodological transparency. This Western paradigm, which underpins the academic tradition, is equally effective in drawing out the deeper meanings of traditional evidence, as in myths, historical narratives and whakapapa. Te Maire Tau, for instance, shows that the story associated with Moki, the Ngāi Tahu war leader who invaded the Canterbury area, was told as if it was a story about Māui. It was a way of situating Moki as a hero, but also as a person who was operating in a way that was perfectly correct, tika, from a Māori perspective. The story was socially and pedagogically reinforcing. Research of this kind is undoubtedly Māori scholarship at work, but its basic epistemology is in the Western scientific tradition. Philosophical and substantive challenges to that tradition from Māori should certainly be articulated and debated, but for me, at least, it is difficult to imagine any other discourse in which this can occur in a scholarly way than in that which is at issue.

Achievements

I have published 25 books and about 300 papers. Five of the books might be regarded as useful contributions to Māori scholarship. *Prodigious Birds: moas and moahunting in prehistoric New Zealand* (1989) was the first comprehensive review of the early hunting and foraging phase in pre-European New Zealand, and it also opened a new phase of research on our extinct avifauna. I edited *Traditional Lifeways of the Southern Māori* (1994) which made available Herries Beattie's major ethnological project from 1920. *The Welcome of Strangers: An ethnohistory of southern Māori A.D 1650–1850* (1998), was a broadly-based narrative of Ngāi Tahu society and its transformation under European contact. *Ngāi Tahu: a migration history* (2008), edited with Te Maire Tau, was based upon an unpublished narrative of Ngāi Tahu history, written 80 years ago by Hugh Carrington. *Tangata Whenua: An Illustrated History* (2014) by Judith Binney, Aroha Harris, and me, provides the first wide-ranging and detailed synthesis of Māori history from origins in Asia 5000 years ago up to the first decade of the 21st century. It won the Royal Society of New Zealand Science Book Prize, 2015.

In Old Court of Corpus Christi College after conferral of Sc D at Cambridge, 2002.

At the ancestral village site in Sealers Bay, Whenua Hou (Codfish Island) western Foveaux Strait, 2007. Atholl standing next to Harold Ashwell's statue, *Hine a kete*, which commemorates the Māori partners of the Pākehā sealers.

One of my smaller works, *Race Against Time: the early Māori-Pākehā families and the development of the mixed-race population in southern New Zealand* (1991) is seen as a foundation of recent historical interest in mixed-descent communities. It was given as a Hocken lecture in 1990, and it wasn't entirely popular, as many people, including in my rūnanga, didn't want to speak about Māori-Pākehā intermarriage. I never quite understood that because in the south there was a lot of intermarriage. In the 1840s, one of the early surveyors said that approximately 50% of southern Māori women were married to Europeans already. The result of that was a large group of people who, like me, had a relatively small amount of Māori ancestry and stood somewhat uneasily between an exclusively Pākehā population and a population of Māori who had strong and diverse family connections to Māori culture and activities. We recognised and were proud of our Māori ancestry, but we didn't necessarily have a close connection with things Māori, such as marae. In a way, we were a bit like the later urban Māori in places like South Auckland. We were disconnected from those things. We didn't go to tangi. Those things that strongly define Māori culture, as we know it, were largely closed to us, not deliberately, but simply out of ignorance on our part. As I have said earlier, it was mainly my dealings with the Waitangi Tribunal that brought me back into the rūnanga.

In my primary discipline, archaeology, my contributions to the Māori past have been mainly through the excavation and analysis of midden sites. On the one hand, I wanted to solve some problems about the chronology of Māori arrival in New Zealand, and the various issues that flow from that, notably about voyaging, and on the other hand, I was interested, as ever, in connections between biology and history. My paper on the prehistory of colonisation in New Zealand (1991), set the scene for the current consensus about when people first reached New Zealand, and my work in the outlying islands showed that Norfolk Island, the Kermadecs, and the Auckland Islands were originally part of the Māori world, some 700 years ago. My MA thesis (1973) had devised the first model drawn from evolutionary ecology as an explanation of prehistoric change in the use of food resources, within individual sites and more generally, and this was developed further in publications from 1981 to 1996. For my research in New Zealand's archaeology and anthropology I was awarded the Percy Smith Medal and Elsdon Best Medal, and in 2005 I became a Companion to the New Zealand Order of Merit.

More broadly, I have pursued an interest in seafaring, publishing critiques of various orthodox models despite, I should add, participating in sailing a double canoe of traditional Polynesian type in the Lapita Voyage expedition.

My interests in seafaring history are global. I organised a conference on the topic at Cambridge, which has been published as *The Global Origins and Development of Seafaring* (2009). Seafaring history sits within my general interests in island colonisation, cultural adaptation to islands, and the human impact upon island ecologies. I have followed those interests across the Pacific and Indian Oceans, and to a small extent in the North Atlantic and Baltic (I was guest professor of archaeology for several years at Gotland University) for nearly forty years.

Lapita Voyage: eating porridge in a squall while sailing the traditional double canoe, *Anuta*, in the west Pacific, 2009.

Views of leadership

I have been a research leader rather than an administrative leader. While I recognise the need for administrative leadership, it is not something that appeals to me. I was head of the Anthropology Department at Otago 1991–1993, but I did not welcome moves to elevate me to Assistant Vice-Chancellor (Humanities). Ann Trotter, the incumbent, told me that her research was largely confined to weekends and, to be honest, I was not prepared to sacrifice so much. Soon after I went to the ANU, new policies put the research departments of Prehistory and Biogeography in jeopardy, and we needed to establish the Division of Archaeology and Natural History, and the Centre for Archaeological Research. I was the initial director of both for several years. However, I was not interested in any more senior administrative roles and glad to relinquish those that I had.

Administrative leadership in university departments or divisions and research leadership in major projects are generally collaborative, but not to the extent that is evident in Māori leadership, as I have experienced that. Consultation and consensus in the setting of university departments focus rather tightly upon the disciplinary staff, but Māori leadership always refers to the people, to the outside, to the iwi, to Māoridom as a whole. There's a sense that the enterprise is bigger than that thing that you might be leading, and you see this all the time of course in Māori leaders that are heads of rūnanga. They are not just the head of the rūnanga. They represent the rūnanga to the iwi and to the larger community and that's what distinguishes Māori leadership from leadership in a commercial or an academic sense.

For me, research leadership is one of those things that you do almost unconsciously. You build projects, you make contacts, you obtain funding, you lead expeditions, but you do it all without thinking very much about your role as a leader. It is the intellectual and practical challenges of the research that are compelling. I have always been active in generating research ideas, and getting the work done. Over the years I have led numerous minor research projects and some major collaborative projects such as the Southern Hunters project (1978–92), the Niue Project (1992–96), the South Island Māori Rock Art project (1990–93), the Indo-Pacific Colonisation project (1994–2007), the Southern Margins project (1998–2007), the East Pacific project (2003–06), the Asian Fore-arc project (2000–07) and the Indian Ocean project (2009–14). In a way, all of these projects are continuing because younger colleagues and students take up the same or similar issues, do some independent research and re-work our project conclusions. It is heartening to see that happening and it is, of course, the way in which research scholarship should proceed.

Research leaders have to be strong in a scholarly sense. They have to be critical; they have to be sceptical. Those are the qualities that I try to bring to my research. I believe very strongly in scholarly criticism and scepticism about what we're doing, and about what other people are doing in our field,

Atholl with wife Rosanne and children Kirsten and John, at the launch of *Tangata Whenua* (Bridget Williams Books), Wellington, 2014.
Aaron Smale

so that knowledge proceeds, not by an accumulation of all the things that are happening, but by refining what's happening so that we are constantly trying to cast off as much as we accumulate driving forward. I find myself more strongly committed to this mode of intellectual enquiry than many of my colleagues, and increasingly unhappy that it is being watered down. Scholarly criticism has never been fully accepted in some academic traditions in any case, but it is disheartening to see the extent to which self-promotion of research, often of modest actual accomplishment, and the general preference for style over substance, is infecting universities today. Part of the problem is that university managers in recent times seldom have the academic experience or credentials that they had once, and they are more readily attracted by self-indulgent advertisement than genuine intellectual performance. I suspect this problem has especially damaging implications for Māori scholars, who are often less assertive in that way than others.

Role models

My mother had been dux of Hāwera High School in the 1920s and she wanted to go on to university and become a journalist, but as the only girl in a large farming family her ambitions were unheeded. She had strong ambitions for my four sisters and me to make the most of education. I had good teachers at primary and secondary school. An influential teacher at Nelson College was 'Jerp' Patterson. He was an old man but he was an absolutely inspiring teacher of history. It was mainly British history, that's what we learnt in those days. Nonetheless that sense of the way in which history recaptures the human past, and also the joy of knowing about the past, was something that he imparted to me and probably to many others as well. At university it is harder to pick out role models because you meet a much broader range of people, but I had good mentors in Foss and Helen Leach, and Charles Higham. At Cambridge I enjoyed the seminars run by David Clarke, a bright young man busy creating a methodological revolution, and periodic, vigorous, discussion about Scandinavian prehistory with Graham Clark, a famous professor of archaeology whose parting remark, "Well, Anderson, let us not be hostages to fortune" comes to mind when I feel like giving up on a research project.

Challenges, opportunities and aspirations

There are challenges for emerging and aspiring Māori academics. Tension remains between Western and putatively traditional Māori scholarship, at least in the Humanities, and that is an issue that many of them are going to have to

At the celebration
of *Tangata Whenua*,
Wellington, 2014
Aaron Smale

face. If they are determined to do well in academic terms and get on quickly, almost certainly it will have to be by choosing a route, which favours Western scholarship. There's just no way around it, that I can see, but it probably comes at some cost. There are older ways of thinking, and older things to think about. There are different ways of perceiving life and wisdom, which some of our emerging scholars will have been brought up in, and will understand in a way that I cannot. It will cost them if they have to abandon those older models or, even worse, if they try and put them together with Western scholarship, unless there's some way of doing so that I can't foresee. That's a real challenge and not just for Māoridom. Across the Pacific, and in Australia, it is a seminal problem for academics of indigenous origin. How is the world and wisdom of your ancestors that has come down to you, to be accommodated in the academic world, if at all? It is especially problematic for the Humanities because, much more than in sciences and technology, there are parallel but very different methodologies and bodies of knowledge. I am uneasy about the informal switching that goes on between these currently, but also reluctant to think that an intellectual apartheid can be the only legitimate solution. There is certainly an opportunity here for creating a third way which has intellectual legitimacy on each side.

In my case, I see plenty of opportunities for new and interesting research, in fact far more than I could possibly take up. For example, I'm interested in changes in the primary productivity of the oceans, and how this impacts on the secondary productivity of fish and marine mammals, and ultimately of people. These changes are accessible through research on oxygen isotopes, in shell or in bone preserved in middens, the sites I like most to work in. Research could show how changes have occurred over long periods and large areas. I am interested in how influential such basic factors, most of them related to long-term climatic change, may have been upon the history of seafaring and island colonisation in the global oceans. I would like to do more on historical Polynesian traditions as well. Comprehensive digitisation of whakapapa, place names and other sources, in New Zealand and throughout Polynesia, would make it possible, in principle at least, to trace connections that reflected human migrations, in some cases down to the level of whānau and perhaps individuals. These are ambitious projects, and would require resources beyond my capacity as a retired academic, but perhaps some of our younger Māori colleagues and students might be interested in taking them up.

KUPU WHAKAMUTUNGA

A number of themes emerge from the preceding chapters. The first is the scholars' love of learning, acquired at an early age and carried through in later years to embrace research and scholarship excellence. They recognised that higher education was the key to make change, transform Māori communities and bring wide-ranging benefits to society as a whole. All but one were entering new territory as the first in their family to attend university, to receive a doctoral degree and become a full professor. Apart from the personal benefits, the link between education and socio-cultural benefits has long been recognised. Their positional power as high-ranking professors with academic freedom has enabled them to influence and advance political imperatives as well.

Of significance is that most had teaching backgrounds and knew that Māori students would be better off with the guidance and care of a good Māori teacher. They were passionate about being the difference. Ranginui Walker said, "Here we had these kids with their different culture and the separate culture of the school... I thought to myself there's a lot of teaching to do here". Linda Tuhiwai Smith said

> There's nothing like teaching 30 smart Māori kids in South Auckland and learning how to engage them in learning. In that space you learn more about teaching than you actually teach.

However, primary school only served to whet their appetites. Ranginui Walker echoed others' sentiments when he said,

> I loved it, and I thought that this is where I would like to make a future for myself, in secondary school, but that required a degree.

Teaching became a pathway into university and teaching at tertiary level. What very few of them discuss is how they found the transition from teaching at primary and secondary levels to teaching at tertiary level. Clearly they were able to take their training and skills learned at the lower levels to the highest levels of teaching.

Wally Penetito makes the point that his years teaching before he went to university were important:

> It provided me with a particular kind of base. Other academics I work with in education who have gone from school to university, got degrees, and then went into teachers' college and teaching have a very different approach to learning and teaching than I have.

A career change for Mason Durie from a health professional to an academic "was often a challenge". He "had little formal training in teaching and no real experience as a lecturer. The challenge was how to engage students so that learning became a passion rather than a requirement".

This raises the question of whether tertiary education institutions are teaching the teachers, or making sure the lecturers and tutors engage and actually teach the students. How much notice do the institutions take of student evaluations of the lecturers? Do they provide appropriate in-service training, to make sure lecturers have the appropriate methods and tools to teach? How much money do universities spend on electronic/high-tech teaching aids in the lecture rooms that are under-utilised? And how much money do they invest in training the teachers?

The second theme is the ability to take advantage of opportunities when and where they present themselves. Each scholar epitomises the fact that just sitting and waiting for something good to happen or for dreams to come true will not make it happen. Making the most of opportunity is an active process that requires attention, consideration, action and discipline. It comes in many shapes and sizes. It may be in the form of being the right person with the right friends, in the right place at the right time with the right prerequisite qualifications to enter Oxford University, as was the case with Ngāpare Hopa, and her several 'defining moments'. A successful sojourn as a consultant psychiatrist was a catalyst for change when Mason Durie was visited by a high-level delegation from Massey University to embark on what became a stellar academic career.

Sometimes opportunity is more about smashing down the gates in your way rather than having doors opened for you. Ranginui Walker outlines the long fight by Māori leaders to establish a lectureship in Māori Studies at the University of Auckland, and when the university finally capitulated, it still showed who wielded the real power by appointing a Pākehā to the position of junior lecturer in Māori over the top of more qualified Māori.

Others try to stand in the path of opportunity and steal from you. Ngāhuia Te Awekōtuku appeared to be unfairly robbed of a professorship by colleagues "who sabotaged the process", and a weak university official who seemed reluctant to stand up to them. But the opportunity later presented itself elsewhere and this time Ngāhuia was able to take it up.

Whatever the situation, these up-and-coming leaders were destined for greatness. They all pursued every opportunity to its fullest extent, and in so doing increased their choice of pathways to success and their abilities to contribute widely.

One of the attributes of a leader in the Māori world is, as the whakataukī suggests, 'Kaore te kūmara e kōrero mo tōna ake reka' (the kūmara does not say how sweet it is), i.e. leaders do not blow their own trumpets. One theme that has come through is the scholars' modesty in listing their achievements. Despite this, it's interesting to note what contributions they have made and regard as their most important, or that readily comes to their mind that they are particularly pleased with. For Atholl Anderson, one significant achievement took courage to do and was not well liked. His Hocken lecture in 1990 on the topic of intermarriage "… wasn't entirely popular, as many people, including in my rūnanga, didn't want to speak about Māori-Pākehā intermarriage."

Wally Penetito says, "I started teaching in 1960, and I'm still here. That's been a big achievement for me."

Notwithstanding their modesty, and their reluctance to list all their achievements, each of the scholars has made a major contribution to expanding the literature on Māori and indigenous knowledge. Each has provided seminal works that have not only advanced Māori scholarship by strengthening its status but have provided emerging scholars with textbooks full of relevant information that they themselves did not have while training. Ranginui Walker documents the opposition to having a Māori Studies course when Bruce Biggs was recruited to Auckland University

> because as the French language professor said, Māori is a language with no literature, with no scholarship around it. Dr Geddes … sent Bruce to the library to gather various books, such as *Ngā Mōteatea, Te Paipera Tapu* (Māori Bible), and *Ngā Mahi a Ngā Tūpuna*. He did a collection, and then he tabled them as proof of scholarly literature.

This small collection has now grown as a result of the efforts of these scholars and others. Linda Tuhiwai Smith points out:

> When I did my PhD there was hardly any Māori or indigenous literature that I could use, and now many of my students can write a literature review and 80% of the literature is Māori or indigenous.

A regular occurrence is having to juggle multiple roles as academics and scholars with the concomitant demands of marae, iwi, community, health and other interests. Durie alluded to the importance of balancing work and whānau. Linda Tuhiwai Smith says, what matters when balancing obligations is that you are a good person, and that you are connected to your family. She credits her community service for her promotion to a professorship — "it is getting leadership through service". Maaka regretted not spending more time with her parents but says, "I look at the university now as being the vehicle that allows me to work … with my native Hawaiian community partners".

A common theme is the importance of support networks. Universities are still seen by many as bastions of the elite, designed to continue to educate the children born into privilege to assume their rightful position in life. They are raised knowing that their parents and grandparents attended university to help them retain their privilege, and that they are expected to do the same. Their education prior to university helps them along that path, and when they enter university they are entering a place that holds no surprises for them. Every support is on hand to help them succeed. On the other hand, those who are not born into such privilege often struggle to find their feet. Margie Maaka said,

> I have managed to navigate the system fairly well. Unfortunately, I think a lot of Māori students are unable to navigate the system, and they get chewed up pretty fast.

Those who did manage to work the system relied heavily on their own support systems and networks. The support required was often in the form of their life experiences within the whānau, which provided them with attributes and qualities necessary for academic success. They shared a common bond; it may be whakapapa-based, it may be geographical location or a shared purpose.

Where they were separated from their whānau networks, each quickly found others to compensate. For example, Mason Durie went to Otago, a whole island away from home. In his second year he decided that it would be good to have a Māori club, and linked up with other Māori students from across the university.

> We formed the Māori club; not just a club to socialise, but a club for considering how Māori students might contribute to Māori, beyond getting a degree.

Ngāpare Hopa details her first day at Auckland University, when she met a few other Māori:

> We have been described as the first wave of Māori students to hit Auckland University … We were few in number, studying and hanging out with each other, sharing notes and ideas from lectures and tutorials.

Conversely, Atholl Anderson, who had been largely raised as a Pākehā, distanced from his Māori roots in his formative years, makes little mention of needing to set up or to look for support when he attended university, although his sense of being Māori was evident as he connected with his local iwi.

Wally Penetito, who studied for his undergraduate degree extramurally without the support of peers, did not find it easy learning how to collaborate with others once he entered the university system full-time.

> I've only learned [the things which come with academic life] in the last few years. I'm still learning them now, such as how to collaborate with other people in research projects or writing articles for publication with other people. … I do know that some of the problems I've had are linked to not really being socialised into academia. You have to do that. You need to sit with other people, other colleagues and hear yourself talking about what you do and let them challenge you, because if you can't get past that, well go and find another job. That's what you have to learn to be able to do, and it is tough.

Along with this theme is the noticeable lack of support within the tertiary education institutions when the scholars arrived. The young students were experiencing a huge change in their lives, many coming from sheltered rural backgrounds or boarding schools with a huge support system to a new environment often far from home, a new culture, without all the support they had enjoyed previously.

Even as graduates they recognised the lack of nurturing for graduates. Over time they built up their own support systems among their peers and with older mentors, and became proficient in walking in two worlds and in doing well in both, but they were forced to do this without any support from the institutions, and in at least two cases, with active discouragement or undermining by colleagues.

One heartwarming theme that came through is gratitude. Most expressed their gratitude in different ways to their whānau and particularly those who have come before them paving the way, acknowledging individual teachers and mentors, recognising the financial contributions from iwi trusts, and scholarship funds. They certainly don't try to make out that their success came easily or only as a result of their own hard work. They all mentioned the hard work they had to put in, but they all also expressed gratitude for the help they have received along the way. And they have continued to show that gratitude by giving back to their communities. Maaka said,

> I think indigenous academics can become too comfortable. We can have good lives at an institution of higher learning. We can go to work and do our research, and we don't necessarily need to come out of our offices. But for me, there's no satisfaction in this. ... I like going out to the community. Most of the time I sit with elders, eat with them, laugh and joke with them, try to find out what their needs are and how we can work together... That's scholarship as far as I'm concerned.

As well as giving back personally to their communities, including iwi, many of the scholars expect those they mentor to do the same.

Another theme which came through was intersectionality. Although the term is never used by any of the scholars, intersectionality played a role in their education and careers. Most experienced some form of overt or covert discrimination in their early education, which continued at university. Mostly this was racial, some of it was classist. The female scholars bucked gender norms and social expectations that they would become nurses, teachers or secretaries, and some suffered significant financial hardship as a result. One scholar who is lesbian also identified the additional particular difficulties she experienced in the system. Intersectionality is another area universities are going to have to learn to deal with, not as topics to teach, but for its impact on their students and employees.

A common theme from many of the scholars was their disdain for the system and power structures which made and still make it so difficult for Māori to succeed. Many came into the university system already politicised. Others became so soon after their entry. Groups like Ngā Tamatoa were instrumental in directing that politicisation, and many have continued their activism in other ways by challenging the status quo as transforming agents. Once your eyes are opened to oppression and unfairness it is impossible to close them. They are committed to making a difference, not only in their fields, but within their communities, across the country and globally.

Another theme is Māori in the international arena. Many of the Māori scholars are working on the international stage. Graham Smith identified how

> many indigenous populations in these jurisdictions look to Māori for what's happening here, because we're viewed as being at the forefront if you like — at the cutting edge for indigenous education development.

The responsibility with helping others is making sure you get it right, and you are not stepping on their mana, or being the second coloniser. Graham Smith goes on to say "but that's for them to decide what might be useful — not for us to tell them what they should do." As Maaka, who has spent 30 years in Hawai'i, much of it working with the indigenous people, said:

> My rights, when I work with the community, come from the rights that they wish to accord me at certain times. I work with the community and respect their wishes and I'm very careful not to overstep the bounds. I do not do things that are without their blessing or guidance.

Returning to the main themes of Māori scholarship and leadership, each of the scholars had differing definitions, and some quite sharply divergent opinions. Some of the questions that arise from that discussion are, is there such a thing as Māori scholarship? If there is such a thing, can non-Māori contribute? Is it static, firmly left in the past, or is it dynamic, future-driven? What is the end goal of Māori scholarship? Can Māori scholarship be objective? Should it? Is it a tool to open the basket of knowledge, or is it the basket itself? Is it a tool to self-achievement, or a step towards empowering whānau, iwi and communities? Does it have its own place in academia, or is it inter-disciplinary? Is it a call for action? Is it a challenge to the status quo, or is it going to be co-opted by the status quo? Does it add to the body of knowledge of the scholar, or is it to "elevate others and to make a difference for a better world" as in Ngāhuia Te Awekōtuku's phrase?

Selwyn Kātene as director, MANU AO, and Mason Durie (chair of Te Kāhui Amokura, acting as the governance entity for MANU AO Academy), in 2009.

Each scholar has demonstrated leadership in many ways. In common is the notion that leadership is for the benefit of society at large. It "is about the enhancement of the people, not about individual enhancement," as stated by Margie Maaka. Their role models were few and not necessarily Māori, as Linda Tuhiwai Smith asserted, "they were people I thought were good people, who achieved things." While there's a human tendency to glorify the past there is some truth in Walker alerting us that,

> There had been a real enthusiasm and development in the 1990s at universities in the Māori Studies area and it hasn't been looked at ever since. The whole drive, immense enthusiasm and vitality which were there, somehow seems to be gone now. It dissipated and it hasn't come back at all, and while we tend to think well perhaps a change of leadership is needed or a different personality, there's something else missing. It's not quite there at the moment.

The final theme identified is a voice of caution in line with a statutory duty to be a critic and conscience of society. Ranginui Walker wasn't deterred when the Prime Minister called for his dismissal "for teaching subversive views". Fortunately the University of Auckland "stuck by its principle of intellectual freedom, critic and conscience of society". Walker regarded that as "one of the beauties of working in the academy". Although, he said, "there are very few people who had the guts to come out and espouse that role ... most people are very conforming".

Margie Maaka refers to the way things have regressed for Māori over the last ten years or so, after the gains of the 1980s and 1990s. Many of the scholars point to examples over the years of how successful Māori initiatives are shut down for various reasons by funders, institutions, governments and other power structures. The latest in a long line was the threat to withdraw funding of Ngā Pae o te Māramatanga (New Zealand's Māori Centre of Research Excellence), and prior to that the closure of MANU AO Academy. As Linda Tuhiwai Smith says,

> What I've learned after years of working in the universities is we think we've made space and gains. However, these are old institutions, and when someone moves on, the spaces close. In order to keep those spaces open all the time, we have to have people that fill those spaces and they've got to be good people. They must do the work, be dedicated, and understand what their role is. ... I would want to be known as someone who has opened doors and make spaces, and I would like the next generation to take that seriously. Their job is to keep those spaces open and create new spaces.

PAPAKUPU

Aotearoa	New Zealand
atua	god(s)
haka	posture dance
hākari	meal, feast
hapū	sub-tribe
haukāinga	local people of a marae, home people
hui	meeting
hūpē	snot, mucus
iwi	tribe
kāhui ariki	royal family of the Kīngitanga
kaiako	teacher
kaimanaaki	nurturer
kaimoana	seafood
kāinga	home
kaitakawaenga	liaison officer
kaitiaki	guardian
kaiwhakaruruhau	advisor
kapa haka	performing group
karakia	chant, incantation, prayer
kaumātua	elder
kēhua	ghost
kete	kit, usually made of flax
Kīngitanga	Māori King movement
kōiwi	human bone, corpse
kōrero	speech, discussion
koro	older man, grandfather
koroneihana	coronation
koroua	respected elder man
kuia	respected elder woman
kutu	headlice
mahi toi	art, craft
mana	authority, prestige, power
mamae	pain
Māoritanga	Māori culture, practices and beliefs
marae	open area in front of a traditional house where formal greetings and discussions take place
maunga	mountain, used to identify with a tribal area
mauri	life principle
mōteatea	song of grief

ngā hau e whā	the four winds (symbolically, all tribes or people present)
pā	village
paepae	orators' bench
papatipu	ancestral land, held under customary title without a European title
piupiu	flax skirt
pōhara	poverty-stricken
pōkeka	a rhythmic chant, peculiar to Te Arawa tribes
pōtae	hat
poukai	meeting to demonstrate support of the Kīngitanga
pukumahi	hard-working
rangatahi	young person or people
rangatira	chief, chiefly
raupatu	conquest, confiscation of land
ringa raupā	(blistered hands) a hard worker
rohe	territory
rongoā	medicine
roro	brains
rūnanga	tribal council
rūruhi	grandmother
tamariki	children
reo	language
take	business
tā moko	tattoo
taiaha	a long weapon of hard wood
tautoko	support
tikanga	customs
tuakana	elder brother or sister
tukutuku	decorative latticework
whakapapa	genealogy
waiata	song
whāngai	fostered, adoptive
wharemate	place of mourning
whakawhanaungatanga	process of establishing relationships; camaraderie
whāriki	woven mat

KUPU TOHU

K

Kaa, Arapera 139
Kaa, Hone 97
Kachmankoi, Stephan 144
Kahikina, Mike 184
Kāhui Ariki 7
Kāi Tahu *see* Ngāi Tahu 93
Kamāriera, Hone me Ūnaihi 128
Kanahele: Aunty Aggie 184, 187; Kamaki 184, 188
Kānata *see* Canada
karakia 19, 22, 56, 123, 125-26, 145
Karapu, Rolinda 61
Kātene, Selwyn 7-8, 10-18, 209-16
Kaupapa Māori theory 77, 93, 104, 106-8, 113, 128, 135, 156
Kawakawa Bay 25
Kawerau 118, 126-27
Kāwharu, Hugh 11, 18, 23, 30, 36, 39, 71, 76, 98, 118, 128
Kelston School for the Deaf 104
Kimberley Hospital 67
Kingi, Pauline 32
Kīngitanga 25, 32, 136-37, 153
Klaricich, John 197
kōhanga reo 52, 92, 128, 149
Kōhere, Rēweti 12
Kokohinau Marae 79
Korokī, King 47, 58
koroneihana 137
Kuila, Isaac 155
kura kaupapa Māori 52, 81, 85, 92-93, 102-5

L

Lake, Derek 46
Lambert, Harry 28
Lange, David 69, 79, 151
Langsbury, Kuao 198
Lapita 203-4
Latimer, Graham 33
Laughton: Jim 169; John 169
Leabourn, Jim 167
Leach: Foss 192, 194, 206; Helen 194, 206
Leder, Hans 146
Lewis, Evan (Joe) 95
Lienhardt, Godfrey 143, 148
Lowie, Robert 148

M

Maaka: Golan 175; Margie 173-189, 212, 214-16
Mackenzie Country 196
Macmillan, Harold 144
Maeroa Intermediate 176
Maharey, Steve 75
Mahuika, Api 13
Mahuta, Robert 53-54, 56, 62, 97, 99, 149-53
Mahuta, Tūmate 145
MAI Programme 110, 157
Maketū 57-58
Manawatū 118, 128
Mangakino 166
Māngere 103
Mantell, Colin 71
MANU AO Academy 9, 13-14, 17-18, 67, 115, 165, 215-16
Manuel, Lena 197
Manukau Institute of Technology 84
Māori Advisory Service 165, 167
Māori Affairs Amendment Act 52
Māori Battalion 72, 140
Māori Centre of Research Excellence 90, 110, 186, 216
Māori Congress 37, 74-75
Māori Council 19, 30-31, 33, 37, 69
Māori health 66, 69, 71
Māori Land Law 52
Māori-Pākehā intermarriage 199, 202, 211
Māori Studies 8, 19, 24, 28, 35-37, 39, 53, 63, 71-74, 79, 97-99, 149, 153, 211, 216
Māori Women's Welfare League 149
Mary Annunciata, Sister 43
Mary Bertrand, Sister 43
Mary Leo, Sister 138, 141
Masterton 94-96
Mātaatua 61, 119
Matahina 121
Mataira, Bill 65
Mataira, Kāterina 13
mātauranga Māori 10-12, 72-73, 88
Matthews, John 167
Māui 22, 64, 197, 201
Maungapōhatu 25, 123
Maungārongo 103
Maungawhakamana 126
Maungawhau 103
McCutcheon, Stuart 14
McDonald, Fraser 50

Otago 35, 63, 65-66, 71, 190-94, 198-99, 204, 212
Ōtaki 41, 65, 68
Ōtaki Porirua Trust Board scholarship 65
Ōtākou 191, 198
Ōtara 29, 103, 166
Oxbridge 56, 135

P

Paku, Te Paea 96
Palmerston North Hospital 67
Pamatatau, Mi'i 167
Papakura, Maggie 50
Paparoa (mother of Ngāhuia Te Awekōtuku) 41-42, 48
Parihaka 25, 191
Parkinson, Mervyn 95
pātere 124
Patterson, 'Jerp' 206
Pawley, Andy 99
PBRF *see* Performance-Based Research Fund
Pearson, Bill 139
Penetito: Wally 158-72, 210-11, 213; whānau 171
Penfold, Merimeri 50
Penfold, Vernon 28
pepeha 124
Pere, Rose 13, 167
Performance-Based Research Fund 74, 100
Peters, Winston 51, 97
Piddington, Ralph 24, 30
Pīhama, Leonie 82, 108
Pipiwai 26, 35
Pitman, Mereana 57
Plato 163
Poananga, Atareta 57
Pōhatu, Taina 108
Pohio, Rosemary 38
Poihākena 118
Pōmare: Eru 71; Māui 197
Potae, Hape 167
Pōtakatāwhiti 62
Pōtatau, Hēmi 99
poukai 137, 149
Pou, Naida 101
Princeton 147
Punaruku 27
Purakaunui 197
Pūriri, Brownie 99

Q

Queen Elizabeth II 41, 138
Queen Victoria School 28, 50, 136-39

R

Rakiura 190
Rangihau, John 53-56, 99, 118, 128
Rangi, Iti 101
Ranginui, significance of name 33
Rangitāne 63, 68, 199
Ratana, Iriaka 137
Rauhihi, Ama 57
Raukawa: Te Runanga 69; Te Wānanga o 68-69 *see also* Ngāti Raukawa
raupatu 19, 122, 136, 149-51, 153-54, 166
Reagan, Ronald 146
Reeves, Pāora 149
Rēweti, Maxine 51
Richardson, Ivor 69
Richardson: Pare 71, 128; Pita 128
Rickard, Tuaiwa 137
Riki, Pera 167
Rikys, Peter 31
Ringatū 123, 125-26, 166
Ritchie, James 53-54, 56
Rogers, Garth 99
Rongowhakaata 65
Rosevear, Watson 65
Rotorua: 40, 42-43, 45-49, 51, 53, 56, 58; Girls' High School 45
Royal, Tūroa 139
Royal Victoria Hospital 68
Rua Kēnana 123
Ruamatā 102, 104-5
Rua, Mohi 61
Ruapotakataka 41
Ruapuke Island 195
Ruātoki 23, 77, 118-19, 121-24, 126-28
Ruatōria 77, 83, 86, 92
Russell: Eleanor, Raewyn & Khyla 198
Russell, Naina 195

S

Sacred Heart school 50
Salmond, Anne 99
Sāmoa 56
Sandos, Joe 147
Sapong, Peter 144
Satyanand, Anand 51

D R Selwyn Kātene is Assistant Vice-Chancellor (Māori and Pasifika) at Massey University and prior to that was director of MANU AO Leadership Academy and a senior manager in the public service and pharmaceutical industry. He has published several books including *Turning the Hearts of the Children: Early Māori Leaders in the Mormon Church*, *The Spirit of Māori Leadership* and *Future Challenges for Māori*. His tribal affiliations are Ngāti Toa, Ngāti Tama, Ngāruahine and Ngāti Tūwharetoa.

S IR Tīpene O'Regan is the retired Assistant Vice-Chancellor Māori of the University of Canterbury, and former long-serving Chairman of the Ngāi Tahu Māori Trust Board and chief negotiator for the Ngāi Tahu Claim. A member of many boards, including founding Chairman of Te Ohu Kai Moana, he remains as Adjunct Professor in the Ngāi Tahu Research Centre at the University of Canterbury and as a Fellow of the University of Auckland where he chairs Ngā Pae o Te Māramatanga. He was made a Knight Bachelor in 1994.